American Language Hub

LEVEL 4
Student's Book

LOUIS ROGERS

macmillan education

Contents

Welcome

GRAMMAR
The passive voice

A **Complete the sentences with the passive voice form of the verbs in the box.**

arrest cancel destroy kill release take

1 Apparently, over 700,000 people ________________ by mosquitos every year.
2 A decision ________________ by the management board later in the week.
3 Three men ________________ in connection with an attempted robbery in Soho last week.
4 The band's debut album ________________ on August 27, 1991.
5 'We regret to inform passengers that the 7:36 flight to San Diego, California ________________.'
6 Over 600 homes ________________ in the forest fires that hit the area last month.

Zero, first and second conditionals

B **Choose the correct options (a, b or c) to complete the conditional sentences.**

1 If you don't hurry up, ___ the beginning of the movie.
 a we'll miss b we'd miss c we'd have missed
2 Let me know if ___ any help with anything.
 a you'll need b you need c you'd need
3 If ___ the fire alarm, leave the building by the nearest exit.
 a you'll hear b you'd heard c you hear
4 I can't help you unless ___ me what's wrong.
 a you'd tell b you tell c you'd have told
5 If I had the money, ___ all my food there.
 a I'll buy b I'd buy c I'd have bought
6 If ___ Emily, I'll tell her to give you a call.
 a I see b I'll see c I'd see

VOCABULARY
Word formation

A **Complete the sentences with the correct form of the words in parentheses.**

1 I thought that was a really ____________ (*product*) meeting actually.
2 Just relax. Try not to ____________ (*think*) it.
3 That reminds me, I need to ____________ (*new*) my passport.
4 Sorry, but I think you may have ____________ (*understand*) the question.
5 There's simply no ____________ (*science*) evidence to support that.

Collocations

B **Choose the correct options to complete the collocations.**

1 We're sorry to announce that there are ***serious / severe*** delays on the central line.
2 Many new business owners find it difficult to ***make / create*** a profit in their first year.
3 I'm finding it really difficult to ***stay / remain*** motivated right now.
4 LeBron James has ***made / given*** the decision not to renew his contract with the Cleveland Cavaliers.
5 Scott seems pretty confident that his team will ***reach / make*** their target by June.
6 My brother-in-law actually ***does / runs*** a small business from home.
7 The government has ***launched / released*** a new campaign focusing on mental health.
8 Annoyingly, we got stuck in ***serious / heavy*** traffic on our way back.

C **SPEAK** **Work in pairs. Discuss the questions.**

1 What can you do to help stay motivated at work and in your studies?
2 Do you know anyone that runs a successful business? What do they do?
3 What's the most difficult decision you've ever made?

PRONUNCIATION
Intonation

0.1 **A** **Draw arrows in the parentheses to show whether the intonation rises (↗) or falls (↘) at each point in the sentences. Then listen and check.**

1 Oh, really? ( ) Wow! That sounds great! ( )
2 It's a formal dinner, ( ) so it's important that you look nice. ( )
3 You've been to New York before, ( ) haven't you? ( )
4 Hmm … I'm not sure really. ( ) Maybe tomorrow afternoon? ( )
5 OK. ( ) I'll speak to Alicia and get back to you. ( )

Silent consonants

0.2 **B** **Underline the silent consonants in each word. Then listen and check.**

1 dishonest
2 listen
3 designer
4 climbing
5 muscle
6 knowledge

1 CONNECTIONS

Women in a minimalist photo shoot in Copenhagen, Denmark.

OBJECTIVES

- talk about reactions and feelings
- design and present a meet-up group
- compare, contrast and summarize short biographies
- talk about people that have influenced you
- give your opinion on the role of inherited ability in success
- write a formal letter asking for information

Work with a partner. Discuss the questions.

1 Read the quote. Do you agree with Euripides? Why/Why not?

2 Can online relationships ever be as close as face-to-face relationships? Why/Why not?

3 What are the most important relationships in your life? Why?

- Talk about reactions and feelings
- Design and present a meet-up group

S – skimming for the main ideas   V – feelings   G – question forms   P – intonation in *yes/no* and *wh-* questions

READING

A SPEAK Work in groups. Discuss the questions.

1 What qualities make someone a hero?
2 What type of people would you describe as 'everyday heroes'? Why?
3 Have you ever done anything heroic?

B SKIM FOR MAIN IDEAS Skim read *Inspiring stories of everyday heroes*. Choose the best summary (a or b) for each story. Use the information in the box to help you.

> **Skimming for the main ideas**
>
> Many modern articles, particularly those online, are presented in multiple short paragraphs to make them easier to read in a short amount of time. We can usually understand the main ideas in this kind of article by quickly skimming the text.

1 a A man jumped onto the train tracks to save his baby.
  b A man jumped onto the train tracks to save a woman's baby.
2 a A young couple was saved from a forest fire that broke out in the fields they were driving through.
  b A young couple saved a family from a forest fire that spread to their house.
3 a A group of heroic pedestrians helped pull a schoolgirl out from under the car that had just hit her.
  b A driver heroically pulled a young schoolgirl out from under his car after an accident.
4 a Despite not being a strong swimmer, a young man was able to rescue his dog from strong currents in the ocean.
  b A passerby was able to rescue a dog that had been swept out to sea.

C READ FOR DETAIL Read the article again and answer the questions. Underline the parts of the text that give you the answers.

1 What caused the stroller to start rolling toward the train tracks?
2 Was Jonas Neff in any real danger?
3 How did the fire develop so rapidly?
4 How did the children escape the burning building?
5 What had Becca Edwards been doing before the accident?
6 How did the driver react after the accident?
7 Why couldn't the dog get back to the beach?
8 Why was the rescuer so sure he could help?

D SPEAK Work in pairs. Discuss the questions.

1 How do you think you would react in the situations described in the article? Why?
2 Do you agree with Jonas Neff that he isn't a hero because 'anyone would do the same'? Why/Why not?
3 Why was Becca Edwards lucky that her accident happened on a main road?

Inspiring stories of EVERYDAY HEROES

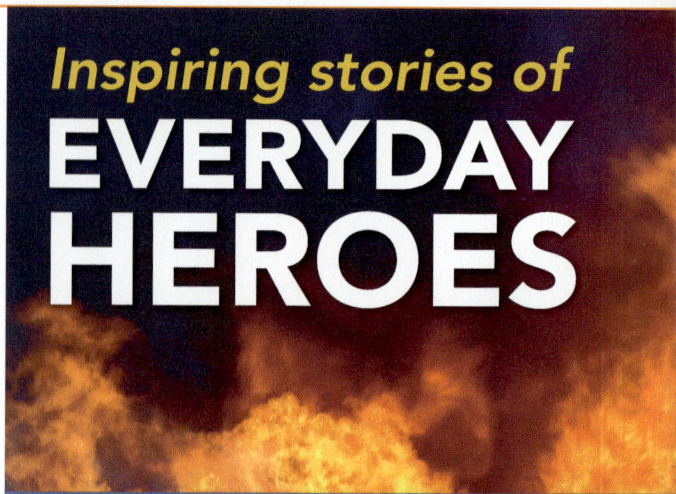

BY EMILY FISCHER | OCT 15, 2018

In an age dominated by movies about superheroes, it's good to know that we can all be heroes in the right context. To inspire you to do something next time you see someone in trouble, here are four real-life stories of normal people who jumped into action without a second thought.

BACK ON TRACK

Reactions are vital in everyday situations. Mother-of-one Christine Thomas was waiting on a crowded platform for her train home, when her phone rang. Expecting an important call, Christine rooted through her bag, not noticing that the brake on her child's stroller had failed and it was rolling toward the platform edge. She looked up, **horrified**, to see the stroller fall off the platform and onto the tracks below. Everyone on the platform froze, too **tense** to move, except Jonas Neff. Jonas jumped down quickly and lifted the stroller and child onto the platform, before pulling himself up just in time to avoid the oncoming train. Interviewed later by local radio, Jonas said, 'I'm not a hero. Anyone else would do the same.' Maybe a little too modest considering that everyone else had been too shocked to move!

ESCAPING THE BLAZE

Everyone can be brave no matter how young or old they are. In the dry heat of the summer, a fire started burning slowly in a farmer's field. As the winds became stronger, the fire spread quickly, surrounding the Sanchez family home. Trapped inside were a grandmother and her two young grandchildren. Spotting the danger as they were driving past, local residents Maria and Javier Hernandez stopped and got out to help. Maria later told local reporters '… I was so **impressed** by the character of such young children. They didn't know who we were but trusted us to catch them as they jumped from the top window. Once they were out, the grandmother jumped too.' The family was clearly upset to lose their home but equally **relieved** to all be alive.

THE STRENGTH OF MANY

Sometimes what you need is a whole group of heroes. **Thrilled** at having just won a local soccer tournament, 10-year-old Becca Edwards was riding her bike home from school one evening when she was hit by a car that had driven through a red light. The car stopped, trapping Becca underneath. **Devastated** by what had happened, the driver could do nothing as Becca screamed for help. Luckily for her, the accident took place on a busy main road. Nine pedestrians ran to help, working together to lift the car up just enough for a tenth hero to pull the schoolgirl out from underneath. Mark Benson, the first paramedic at the scene, said Becca was lucky to be alive and praised the quick response of the passers-by.

DANGER AT THE BEACH

Michael was happily throwing sticks into the ocean for his dog, Linus, when suddenly it all went wrong. Strong currents dragged poor Linus out to sea and he wasn't able to swim back to shore. Terrified that Linus might die, but not a particularly strong swimmer, Michael stood helpless and **frustrated** on the beach. All of a sudden, a man came running past and dived into the water. After a brief struggle, he managed to pull Linus back to the shore where he was met with a huge round of applause from the crowd of onlookers that had gathered. 'Initially, I felt kind of **awkward** on the beach because I didn't know what to do' said the young hero. 'But I'm pretty confident in the water, so I just jumped in. I'm glad I could help out, but I wouldn't recommend swimming in such dangerous currents unless you're confident you can get back. A person's life is much more important than a dog's!'

VOCABULARY

Feelings

A Scan the article again. Complete the definitions with the adjectives in bold.

1. ________________ feeling happy because something bad has stopped or hasn't happened
2. ________________ feeling nervous, worried and not able to relax because of what might happen
3. ________________ feeling embarrassed and not relaxed
4. ________________ feeling very shocked and upset
5. ________________ feeling very shocked or frightened
6. ________________ feeling very happy and excited
7. ________________ feeling admiration for someone because of an unusually good achievement, quality or skill
8. ________________ feeling annoyed or impatient because you can't do or achieve what you want

B Complete the sentences with adjectives from Exercise A.

1. I felt a little ________________ at first because I wasn't wearing a suit like everybody else.
2. I was just really ________________ because the police wouldn't let me help.
3. It'd been a horrible flight and I was pretty ________________ when the plane finally landed.
4. Firefighter Mark Cox was ________________ to receive an award for bravery after the incident.
5. You couldn't help but be ________________ by how quickly he reacted to the danger.
6. The crowd grew ________________ as they waited to see if firefighters would reach the child in time.
7. I was ________________ to hear that my grandmother had died because we were very close.
8. We were all ________________ as the elevator fell 15 floors toward the ground.

C Go to the Vocabulary Hub on page 142.

D SPEAK Work in pairs. When was the last time you felt any of these emotions? What happened?

SPEAKING

SPEAK Work in groups. Read the scenarios (1–3) and discuss what you would do in each and why.

1. You're on a busy train when the woman in front of you suddenly falls over. Her eyes are closed and she doesn't appear to be breathing.
2. You're walking home late at night when you see a group of men shouting at a terrified businessman. You think they might attack him.
3. A fire breaks out in the house across the street. The elderly woman that lives there has difficulty walking and has poor hearing.

a

b

LISTENING

A SPEAK Work in pairs. Read the information about Get Together and discuss the questions.

1. What is the purpose of Get Together?
2. What kind of groups are available?
3. Do you think this is a good idea? Why/Why not?

> ### Get Together
> Home About us Contact Login Sign up
>
> **Get Together** helps connect millions of people with similar interests around the world. The basic idea is simple – find people in your local area that share your passion and form a group. Meet regularly to play together, learn new skills or just make new friends.
> Our members have rediscovered their passion for reading, trained for triathlons, even changed their careers – the possibilities are endless. Whatever you're interested in, you're sure to find a group that suits you.
>
> | Members | Groups | Countries |
> | --- | --- | --- |
> | 25 million | 185,967 | 148 |

1.1 **B LISTEN FOR MAIN IDEAS** Listen and match the conversations (1–3) to the pictures (a–c).

Conversation 1 ___ Conversation 2 ___ Conversation 3 ___

1.1 **C LISTEN FOR DETAIL** Listen again. Are these sentences true (T) or false (F)? Correct the false sentences.

1. a Both speakers at the ukulele group regularly go to meet-ups. *T / F*
   b They have played the ukulele for the same amount of time. *T / F*
2. a The man's apartment is in a convenient location. *T / F*
   b The man has done a 10K race before. *T / F*
3. a Martin needs to return the registration form as soon as possible. *T / F*
   b Martin and Yumi both enjoyed the Haruki Murakami novel *Norwegian Wood*. *T / F*

D SPEAK Work in groups. Discuss the questions.

1. What are the benefits of joining a group like this?
2. Do you think this is the best way to meet new people in your area? Why/Why not?
3. What Get Together groups would you like to join in your area? Why?

GRAMMAR
Question forms

1.2 **A** Listen to extracts from the conversations again. Complete the questions.

1 Sarah: Yeah, same really. It just seemed like a fun thing to do. Anyway, ______________ ______________ the group tonight?
Mark: Uh, Lucy, I think. She's actually a professional musician, so we're in good hands.

2 Fyodor: Well, I like Rochester, but my apartment is a really long way from the train station and I don't really get along with my roommates.
Alana: Fair enough. ______________ ______________ like them?
Fyodor: Well, one of them works night shifts so he always comes home really late and the other just spends all his time in his room.

3 Fyodor: I suppose so. Who ______________ ______________?
Alana: A couple of friends I've known since college. They can definitely be annoying sometimes, but I wouldn't want to live with anyone else.

4 Martin: Excuse me, ______________ ______________ where I sign in for the book club Get Together?
Yumi: Uh, yeah, right here actually. I'm running the group tonight. Can I take your name, please?

B WORK IT OUT Choose the correct options to complete the rules.

Question forms

Indirect questions

We use indirect questions when we want to be more polite. They usually start with phrases like *Could you tell me …?, Do you know …?* and *Would you mind …?* In indirect questions, we use the same word order as a statement (i.e. [1]***verb + subject / subject + verb***) and we don't use the auxiliary *do*.

Questions with prepositions

If a verb is followed by a preposition, the preposition comes at the [2]***beginning / end*** of the sentence.

Subject questions

When we ask about the subject of a sentence, we use the same word order as a statement, and the question word (e.g. *when, who, what, which*, etc) replaces the [3]***subject / object***.

Negative questions

When we ask negative *wh-* questions, we [4]***use / don't use*** the auxiliary verb, even in subject questions.

C Go to the **Grammar Hub** on **page 122**.

D PRACTICE Reorder the words to make questions.

1 would / most like to meet / which / you / famous person
____ ?

2 is / can / ask / your earliest memory / I / what
____ ?

3 think / you / is more important / diet or exercise / do
____ ?

4 English / you / why / are / studying
____ ?

5 your job / what / like about / you / don't
____ ?

E SPEAK Work in pairs. Discuss the questions in Exercise D.

PRONUNCIATION

Intonation in *yes/no* and *wh-* questions

A (1.3) Listen to the questions from the conversations. Draw arrows to show whether the intonation rises (↗) or falls (↘) at the end of each question.

1 Have you been playing long? ___
2 Where were you living before? ___
3 Who do you live with? ___
4 Have you had time to finish the book yet? ___

B (1.4) Circle the arrows to predict which intonation will be used in each question. Then listen and check.

1 Is there an application fee? [↗] / [↘]
2 What kind of event could we run? [↗] / [↘]
3 How often does the group meet? [↗] / [↘]
4 Do you need any special equipment? [↗] / [↘]
5 Is everyone happy with that? [↗] / [↘]

SPEAKING HUB

A PLAN Work in groups. Brainstorm a list of things you like doing or are interested in.

B PREPARE Choose one of your ideas from Exercise A to use as the focus of a new meet-up group. Write notes about:

- what you'll actually do at the meet-ups
- where / how often you'll meet
- what special events you might organize
- how much members will need to pay and why

C PRESENT Present your ideas to the class. Ask other groups follow-up questions to get more information.

D DISCUSS As a class, discuss which meet-up groups would work best in your area and why.

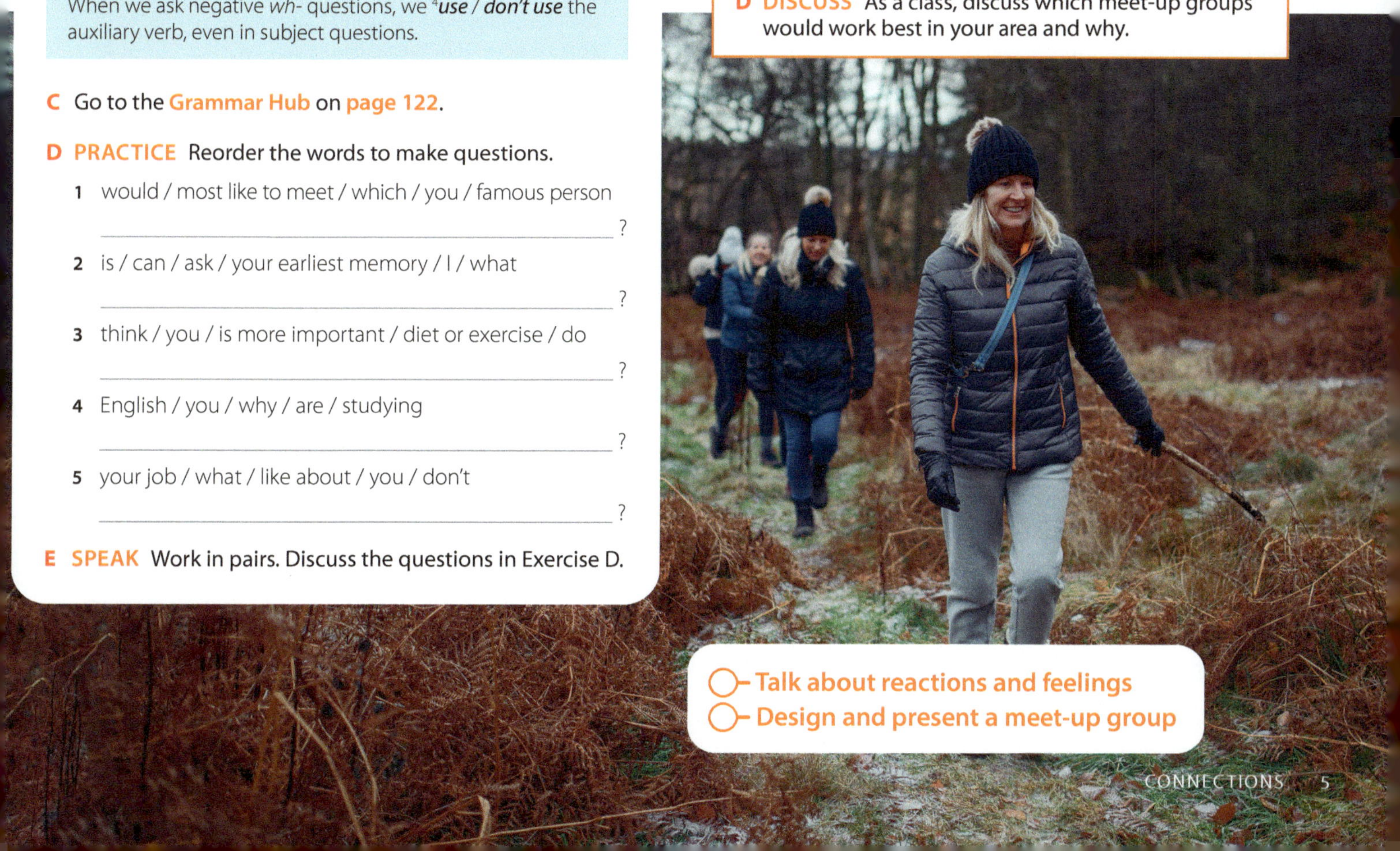

Talk about reactions and feelings
Design and present a meet-up group

1.2 Who we are

- Compare, contrast and summarize short biographies
- Talk about people that have influenced you

G – tense review
V – personality adjectives; noun suffixes
L – listening for the main ideas
P – connected speech: final consonant and initial vowel

READING

A SPEAK Work in groups. What do you know about the people in the article below?

B READ FOR GIST Read *The long road to success* and choose the sentence (1–3) that best describes the connection between the two people.

1 famous people that had difficult childhoods
2 famous people that overcame challenges to succeed
3 famous people that failed in college

C SCAN Scan the article again and check (✓) the person that each sentence is about.

Which person …	Stephen Hawking	Vera Wang
1 had an unusual childhood?		
2 didn't meet their academic potential?		
3 had a significant change in their career?		
4 was inspired to start a new business?		
5 lived much longer than people expected?		
6 is very rich and successful today?		

The long road to success

It's easy to think that the rich and famous have always lived a privileged life, but many have overcome great adversity to get to where they are today. When life presents us with challenges, how we react can determine how successful we become.

Stephen Hawking

What was his early life like?
Keeping bees in the basement of their crumbling St. Albans home, making fireworks in the greenhouse and driving around in a former London taxi, the Hawking family was certainly a little eccentric. In fact, they frequently ate dinner in silence [1]while each of them was reading a book.

Was he always a gifted academic?
At school, Hawking was thought of as bright but not brilliant. In his first year of high school, [2]he was the third worst student in the class. He also admitted to being a lazy student at Oxford University, only spending about an hour a day studying.

When did his condition develop?
Hawking first recognized something was wrong when he started to occasionally trip and fall while studying for a PhD at Cambridge University. At 21 years old, he was diagnosed with amyotrophic lateral sclerosis (ALS), and given just two years to live.

How did this affect him?
Hawking said that before he was diagnosed with ALS, he had been bored with life. Being told that he would not live to complete his PhD encouraged the young physicist to focus on his studies.

What made him famous?
Hawking is most famous for his research into black holes. By his early thirties, he had won many awards and went on to publish numerous papers and books, including *A brief history of time*. He was still proposing groundbreaking ideas about space and time until his death 50 years later.

Glossary

ALS (n) amyotrophic lateral sclerosis is a serious disease that affects nerve cells and causes muscles to become smaller and weaker

Vera Wang

Did she always want to work in fashion?
From the age of eight years old, Wang wanted to become a professional figure skater. After years of training and competing, she realized that no matter how hard she trained, she would never make the Olympic team. She gave up figure skating and moved to Paris to study Art History. It was there in the French capital that Wang realized she wanted to pursue a career in the fashion industry. After [3]she had completed her year in another country, Wang moved back to the US where she worked as a sales person at Yves Saint Laurent. It was at this point she met *Vogue* fashion director Frances Stein, who told Wang to give her a call when she graduated. A year and a half later she did, and spent the next 17 years working as an editor at the magazine.

How did she get into fashion design?
Wang left *Vogue* in 1982 and lived in Paris for several years before taking a position as design director at Ralph Lauren in New York. When planning her wedding in 1989, she was so disappointed by the lack of fashionable wedding dresses that she decided to design her own. A year later, she opened her own bridal shop, from which [4]she has built a fashion empire worth millions. [5]Today, she is worth over $600 million and is considered one of America's most successful self-made millionaires. Her clothes are worn by everyone from Michelle Obama to Kim Kardashian. She remains heavily involved in her company and is known for working long hours and holding frequent meetings to ensure she knows [6]exactly what's happening.

D READ FOR DETAIL Read again. Complete the sentences with no more than two words from the article.

1 Stephen Hawking was considered a ________ student at Cambridge University.
2 Before finding out about his illness, he only studied for ________ each day.
3 He was told he would live for just ________ more years.
4 He was given a lot of ________ for his early work.
5 Vera Wang gave up her dream of becoming a professional ________ after realizing she would never make the Olympic team.
6 She worked as a ________ before joining Vogue shortly after graduation.
7 She left Vogue in 1982, after ________ working as an editor.
8 Her personal fortune is thought to be more than ________.

E SPEAK Work in pairs. Can you think of anyone else that has overcome huge challenges in order to succeed?

GRAMMAR

Tense review

A Scan the article again. Match the highlighted sentences (1–6) to the tenses below.

___ simple present ___ past progressive
___ simple past ___ present progressive
___ past perfect ___ present perfect

B WORK IT OUT Complete the rules with the tenses in Exercise A.

Tense review

We use the [1] ________ to talk about past states or completed actions in the past.

We use the [2] ________ to talk about things happening now or around now.

We use the [3] ________ to talk about a state or action that started in the past and is still happening now.

We use the [4] ________ to talk about something that is generally true.

We use the [5] ________ to talk about an action in the past that was in progress when something else happened.

We use the [6] ________ to talk about a past action that occurred before another past action.

C Go to the Grammar Hub on page 122.

D PRACTICE Complete the text with the correct form of the verbs in parentheses.

Saroo Brierley

Saroo Brierley [1] ________ (*be*) born in Ganesh Talai, a suburb in Khandwa, India. His family was poor and regularly had to beg for food and money. When he was five, Saroo [2] ________ (*take*) a train with his older brother, Ghuddu, from Khandwa to the city of Burhanpur, where Ghuddu had a job cleaning trains at night. By the time they arrived, Saroo was so tired he fell asleep on the platform. Ghuddu told him to wait there but when he [3] ________ (*not return*), Saroo grew impatient and got on a train that [4] ________ (*wait*) at the platform. He fell asleep and when he woke up, he realized that he [5] ________ (*travel*) to Kolkata by mistake – 1,500 km away from home.

After living on the streets for three weeks, he was placed in a local orphanage. An Australian family adopted him and he [6] ________ (*spend*) the next 25 years living in Australia. Saroo wanted to find his family. Using his memories and Google Earth, Saroo eventually [7] ________ (*find*) his hometown in India.

Before his story was turned into an internationally successful book and movie, Saroo [8] ________ (*help*) his dad run a business. Now he [9] ________ (*work*) as a motivational speaker until he decides what to do next. Since living in Australia, Saroo [10] ________ (*have*) a happy life and always feels lucky.

E SPEAK Work in pairs. Discuss the questions.

1 What challenges do you have in your life right now?
2 What is the biggest challenge you have ever faced? How did you deal with it?

SPEAKING

A PREPARE Student A – Go to the Communication Hub on page 149. Student B – Go to the Communication Hub on page 152.

B SPEAK Tell your partner about the person you read about.

C DISCUSS Work in groups. Discuss the questions.

1 What are the similarities between the two people you read about?
2 Who do you think had bigger challenges to overcome? Why?

LISTENING

A SPEAK **Work in pairs. Tell your partner about your closest friends. How are they similar/different? Is it important to have different types of friends? Why/Why not?**

1.5 **B LISTEN FOR MAIN IDEAS** **Listen to an interview about friendship, personality and success. Put the following topics in the order they are discussed. Use the information in the box to help you.**

> **Listening for the main ideas**
>
> Talks, speeches and interviews usually contain multiple main ideas, based around one central theme. Speakers frequently introduce each new idea or point with phrases such as *the next is*, *another one is*, *the last is*, etc. Identifying these phrases can help you focus on the key information that follows.

___ a work colleague who makes you laugh
___ a complete opposite of you
___ a best friend you can rely on
___ a very honest friend who tells you the truth
___ a neighbor in your community
___ a friend who is not afraid

1.5 **C LISTEN FOR DETAIL** **Listen to the interview again. Choose the correct options (a, b or c) to complete the sentences.**

1. According to research, we can only maintain a friendship group of …
   - **a** several hundred people.
   - **b** no more than 50 people.
   - **c** no more than 20 people.
2. Open-minded adventurers are people who …
   - **a** are always making new friends.
   - **b** don't find new situations stressful.
   - **c** like habit and routine.
3. It's important to have a friend who …
   - **a** will constantly praise you.
   - **b** is very flexible.
   - **c** will be brutally honest with you.
4. Moving a lot affects our relationships with …
   - **a** our neighbors.
   - **b** our colleagues.
   - **c** our relatives.
5. Successful people …
   - **a** prioritize work over everything else.
   - **b** work longer hours than their colleagues.
   - **c** feel part of a group.

D SPEAK **Work in groups. Discuss the questions.**

1. What positive and negative effects does social media have on our relationships?
2. How well do you know your neighbors/colleagues/classmates? Do you consider any of them friends?

VOCABULARY

Personality adjectives

1.6 **A** **Complete the extracts with the personality adjectives in the box. Then listen and check.**

> arrogant down-to-earth easy-going loyal
> open-minded self-centered stubborn witty

1. We all need a ______________ best friend. Someone who will support us no matter what happens.
2. This person is an ______________ adventurer. They always force us into new and different situations.
3. They are ______________ and open to new ideas, cultures and activities. None of these things stress them out.
4. No, these people aren't ______________. They just have a lot of self-belief.
5. They'll tell you when you're being ______________ and should think about others more.
6. Or they'll tell you you are being ______________ and need to be more flexible.
7. She's very ______________. She just does everything in this very sensible, practical way. I guess she is a helpful person to have around!
8. Having no ______________ people to have a laugh with would make work very boring.

B Choose the correct adjectives to complete the sentences.

1 My neighbor is really ***easy-going*** / ***open-minded***. He's always willing to consider new ideas or opinions.

2 In a difficult situation, she stays calm. She's so ***loyal*** / ***down-to-earth*** and knows exactly what to do.

3 She never gets stressed. She's so ***easy-going*** / ***witty***.

4 I find her really ***arrogant*** / ***self-centered***. It's like she thinks she is better than everyone.

5 Even when I've done stupid things, she has always been ***loyal*** / ***down-to-earth*** and supported me.

6 There's no point arguing with him. He's just so ***stubborn*** / ***arrogant*** and won't change his mind.

7 I think she's really ***easy-going*** / ***witty*** actually. She's always making relevant jokes.

8 Stop being so ***self-centered*** / ***stubborn***. Try to think about other people for once!

C Go to the Vocabulary Hub on page 143.

D Complete the personality quiz.

What kind of person are you?

Rate yourself on a scale of 1–5.
1 = Strongly disagree 5 = Strongly agree

You find it easy to stay focused even when you are under pressure.	1 2 3 4 5
You usually start conversations.	1 2 3 4 5
You rarely do something just out of curiosity.	1 2 3 4 5
You feel more important than other people.	1 2 3 4 5
Getting what you want is more important than keeping others happy.	1 2 3 4 5
Making other people laugh is important to you.	1 2 3 4 5
You try to win arguments even when you might be wrong.	1 2 3 4 5
You don't believe in hiding your feelings to keep people happy.	1 2 3 4 5

E SPEAK Work in pairs. Describe your partner's personality using their answers to the quiz in Exercise D. Do you agree with their description of you?

PRONUNCIATION

Connected speech: final consonant and initial vowel

1.7 **A** Listen to the sentence and draw (‿) between any words that link together.

Most people spend at least 50 percent of their waking hours at work.

B Work in pairs. Look at the example in Exercise A and discuss the questions.

1 Does the first word end in a consonant or a vowel sound?

2 What sound does the next word begin with?

1.8 **C** Read the sentences. Draw (‿) to predict which words are connected. Then listen and check.

1 They are open-minded and friendly.

2 She achieved a lot despite having a difficult childhood.

3 He built a successful business at a young age.

4 We spent a lot of our time together going for walks in the country.

5 We hung out at the beach, went out at night and played games online together.

VOCABULARY

Noun suffixes

We use the following suffixes to change adjectives to nouns:
-ion (e.g. *ambitious* > *ambit**ion***)
-ity/-ty (e.g. *flexible* > *flexibil**ity***)
-ence (e.g. *different* > *differ**ence***)
-ness (e.g. *stubborn* > *stubborn**ness***)
-ism (e.g. *pessimistic* > *pessim**ism***)

Complete the sentences with the noun form of the adjectives in parentheses. Use the information in the box to help you.

1 I think what I value most in a friend is ________ ________ (*loyal*).

2 ________ (*optimistic*) is a great quality for a close friend to have.

3 Her ________ (*determined*) to succeed had a great influence on me.

4 Frankly, I was amazed by his ________ (*arrogant*).

5 She took ________ (*responsible*) for her actions.

6 He always gave me the ________ (*confident*) to try new things.

SPEAKING HUB

A PREPARE Make a list of people that have had a big influence on you (e.g. a teacher, your best friend, a grandparent, etc).

B PLAN Choose one of the people in Exercise A to tell your partner about. Use the following questions to write notes:

1 What was their personality like?

2 Why did they have such an influence on you?

3 What things did you do together?

C SPEAK Work in pairs. Use your notes from Exercise B to talk about the person you chose. Ask follow-up questions to find out more about them.

D DISCUSS As a class, discuss the types of people that influenced you. What personality traits do they share?

- Compare, contrast and summarize short biographies
- Talk about people that have influenced you

1.3 Keeping it in the family

A – idioms: family S – developing and introducing new topics

The Special Olympics

COMPREHENSION

A Work in pairs. Successful athletes are usually not the only person in their family to compete at the highest level. Why do you think this is?

B Watch a news report about a competitor at the Special Olympics. The report focuses on this person because …

1 he is competing at the highest level in his sport.
2 his great grandfather was also a successful athlete.
3 he is competing in multiple events.

C Watch again. Complete the sentences with no more than three words from the report.

1 Daniel Wolff won the ________________ event at the Special Olympics in 2015.
2 His great grandfather won a ________________ at the Berlin Olympics in 1936.
3 Daniel's grandfather describes his achievement as '________________'.
4 This year's Special Olympics has drawn crowds of ________________ people.
5 ________________ people in Daniel's family have come to watch him compete.

D Are these sentences true (T) or false (F)? Correct the false sentences. Then watch the report again to check.

1 Daniel's grandfather believes that sporting ability is genetic. *T / F*
2 Daniel was confident before the event that he would win. *T / F*
3 The reporter believes Daniel had a good level of support at the event. *T / F*
4 His father didn't think it was fair to leave his children at home. *T / F*
5 The 400 meters is the only event Daniel is taking part in. *T / F*

AUTHENTIC ENGLISH

A Work in pairs. Read the extract from the report. What do you think the expression in bold means?

Daniel Wolff crosses the line to win the 400 meters and shows that athletic success really can **run in the family**.

B Read the information in the box and check your answer to Exercise A. Why is this idiom appropriate for the report?

Idioms: family

Idioms are a group of words whose meaning is different from the meaning of the individual words. Since this can make them difficult to remember, one way to record new idioms is to group them by topic. Some common idioms in English are connected to the topic of family:

You have to choose your brother. Remember – ***blood is thicker than water!*** (= used to say that family relationships are always more important than any others)

Athletic ability ***runs in the family*** *– both he and his father played for their country.* (= if an ability, quality, disease, etc runs in the family, many family members have it)

C Read the sentences (1–3) and try to guess the meaning of the idioms in bold.

1 His grandfather was also a famous author – writing must **be in the blood**.
2 She **followed in her** mother's **footsteps** and trained to become a doctor.
3 He **is the spitting image of** his father at that age.

D Work in pairs. Discuss the questions.

1 Do you think any of your skills, abilities, etc are in your blood?
2 Have you followed in the footsteps of anyone in your family?
3 Have you ever been told you are the spitting image of someone?

Family matters

SAM MALCOLM AMANDA HARRY EMILY

A Work in pairs. What job do you have now or want to have in the future? What makes you particularly suitable for it?

B Watch the video. What runs in Harry's family? What runs in Sam's family?

SPEAKING SKILL

A Watch the video again and complete the extracts from the conversation.

Sam: And I must remember to get the paper towels for the toilets. [1] ______________________, did the hand soap arrive in the delivery?

Sam: I'm just so excited about getting this new café off the ground – I don't want to forget anything. Anyway, how are you getting on?

Sam: Oh really? You're not going to blame your upbringing are you?
Harry: [2] ______________________ because untidiness really does run in my family. I mean, you should have seen the state of our house when I was growing up!
Sam: [3] ______________________ things that run in the family, I actually saw this really heartwarming story on the news …

B Work in pairs. Discuss the questions. Then read the information in the box to check your answers.

1 What is the function of the phrases you wrote in Exercise A?
2 What is different about *anyway*?

Developing and introducing new topics

Developing topics

During a conversation, a speaker may say something that reminds us of relevant information or a related topic. To introduce our idea, we can use the following expressions:

Speaking/Talking of which …, Talking of [topic] …, Actually, that reminds me of …, Strange you should mention that (because) …

Introducing new topics

We use *anyway* to introduce a completely unrelated topic.

Anyway, I think we should …

C Work in pairs. Student A – Talk about one of the topics below. Student B – Listen and either develop or change the topic. Then swap roles.

- a movie that you saw recently
- a news item you read recently
- a restaurant you went to recently
- an interesting thing that happened to you recently
- a trip you went on recently
- an athletic event you saw recently

SPEAKING HUB

A PREPARE Work in pairs. Brainstorm a list of factors that affect our abilities and skills.

B PLAN Work in two groups. You are going to debate the following:

Practice has no effect on ability – we inherit our abilities from our parents.

Group A – You agree with the idea above.

Group B – You disagree with the idea above.

Plan your arguments. Think about how to support your position, as well as what the other group might say.

C SPEAK Hold your debate.

D REFLECT Which group put forth the more persuasive argument? Which side do you agree with?

Give your opinion on the role of inherited ability in success

➤ Turn to page 154 to learn how to write a formal letter asking for information.

Unit 1 Review

VOCABULARY

A Choose the correct options (a, b or c) to complete the sentences.

1 They were ___ to arrive at the airport just in time for their flight.
   a relieved   b devastated   c furious
2 I was completely ___ when we lost the World Cup final on penalties.
   a thrilled   b relieved   c devastated
3 Louis was ___ to find out his daughter had been offered a place at Yale University.
   a disgusted   b thrilled   c horrified
4 I'm pretty ___ by your lack of enthusiasm.
   a frustrated   b impressed   c relieved
5 Everyone sat in ___ silence as I broke the bad news.
   a relieved   b disgusted   c stunned

B Complete the sentences with the adjectives in the box.

easy-going   loyal   optimistic   sensitive   stubborn   witty

1 Why does he have to be so ______________ all the time? Not everything in life is good!
2 This girl I met at the party was so ______________. I was laughing all night!
3 I don't think I've ever seen him get stressed or upset. He's so ______________.
4 The team has a lot of ______________ fans. They're still buying tickets – even at $120 a game!
5 Stop being so ______________ and just admit that you're wrong!
6 How can we break the news to her? She's such a ______________ person.

C Complete the text with the correct form of the words in parentheses.

Perfectionism

Do you find it hard to live up to your own [1]______________ (*expect*)? Do you experience [2]______________ (*frustrate*) when you work with lazy people? If so, you might be a perfectionist. The positive thing about working with a perfectionist is their [3]______________ (*reliable*), [4]______________ (*dedicate*) and [5]______________ (*professional*). However, if you are a perfectionist, don't assume everyone will want to work with you because of these characteristics. Your constant criticism of other people can affect their [6]______________ (*confident*). Your [7]______________ (*stubborn*) and inability to admit you might be wrong are not attractive either. You probably won't be worried about that, though, because you're likely to be convinced of your own [8]______________ (*superior*).

GRAMMAR

A Choose the correct options to complete the sentences.

1 Could you tell me ***where is the reception desk / where the reception desk is***, please?
2 So why ***didn't you / you didn't*** like the movie?
3 Really? So, ***what was happening / what happened*** then?
4 Who ***Javier is meeting / is Javier meeting***?
5 Which candidate ***are you going to vote for / are you going to vote***?
6 Why ***you don't come / don't you come*** out this evening?
7 ***You haven't / Haven't you*** finished the homework yet?
8 Do you mind telling me ***how old you are / how old are you***?
9 Can I ask what you think ***you are doing / are you doing?***
10 Why ***you are so / are you so*** worried about it?

B Complete the conversations with the correct form of the words in parentheses.

1 **A:** ______________________ (*you / ever / be*) to Japan?
  B: Yes, I actually ______________________ (*teach*) English in Tokyo for three years after college.
2 **A:** ______________________ (*you / know*) Yara?
  B: Yes, I ______________________ (*know*) her since college.
3 **A:** Why ______________________ (*be / you*) at work today? I thought you had an important meeting.
  B: I ______________________ (have) a tough week, so I decided to take a day off.
4 **A:** What ______________________ (*you / do*) when you heard the news?
  B: I ______________________ (*just / put*) Mia to bed when my brother called.
5 **A:** ______________________ (*you / find*) a new job yet?
  B: Maybe. I actually ______________________ (*have*) an interview last week.
6 **A:** Where ______________________ (*you / go*) when you had the accident?
  B: I ______________________ (*drive*) to work.
7 **A:** Oh no! My yoga class ______________________ (*start*) in five minutes and I can't find my mat!
  B: Calm down. Try to think. Where ______________________ (*you / last / see*) it?
8 **A:** I kept getting lost when I ______________________ (go) to Berlin last week.
  B: It's difficult to learn your way around a place you ______________________ (*never / go*) to before.

2 LIFESTYLES

Plunge boldly into the thick of life, and seize it where you will, it is always interesting.

Johann Wolfgang von Goethe

Underwater view of a boy jumping into a swimming pool.

OBJECTIVES

- talk about health and lifestyle choices
- plan and conduct a lifestyle survey
- conduct an interview about lifestyle changes
- debate the impact of smartphones
- give your opinion on food choices
- write an article giving advice

Work with a partner. Discuss the questions.

1 Read the quote. What do you think Goethe means? Do you agree with him? Why/Why not?

2 Do you dive into the unknown or do you play it safe?

3 What is most important to you in life?

2.1 A full life

- Talk about health and lifestyle choices
- Plan and conduct a lifestyle survey

V – health and fitness
G – present perfect and present perfect progressive
L – listening for reasons
P – connected speech: present perfect progressive

VOCABULARY
Health and fitness

A SPEAK Work in pairs. Brainstorm a list of things that have positive or negative effects on our health.

B Complete the definitions (a–f) with the words in bold.

1 A lack of healthy lunch options has led to worrying levels of childhood **obesity**.
2 Drinking a lot of coffee can cause **anxiety** and negatively affect sleep.
3 Fatty foods like butter and cheese can increase levels of **cholesterol**.
4 She suffered from **depression** after losing her job.
5 There are around 500 **calories** in an average slice of chocolate cake.
6 My husband's been under a lot of **stress** at work recently.

a ______________ (n) a unit for measuring how much energy you get from food
b ______________ (n) a type of fat in the blood that can cause heart disease if you have too much
c ______________ (n) a condition in which someone is too fat in a way that is dangerous for their health
d ______________ (n) a medical condition in which a person is so unhappy they cannot live a normal life
e ______________ (n) pressure or worry caused by problems in everyday life
f ______________ (n) the feeling of being very worried that something bad is going to happen

C Complete the sentences with words from Exercise B.

1 I suffer a lot from ______________ in the winter. I'm much more positive in the summer months.
2 Keeping your diet low in fatty foods can help lower ______________.
3 Nuts have more ______________ in them than you might think.
4 ______________ is a huge problem in my country. Almost a quarter of the population is dangerously overweight.
5 ______________ is one of my biggest issues. I worry so much about everything.
6 I worry about my ______________ levels. I'm under too much pressure at work.

D Go to the **Vocabulary Hub** on **page 143**.

E SPEAK Work in pairs. What effects do the following have on our health?

- junk food
- smoking
- lack of exercise
- poor work–life balance

READING

A PREDICT Work in pairs. Look at the pictures (1–6) and the corresponding sub-headings in the article. Discuss how you think each of these things might help people to live longer.

B SCAN Read *Six ways to live longer* and check your predictions from Exercise A.

C READ FOR DETAIL Read the article again and answer the questions. Underline the parts of the text that give you the answers.

1 Why might owning a pet be good for your physical health?
2 What is different about the Japanese diet?
3 Why do people who think about details tend to live longer?
4 What charitable activity can help you live longer?
5 What does singing reduce?
6 What don't negative people pay attention to?

D SPEAK Work in pairs. Discuss the questions.

1 Why do you think owning a dog might reduce the risk of heart disease?
2 Why do you think 'smaller plates' have a positive effect on Japanese health?
3 Which of the suggested lifestyle changes in the text would you be happy to make? Why?
4 What other changes could you make to improve your overall health?

1

SIX WAYS TO LIVE LONGER

For the first time, people are expected to live a shorter life than their parents. Higher levels of obesity, a reliance on processed foods and more sedentary lifestyles are all taking their toll. If we want to live longer and healthier lives, there are many things we can do to slow the aging process and it doesn't just involve eating more healthily and going to the gym.

1 GET A PET

If exercise isn't your thing, then maybe you should consider getting a pet. Scientists in Sweden found that people who owned a dog had a much lower risk of various heart diseases and other illnesses. Dogs obviously need walking but having a pet is also good for many mental health issues such as lowering stress, fear and anxiety.

2 MOVE TO JAPAN

A dramatic solution would be to move to a new country. The Japanese lifestyle is arguably much healthier than in many other countries. First, they eat a lot less fat and lower their cholesterol by eating less dairy and swapping red meat for fish. They also make healthier food choices by eating seaweed, a lot of vegetables and by eating fewer **processed foods**. They use smaller plates and have a lower **calorie** intake than most other countries. Therefore, Japan has a very low obesity rate, with just under 4% of the population considered obese.

3 THINK OF THE DETAILS

People who think carefully about everything and pay a lot of attention to detail tend to live longer. Those who are careful with money, put everything in its right place and focus on details don't comfort eat as much as other people, and sleep better. People who carefully think things through deal better with stress and generally see the positives in most situations. They also have less risky lifestyles.

4 HELP OTHERS

In general, having strong social ties is a good predictor for living a longer and healthier life. People who take care of others are much more likely to make and keep friends throughout their life. Not only will you feel better if you help others but you will also live longer. A study in the US found that people who volunteer regularly in their lifetime live significantly longer than those who don't.

5 SING

People who regularly sing, especially in groups, tend to have a longer life expectancy. Researchers at Harvard and Yale universities in the US found that singing in a choir makes you happier and healthier than others. Singing can reduce stress levels and also helps to improve your immune system so that you are better able to fight illnesses.

6 DON'T COMPLAIN

Positive people live longer. If you're an optimist, then you are likely to live 12 years longer than a pessimist. Researchers at the US Mayo Clinic found that pessimists are more likely to get viral illnesses and they are much less likely to check their own physical health. Positive people also have a lower risk of suffering from heart disease and are better able to cope with stress.

SPEAKING

A DISCUSS Work in groups. Discuss the questions.

1. Why do you think so many people continue to do things that are widely known to be harmful to their health?
2. Do you think it is more important to focus on your physical or mental health? Why?
3. What can be done to reduce the risk of obesity, heart disease and other illnesses that are all associated with modern lifestyles?
4. What could be done to increase life expectancy in your country?

B PRESENT Present the main conclusions of your discussion to the rest of the class. Explain your reasoning.

LISTENING

A SPEAK Work in pairs. Look at the pictures (a–f) and discuss the questions.

1 Which of these things would you find difficult to give up? Why?

2 What are some of the potential benefits of giving these things up?

3 What other things do people typically try to give up?

4 Have you ever tried to give anything up? How successful were you?

B PREDICT People frequently decide to give things up at the start of a new year. How successful do you think they are? What percentage of people do you think break their New Year's resolution after:

a a month? b a year?

2.1 **C LISTEN FOR GIST** Listen to the first part of a radio show about lifestyle changes and check your predictions from Exercise B.

2.2 **D LISTEN FOR MAIN IDEAS** Listen to the next part of the radio show. Match the speakers (1–5) to the things that they have given up from Exercise A. There is one more option than you need.

Speaker 1 ______________

Speaker 2 ______________

Speaker 3 ______________

Speaker 4 ______________

Speaker 5 ______________

2.2 **E LISTEN FOR REASONS** Listen to the interviews again. What reason(s) does each speaker give for their lifestyle change? Write notes. Use the information in the box to help you.

Listening for reasons

In interviews, speakers are frequently asked to explain their reasons for a particular action or belief. Reasons are usually signaled with:

- **Fixed words and expressions** (e.g. *because (of), since, that's why, due to the fact that, in order to, etc*). ***Since*** *my family still lives in the area, we decided to move back there.*
- **Infinitives of purpose**
  I stopped eating red meat ***to help*** *reduce my blood pressure.*

However, speakers don't always explicitly state their reasons for something. Sometimes we need to guess the implied meaning from context:

I just remember reading a lot of articles about the impact smoking can have, not only on your health, but on the health of everyone around you. I quit last summer, and I feel much, much healthier.

(= We can guess from the context that the speaker stopped smoking because of the articles they read.)

GRAMMAR

Present perfect and present perfect progressive

A **Work in pairs. Read the extracts from the radio show and answer the questions.**

1 Which sentence describes a finished action? Which describes an unfinished action?

a Yeah, I've actually given up coffee.

b We've been spending more time together as a family.

2 Which sentence focuses on the present effect and which focuses on the action itself?

a I've managed to lose a little weight.

b We've been living without smartphones and tablets for six months now.

3 Which sentence is a temporary action and which is permanent?

a My car's in the garage right now, so I've been riding my bike to work for the past two weeks.

b Well, this is going to sound weird, but I stopped using shampoo.

4 Which sentence focuses on frequency? Which focuses on duration?

a I've only had three chocolate bars this month!

b I've been living without coffee for months now.

B WORK IT OUT Choose the correct options to complete the rules.

Present perfect and present perfect progressive

a finished vs unfinished
We use the present [1]*perfect / perfect progressive* for finished actions with a present effect, and the present [2]*perfect / perfect progressive* for unfinished actions.

b result vs action
We use the present [3]*perfect / perfect progressive* to emphasize the result of an action, and the present [4]*perfect / perfect progressive* to highlight the action itself.

c temporary vs permanent
We use the present [5]*perfect / perfect progressive* to suggest that something is permanent, and the present [6]*perfect / perfect progressive* to suggest something is temporary.

d frequency vs duration
We use the present [7]*perfect / perfect progressive* to say how much / many times something has happened, and the present [8]*perfect / perfect progressive* to say how long something has continued to happen for.

C Go to the **Grammar Hub** on **page 124**.

D PRACTICE Complete the sentences with the present perfect or present perfect progressive of the verbs in parentheses. If both are possible, use the present perfect progressive form.

1 I ____________________ (*stop*) working 12 hours a day.
2 She ____________________ (*try*) to spend less time on social media but she's finding it hard.
3 I ____________________ (*work*) at a restaurant to pay my college fees.
4 I ____________________ (*be*) to the gym five times this week.
5 I ____________________ (*exercise*) all morning. I can't wait for lunch.
6 I ____________________ (*give up*) junk food and now I feel great!

E SPEAK Work in pairs. Use the prompts to ask and answer questions in the present perfect or present perfect progressive.

1 How many times / you / check / social media today?
2 What / you / give up / in the last ten years? Why?
3 What / you / do / recently in order to be healthier?

PRONUNCIATION

Connected speech: present perfect progressive

2.3 **A** Listen to three extracts from the radio show. Is there a pause between the words in bold? Is the strong or weak form of *been* used?

1 **We've been spending** more time together as a family.
2 Absolutely! **I've been living** without coffee for months now.
3 **I've been riding my bike** to work for the past two weeks.

2.4 **B** Listen and complete the sentences.

1 ____________________ working really hard recently.
2 ____________________ using my phone too much lately.
3 ____________________ eating less junk food.
4 ____________________ spending more time together.
5 ____________________ going to the gym a lot lately.

2.4 **C** Listen again and repeat the sentences.

SPEAKING HUB

A PREPARE What have you been doing too much of recently? What have you not been doing enough of recently? Write notes about:

- use of technology
- exercise
- diet
- family

B PLAN Work in pairs. Write six questions you could ask other students about their habits. Use your notes from Exercise A to help you.

1 *What unhealthy foods have you been eating too much of?*
2 *How often have you seen your family this month?*

C SPEAK Ask other students in the class your questions. Try to give each other advice on changes you could make.

A: *How often have you seen your family this month?*
B: *I haven't seen them at all! I'm just so busy all the time.*
A: *Well maybe you could try calling them once a week? You don't need to talk for long, but it's important to stay in touch.*

- Talk about health and lifestyle choices
- Plan and conduct a lifestyle survey

2.2 Change

- Conduct an interview about lifestyle changes
- Debate the impact of smartphones

G – *used to, would, get used to, be used to*
S – identifying assumptions
P – catenation: *used to*
V – adverbs of stance; adverb + adjective collocations

LISTENING

A SPEAK Work in pairs. You're going to listen to an interview with a family that has moved from the city to a remote island. What do you think would be the advantages and disadvantages of such a move?

2.5 **B LISTEN FOR GIST** Listen to the interview. Which members of the family are happy with the move? Which aren't?

2.5 **C LISTEN FOR DETAIL** Listen to the interview again. Choose the correct options (a, b or c) to complete the sentences.

1 Frank made the decision to leave New York because …
  a he found his job too demanding.
  b he found his lifestyle uneventful.
  c he couldn't afford to live there.

2 Since moving to the island, the family …
  a largely eats food that is home-grown or caught.
  b has to spend a lot of money at the local store.
  c generally has a much better diet than before.

3 Frank says that the family's new lifestyle …
  a was surprisingly easy to adapt to.
  b is less physically demanding.
  c has tested them financially.

4 Katie cannot stream media on the island because …
  a the mountains affect her phone signal.
  b the internet connection is terrible.
  c the family cannot afford the internet.

5 Katie is homeschooled by her mother because …
  a there isn't a good school on the island.
  b she is planning to take US exams.
  c it gives her more time to gather food.

6 Frank thinks his son enjoys life on the island because …
  a there are lots of young children to play with.
  b he's allowed to play outside all day.
  c he hated growing up in New York.

D SPEAK Work in pairs. Imagine moving to a small island far away from where you live. What would you miss? What would you be happy to leave behind?

GRAMMAR

used to, would, get used to, be used to

A Work in pairs. Match the extracts from the interview (1–4) to their meaning (a–d).

1 I **used to work** long hours and it was stressful.
2 I'**m used to getting up** at 6 o'clock every day…
3 Financially, it has also been much harder but we'**re getting used to** it.
4 Back in New York **he'd complain** about his job constantly.

a This situation is still strange, but it's becoming more familiar.
b This habit was true in the past but isn't true now.
c This situation was true in the past but isn't true now.
d This was strange at first but is normal for me now.

B WORK IT OUT Complete the rules with the words in the box.

be used to	get used to	used to / didn't use to	would

used to, would, get used to, be used to

We use [1] ______________________ + base form to talk about finished habits and states: things that were true in the past but aren't true now.

We can also use [2] ______________________ + base form to talk about finished habits and routines, but not to talk about states.

We use [3] ______________________ to talk about something that was unfamiliar but is not unfamiliar now.

We use [4] ______________________ to talk about something that is still unfamiliar and not a current habit.

C Go to the **Grammar Hub** on **page 124**.

D PRACTICE Complete the sentences with *used to*, *would*, *be used to* or *get used to* and the verbs in parentheses.

1. I ______________ (*look*) very different when I was younger.
2. I ______________ (*not / like*) mornings but now I enjoy getting up early.
3. When I was a teenager, I ______________ (*eat*) a lot of junk food.
4. I ______________ (*work*) long hours now. I've done it for years.
5. I am ______________ (*cook*) for myself but I'm still not great at it.
6. When I was younger, I ______________ (*play*) video games for hours.
7. I ______________ (*not / drive*). I only passed my test recently.
8. I've decided to cut down on sugar. I ______________ (*eat*) less but it's a little boring!

E PRACTICE Rewrite the sentences in Exercise D so they are true for you.

F SPEAK Work in pairs. Discuss your sentences from Exercise E. Ask follow-up questions for more information.

PRONUNCIATION

Catenation: *used to*

A (2.6) Listen to these extracts from the interview. Do we pronounce the final /d/ in *used to*? Do we use the strong or weak form of *to*?

1. I used to dream of living a quieter and more peaceful life.
2. I'm getting used to being isolated from everyone.
3. I guess I'm not used to it yet.

B (2.7) Listen and repeat the sentences.

1. She used to have long hair.
2. Have you gotten used to living on your own?
3. I'm used to getting up early every day.
4. I actually used to drink a lot of coffee.
5. Don't worry, he's used to it by now.

SPEAKING

A PREPARE Think about how your life has changed in the last ten years. Make a list of positive changes in these areas:

- where you live
- family
- work
- education
- free time
- health

B PLAN Write notes about the three biggest changes in Exercise A. Use these questions to help you:

- What prompted the change?
- How has the change affected your life?
- Are you used to the change yet?

C SPEAK Work in groups. Take turns explaining your changes. Ask follow-up questions for more information.

READING

A SPEAK Work in groups. What are some of the positive and negative effects of social media?

B SCAN Read *The big debate* quickly. Which of your ideas from Exercise A are discussed?

C READ FOR GIST Read the article again. Choose the most appropriate debate question (1–4) for the article.

1 Should social media be banned?
2 Have relationships in society gotten worse?
3 Has social media made us less social?
4 Should we reconnect with the people around us?

THE BIG DEBATE

PETE LOMAS, PSYCHOLOGIST

Admittedly, the internet is pretty much the greatest invention of all time. However, I'd argue that social media is the worst invention to appear in this internet era. It seems to me that despite being 'in contact' with more and more people, we are in fact losing contact – meaningful contact – with most people in our lives.

[a]Beyond question, we're less comfortable in social settings than we once were. **Sadly**, we have all sat around a table where no one is really talking as they skim through their social media. Research by Ofcom has found that 51% of adults and 65% of teenagers have used their smartphone while socializing. **Frankly**, this is going to have a negative impact on our relationships. In fact, in some countries, groups of friends now have a rule – if you check your phone during dinner in a restaurant, then you have to pay for everyone. Are we really in a position where we need to fine people to get them to pay attention to us?

[b]Unfortunately, it's not just affecting how we interact but it is also making us feel worse, not better. **Naturally**, constant communication transforms how you feel, especially if you monitor emails, text messages and status updates. There is even an acronym for this phenomenon: FOMO – 'fear of missing out'. [c]As I see it, anything social should make us feel involved but social media is clearly making some people feel left out rather than part of something.

Social media should be renamed anti-social media. [d]In an already isolated world, social media is cutting us off from the world around us even further.

AMY DAY, APP DEVELOPER

From my perspective, social media has **undoubtedly** enhanced our relationships with others. It is true that not all of our online relationships are as close as our face-to-face connections but, on the other hand, it has allowed us to reconnect with lost friends, maintain connections and build new ones.

[e]From my point of view, modern life had already made us all fairly isolated individuals. We work long hours. We commute long distances. We move to cities where we know nobody, just for work. Our families all move around, not just in the country we live in, but also to different countries. I'm sure that social media has **simply** emerged from the pressures of modern life and our desire to connect with others despite these obstacles.

Apparently, we are giving up face-to-face relationships with people in favor of less personal social media ones. In all honesty, I don't think this could be further from the truth. According to research by Marketing Charts using data from Nielsen, in the space of five years, TV viewing by 18–24 year olds has fallen from 25 hours a week to **merely** 12. Those aged over 50 still watch over 40 hours a week and this figure isn't declining. Young people are clearly giving up anti-social activities in favor of other ways of interacting.

People who argue that social media has made us less interactive with the world around us clearly have the image in their mind of people on a train with their heads down looking at their phones. These people aren't choosing to be antisocial. [f]Far from it – they are choosing to interact with the people they deem important in their own lives.

D IDENTIFY ASSUMPTIONS Read the article again. Match the sentences in the text (a–f) with the assumptions (1–6). Use the information in the box to help you.

Identifying assumptions

Writers frequently make assumptions about what groups of people think or the opinions of others. These are signaled with phrases such as *As we all know …*, *Without a doubt …* and *Beyond question …*, which are used to try to convince the reader of a certain point of view.

The assumption can also be implied rather than stated directly. For example:

It seems to me that despite being 'in contact' with more and more people, we are in fact losing contact, meaningful contact, with most people in our lives.

(= assumes that online contact is not meaningful.)

1. Previous generations were all good at socializing. ___
2. Nobody that uses social media feels like they're part of a group. ___
3. Social media makes nobody feel positive. ___
4. The world was disconnected before social media. ___
5. Everyone on their phone is using social media. ___
6. Everyone in the modern world felt disconnected anyway. ___

E SPEAK Work in groups. Which of the assumptions in the text do you agree with? Which do you disagree with? Why?

VOCABULARY
Adverbs of stance

A Scan the article again. Complete the definitions with the adverbs in bold.

1. ________________ used to say that something is true even though it may weaken your argument
2. ________________ based only on what you have heard, not on what you are certain is true
3. ________________ used to emphasize that you are about to give your honest opinion, even though the person you are talking to might not like it
4. ________________ used to emphasize that something is small or unimportant
5. ________________ in the way that you would expect
6. ________________ used to say that something is certainly true or is accepted by everyone
7. ________________ used to show that you think something is bad or wrong
8. ________________ used to emphasize that you are saying something in a plain and straightforward way

B Choose the correct options to complete the sentences.

1. ***Naturally / Sadly***, all new developments come with both advantages and disadvantages.
2. ***Merely / Admittedly***, I see less of my friends in person now.
3. ***Frankly / Apparently***, we have a weaker sense of community than we used to, but I'm not sure I agree.
4. Social media is ***merely / apparently*** another method of communication.
5. ***Simply / Frankly***, I think social media enhances relationships.
6. The internet has ***undoubtedly / apparently*** enhanced many aspects of our lives. I don't think anyone could question that.
7. I think many people regret the breakdown of communities. ***Sadly / Naturally***, many communities are not as close as they once were.
8. It's very ***simply / merely*** the best solution to the problem.

VOCABULARY

Adverb + adjective collocations

Some adverbs and adjectives are commonly used together. For example, we say *strongly opposed* NOT ~~*deeply opposed*~~ or ~~*utterly opposed*~~. Learning these collocations will help make your language sound more natural.

Complete the sentences with the adverbs in the box.

absolutely bitterly deeply highly ridiculously

1. It is ________________ likely that more and more of our relationships will be conducted using phones.
2. It is ________________ ridiculous to say that smartphones have been negative for relationships.
3. I think society should be ________________ concerned about the negative impact of smartphones.
4. Smartphones make it ________________ easy to stay in touch with people.
5. I was ________________ disappointed when my friend started checking her phone during dinner.

SPEAKING HUB

A PLAN Work in pairs. How do you use technology to support your relationships?

B PREPARE Work in two groups. You are going to debate the following:

Smartphones have had a negative impact on our personal relationships.

Group A – You agree with the statement above.

Group B – You disagree with the statement above.

Plan your arguments. Think about how to support your position, as well as what the other group might say.

C SPEAK Hold a class debate.

- Conduct an interview about lifestyle changes
- Debate the impact of smartphones

2.3 Clean eating

A – adding emphasis S – backchanneling and lexical repetition

Ella's story

COMPREHENSION

A Work in groups. Look at the picture and discuss the questions.

1 You are going to watch a video about clean eating. What do you think this term means? Why?

2 Do you pay close attention to your diet? Why/Why not?

3 Who or what influences the food you eat?

Glossary

gluten (n) a natural, sticky substance found in some foods (e.g. wheat)
vegan (n) someone who doesn't eat anything made from animals or fish, including eggs, milk and cheese

B Watch the interview with Ella Mills and answer the questions.

1 Why is Dr. Yeo interviewing Ella Mills for the program?

2 What do all of Ella's recipes have in common?

3 What made Ella decide to change her diet?

4 What did Ella give up as part of her change in diet?

C Watch the interview again. Are these sentences true (T) or false (F)? Correct the false sentences.

1 Ella's first cookbook wasn't very successful when it was originally published. T / F

2 Ella decided to become a vegetarian more than ten years ago. T / F

3 Ella felt that her original medical treatment wasn't working effectively. T / F

4 Ella was initially doubtful that a change in diet could improve her condition. T / F

5 The fact that many others could identify with her experience encouraged Ella to continue sharing her story online. T / F

D Work in groups. Discuss the questions.

1 Because Dr. Yeo refers to 'Professor Google' in the video, what do you think his attitude is toward seeking medical advice online?

2 Do you think it's a good idea to search for medical advice online? Why/Why not?

AUTHENTIC ENGLISH

A Work in pairs. Read the extracts from the interview (1–4). Underline the words and phrases used to make the sentences more emphatic.

1 … and her debut cookbook was the fastest-selling ever in the UK.

2 I was the least vegetarian person you would have ever met in your life.

3 … and I came across lots of stories of people who'd used a change in diet and lifestyle to help manage all kinds of conditions, which I was, to be honest, incredibly skeptical of …

4 Her story of how she changed her diet to change her health has proved hugely influential.

B Read the information in the box and check your answers to Exercise A. How else can you make what you say more emphatic?

Adding emphasis

In informal spoken English, speakers frequently use superlatives, adverbs of degree, *ever/never* and expressions like *in your life* to exaggerate or make their sentences more emphatic. Doing so helps maintain the interest of the listener or highlight the importance of what's being said.

C Work in pairs. Take turns talking about the following topics. Use the techniques in Exercise B to make your descriptions more emphatic.

1 a terrible meal you once had

2 an amazing movie you've seen

3 a terrifying experience

The worst meal I've ever had was when I was on vacation in Thailand. I was with my …

You are what you eat

SAM MALCOLM AMANDA HARRY EMILY

A Work in pairs. Discuss what you had for breakfast and what you think your partner's choices say about them.

B Watch the video. What are the differences between Emily and Malcolm's attitudes toward food?

SPEAKING SKILL

A Watch the video again. Complete the box with examples from the conversation.

Backchanneling and lexical repetition

Backchanneling

Giving signals to show we are interested in what the other speaker is saying is called backchanneling.

To show interest, we say things like *I see* or just make noises like [1] ________, ________.

To show surprise, we say single words like [2] ________, ________, ________.

Lexical repetition

Another way to show we're engaged is lexical repetition. Sometimes this means using the same words as someone else. For example, when Emily first talks about clean eating, Malcolm starts his next turn by saying *clean eating* to show that he is following the topic. Another form of lexical repetition is to rephrase what has been said.

Emily: *For me, it's about eating mindfully – I mean, really thinking about what you're putting into your body and how your body uses the energy.*

Malcolm: *I see. So it's just about trying to eat* [3] ________________________________?

Emily: *Yeah, making sure your body is getting* [4] ________________________________.

B Work in pairs. Student A – Make a comment about one of the topics below. Student B – Rephrase your partner's comment to show you're engaged. Then swap roles.

- the weather today
- a type of food you like
- a movie you like
- a country you've been to
- a city you know
- what you are wearing
- a singer or band

A: It's nice and sunny today.
B: Oh, it's beautiful, isn't it?

SPEAKING HUB

A PREPARE Brainstorm a list of the advantages and disadvantages of becoming a vegan.

B PLAN Do you think you could become a vegan? Why/Why not? Use your ideas from Exercise A to write notes.

C DISCUSS Work in pairs. Discuss whether or not you would be prepared to become a vegan. Explain your reasoning.

A: I don't think I could ever be a vegan. I enjoy eating meat too much.
B: But what about the health benefits? A lot of people believe that vegans have a much longer, healthier life.

Give your opinion on food choices

➤ Turn to page 155 to learn how to write an article giving advice.

Unit 2 Review

VOCABULARY

A Match the causes (1–6) to their effects (a–f) to form full sentences.

1 High-**calorie** diets ...
2 Regular **physical** exercise ...
3 Strong friendship groups can **reduce the risk of** ...
4 A low-calorie diet may **slow the aging process** ...
5 Eating heavily **processed foods** may result in ...
6 Maintaining a good **level of fitness** could be positive ...

a can result in reduced levels of **stress**.
b **depression** occurring.
c a person's **cholesterol** levels rising.
d could lead to higher levels of **obesity**.
e for a person's **mental health**.
f and lead to a longer **life expectancy**.

B Replace the words in italics with adverbs from the box.

admittedly apparently frankly merely naturally sadly simply undoubtedly

1 I didn't say you had to do it, I *only* suggested you might want to.
2 Have you heard about Mark and Emily? *I'm not sure, but I was told* they're having a baby!
3 That's *just* not true! We sent them multiple emails asking for more time.
4 Tom didn't get the job. *As you'd expect*, he's pretty disappointed, but I'm sure he'll get over it.
5 *It's obvious that* stress has played a large part in her decision.
6 *To be honest*, I think you need to spend more time with your family.
7 *It's true that* I don't exercise enough.
8 *I'm disappointed that* we can't go on vacation this summer.

C Choose the best adverbs to complete the collocations.

1 I'm ***bitterly / deeply*** concerned about his mental health right now.
2 You should try the 'couch to 5K' running plan. It's ***highly / ridiculously*** easy.
3 This diet is ***absolutely / deeply*** terrible. I don't see how anyone can stick to it.
4 I was ***bitterly / absolutely*** disappointed when I heard I didn't get the job.
5 It's ***ridiculously / highly*** likely that she'll pass the exam and get into the university.
6 It was ***bitterly / deeply*** cold outside and I'd forgotten my winter coat.
7 Have you ever seen *The Shining*? It's ***highly / absolutely*** terrifying!
8 The actor admitted he was ***deeply / ridiculously*** ashamed of his behavior.

GRAMMAR

A Complete the conversations with the present perfect or present perfect progressive form of the verbs in the box.

decorate have live reply send travel

1 **A:** We must be almost there by now – we ______________ for hours!
B: Don't worry, not long to go!
2 **A:** Have you managed to get in touch with Andy yet?
B: No! I ______________ him half a dozen emails, but he still ______________.
3 **A:** Where are you staying right now?
B: I ______________ with my parents while I look for a new apartment.
4 **A:** What are you working on?
B: The same thing! I ______________ the same house for weeks now!
5 **A:** Do you want to go out for coffee?
B: No, I'd better not. I ______________ three already this morning.

B Complete the letter with *used to*, *would*, *be used to* or *get used to* and the correct form of the verbs in the box.

arrive be (x2) drive go know live run

Before the internet

In the past, if someone 'followed' you, then you [1]______________ quickly in the opposite direction. 'Going viral' [2]______________ a bad thing and 'trolls' were only toys and not unpleasant people. Arguments [3]______________ on for a long time because no one could quickly find the answer on their phone. People [4]______________ everyone's phone numbers by heart. If you wanted to meet your friends, they [5]______________ on time, otherwise it was impossible to find them later. Today, people [6]______________ without a map and never having to plan their trips. We all seem to have [7]______________ in a world where people speak to their devices as if they're human! I have to say that of all these changes – one thing I'll never [8]______________ is these devices spying on me!

Richard Solomon

Cleveland, Ohio

C Work in pairs. Discuss the questions.

1 What did you used to look like when you were younger?
2 What's something that you used to hate, but now love?
3 Do you think you're used to speaking in English yet?
4 What would someone have to get used to if they lived in your country?

3 SURVIVAL

> Courage is knowing what not to fear.
>
> Plato

Nearing the summit of the Totem Pole in Tasmania, Australia.

OBJECTIVES

- create a collaborative story
- tell a personal anecdote
- discuss priorities in a survival situation
- talk about fears and offer advice
- describe a trip or journey
- write a short story

Work with a partner. Discuss the questions.

1 Read the quote. What do you think Plato means?

2 Look at the picture. What would you be afraid of if you were alone in this place?

3 What skills and strengths do you have to survive a challenging situation?

3.1 Staying alive

- Create a collaborative story
- Tell a personal anecdote

S – following the sequence of a narrative
V – descriptive verbs
G – narrative tenses
P – dramatic storytelling techniques

READING

A SPEAK Work in pairs. Discuss how you might survive in the following situations.

1. Your plane crashes in the jungle and you're lost without a phone.
2. On a climb in the Alps, you trip and break your ankle.
3. Your boat sinks, but you manage to swim to a desert island.
4. While driving through the Sahara, your jeep breaks down, miles from any towns.
5. There's a fire in your office building and you're on the top floor.

B READ FOR GIST Read *Nigerian cook survives for three days in an underwater air bubble* and answer the questions. Write notes.

1. Who is the main focus of the story?
2. What happened to the Jascon-4?
3. How did the ship's cook survive for three days?
4. What happened to the other crew members?
5. How was the cook eventually rescued?

C FOLLOW THE SEQUENCE OF A NARRATIVE Read the article again. Put the events in the order they happened. Use the information in the box to help you.

Following the sequence of a narrative

Articles describing the sequence of past events don't always present the information in chronological order. To help you identify the order in which things happened, look for:

Time expressions

Writers use a combination of specific time expressions (e.g. *at 5 am, on May 26th*, etc) and phrases (e.g. *24 hours later, over the next three days*, etc) to highlight key points in the narrative.

Tenses

Identifying which tense has been used and why (e.g. past perfect to show that one action happened before another) will also help you to understand when events happened in relation to each other.

___ He woke up and went to the bathroom.
___ He found some equipment.
___ He gave the divers a huge shock.
___ He thought he heard sharks outside.
___ He stopped the water coming in.
___ The boat was turned over by a powerful wave.
___ He opened the door and went into the passageway.
___ He knocked on the wall with a hammer.
___ He spent two days recovering.

Nigerian cook SURVIVES for THREE DAYS in UNDERWATER AIR BUBBLE

Harrison Okene was trapped 30 meters below the surface in freezing waters.

Harrison Okene was a happy young man who was about to get married in a few days. At the time, he was working as a cook on a boat and before getting married, he had to go on one last trip. Unfortunately, it quickly turned into a nightmare.

The events started to unfold at 5:00 am on May 26th. The crew of the Jacson-4 had been sleeping while the boat was resting 20 miles off the Nigerian coast. While a violent storm was raging, Okene got up to go to the bathroom. As he was standing in the bathroom, a huge wave hit the boat. It turned over and plunged 30 meters below the surface, with Okene and the rest of the crew still inside. Water quickly began to fill the cabin, blocking the bathroom door as the boat sank into the ocean. Using all his strength, Okene forced open the door and headed out into the passageway. Wearing nothing but pajamas, he waded through the passageway in total darkness toward the only light he could see. Quickly he grabbed a drink and a few tools and made it to the light. Stuck in a small pocket of air, he blocked the sides with furniture to keep the water out. Unknown to Okene, all of his crewmates had already drowned. With hardly any air to breathe, time was running out. Hungry, cold and tired, Okene thought he could hear sharks circling the boat and started to lose hope. However, his luck was about to change.

When a rescue crew arrived, they assumed everyone had died since the boat had been resting on the seabed for 60 hours. Realizing the sounds he had heard were human, Okene started banging on the wall with a hammer. Thinking he wouldn't be discovered, he jumped into the water and began swimming through the ship. Seeing a rescue diver swim past him, Okene reached out to touch the man on the shoulder. Although initially terrified, the diver realized he'd found a survivor and called for support. Shortly afterward, Okene was strapped to diving equipment and taken back to the surface where he spent two days in a decompression chamber.

GRAMMAR

Narrative tenses

A Complete the sentences with the correct form of the verbs in parentheses. Then scan the article again to check your answers.

1. At the time, he ________________ (*work*) as a cook on a boat.
2. While a violent storm ________________ (*rage*) outside, Okene got up to go to the bathroom.
3. It ________________ (*turn*) over and plunged 30 meters below the surface, with Okene and the rest of the crew still inside.
4. Unknown to Okene, all of his shipmates ________________ (*already / drown*).
5. When a rescue crew arrived, they assumed everyone had died, as the boat ________________ (*rest*) on the seabed for 60 hours.

B WORK IT OUT Choose the correct tenses to complete the rules in the box.

Narrative tenses

We use the [1]***simple past / past perfect*** for completed actions that are the main events in a story.

We use the [2]***past progressive / simple past***:

- for actions in progress at a particular point in time.
- when a longer action is interrupted by a shorter action.
- to set the scene of a story.

We use the [3]***past perfect / past perfect progressive*** for completed actions that happened before the main event.

We use the [4]***past perfect / past perfect progressive*** for longer actions that started before other events and continued up to these events.

C Go to the **Grammar Hub** on **page 126**.

D PRACTICE Complete the text with the correct form of the verbs in parentheses.

NEWS SPORT CULTURE LIFESTYLE SEARCH

7-YEAR-OLD JAPANESE BOY SURVIVES FOR OVER A WEEK ALONE IN THE WOODS

FAMILY DAY OUT TURNS TO DISASTER

A family day out looking for wild vegetables quickly turned to disaster when a boy's parents decided to punish his bad behavior. Yamato Tanooka [1] ________________ (*throw*) stones at cars as he waited for his parents. Spotting his behavior, his father quickly [2] ________________ (*become*) very angry and [3] ________________ (*yell*) at him. To punish their son, Mr. and Mrs. Tanooka [4] ________________ (*leave*) him on the side of the road and [5] ________________ (*drive*) a few hundred meters away. By the time they [6] ________________ (*drive*) back to the spot, Yamato [7] ________________ (*already / leave*). His father [8] ________________ (*call*) the police and [9] ________________ (*say*) he [10] ________________ (*become*) separated from his son while they [11] ________________ (*pick*) wild vegetables. In the meantime, Yamato [12] ________________ (*walk*) off into the woods, upset that his father [13] ________ him ________ (*tell off*). When the army finally [14] ________________ (*find*) Yamato, he [15] ________________ (*live*) for six days on his own in woods that are home to brown bears. Yamato told reporters that he [16] ________________ (*walk*) for five hours through the woods when he found an old army cabin. Afraid of the dark, he decided to hide there and wait for his parents to find him.

E PRACTICE Work in groups. Write the first sentence of a dramatic story. Pass your sentence to the student on your right. Add another sentence to the story you have just received. Keep doing this until your story is complete.

SPEAKING

A PREPARE Go to the **Communication Hub** on **page 150**.

B PRESENT Choose one person to tell your story to the class. Listen to the other stories and ask questions about the details.

LISTENING

A Label the pictures (1–6) with the activities in the box.

bungee jumping free running free climbing
potholing skydiving whitewater rafting

B SPEAK Work in pairs. Discuss the questions.

1 Which of these sports do you think is the most dangerous? Why?

2 Why do you think some people enjoy doing dangerous sports like these?

3 Have you ever done any of these sports? Would you like to? Why/Why not?

3.1 **C LISTEN FOR GIST** Listen to a radio talk show about extreme sports and answer the questions. Write notes.

1 Which of the sports from Exercise A do the speakers talk about?

2 How many of the speakers have been injured while doing their sport?

3.1 **D LISTEN FOR DETAIL** Listen again and choose the correct options (a, b or c) to complete the sentences.

1 Paul started free climbing when he was …
   a 10 years old. b 17 years old. c 27 years old.

2 Paul thinks climbing without safety equipment …
   a is a terrible idea.
   b is a good challenge.
   c allows him to go higher.

3 Paul was most scared when …
   a he was caught in strong winds during a climb.
   b the bridge he was crossing on broke.
   c a snake shot out of a crack in a rock.

4 Hayley thinks that …
   a potholing is more challenging than rock climbing.
   b rock climbing is too challenging.
   c potholing is more like walking than climbing.

5 Hayley was lost underground for …
   a a few minutes. b a few hours. c a few days.

6 Lee started free running …
   a because his friends were doing it.
   b because he saw a video of people doing it.
   c because he wanted something more challenging than gymnastics.

7 Lee most enjoys …
   a the physical challenge of free running.
   b the way free running makes you look at a city.
   c the risks involved in free running.

8 Lee says that …
   a you should push yourself beyond your limits.
   b you need to be very competitive to be good at free running.
   c you should only do what you know you are capable of.

E SPEAK Work in groups. Discuss the questions.

1 Who do you think had the most frightening experience. Why?

2 Which of the sports would you like to try? Why?

1 ____________

2 ____________

4 ____________

3 ____________

VOCABULARY
Descriptive verbs

A **Work in pairs. For each extract, choose the option that makes the same sound as the verb in bold.**

1 I can still remember the snow **crunching** under our feet as we walked together.
   a old leaves under your feet
   b your feet in an empty hospital hallway
2 Sometimes the wood **groans** under your weight, which can be a little scary, but so far none have ever actually broken!
   a grass under your feet
   b floorboards under your feet
3 I am terrified of snakes, so I just froze as it started to **hiss** and arch backwards.
   a the wind closing a door
   b air slowly escaping from a tire
4 It can be silent for just a few minutes and all you can hear is water **trickling** around you.
   a a slow-running tap
   b a large, powerful river
5 I can still hear my ankle **snap** as I landed.
   a a branch breaking
   b a window breaking

B **Complete the sentences with the correct form of the verbs in Exercise A.**

1 The snake ________________ and slithered back into the undergrowth.
2 The leaves were ________________ under our feet as we crept slowly through the forest.
3 I could hear the branch of the tree ________________ under my weight before it ________________ and I fell to the ground.
4 Every time it rained, I could hear water ________________ down the wall behind my bed.

C Go to the **Vocabulary Hub** on **page 144**.

D **SPEAK Work in pairs. Use descriptive verbs to make this story more interesting.**

I was walking through the forest with fallen leaves under my feet. The trees were blowing in the wind. Suddenly, I heard a branch break behind me. I turned to see a huge dog running toward me.

5 ________________

PRONUNCIATION
Dramatic storytelling techniques

3.2 **A** **Listen to this extract from the talk show. Mark the pauses with (/) and underline any words that are emphasized.**

Well, a few years ago I was in South Africa with a few of my friends and we'd almost finished the first part of an all-day climb. I was just pulling myself up when I saw a huge snake right in front of me. I am terrified of snakes, so I just froze as it started to hiss and arch backwards. I waited for another few minutes, not moving, and then it just seemed to get bored and slithered back into a crack in the rock. It was the most terrifying moment ever and it had nothing to do with climbing!

3.2 **B** **Listen to the story again. When does the speaker speed up and slow down? Why do you think he does this?**

C **Read the story extract. Predict where you think the pauses will be, which words the speaker will stress and when they will speed up.**

So a few months ago I was staying at my parents' house when this strange thing happened. We were all enjoying the warmth of the crackling fire as the trees creaked in the wind outside. Suddenly, we heard glass smashing upstairs and something heavy banged on the floor. We rushed upstairs to find that a huge branch had crashed through the roof of the house.

3.3 **D** **Listen and check your answers to Exercise C. Then, practice telling the story with a partner.**

SPEAKING HUB

A **PLAN** **Think of the most amazing, terrifying or embarrassing moment in your life. Write notes about:**

- where you were
- who you were with
- what happened

B **PREPARE** **Work in pairs. Tell your stories and work together to make them more dramatic or exciting.**

C **PRESENT** **Work in small groups. Tell your stories as dramatically as you can. Ask questions to get more information.**

6 ________________

Create a collaborative story
Tell a personal anecdote

3.2 Fear and danger

- Discuss priorities in a survival situation
- Talk about fears and offer advice

G – alternatives to *if* in conditionals
S – listening for definitions, examples and explanations
P – intonation in conditional sentences
V – phrasal verbs to describe problems; dependent prepositions: adjectives

READING

A SPEAK Work in groups. Discuss what you would do in the following situations.

1 You're caught in some quicksand in the desert. As you're sinking you see a large stick nearby.

2 You're attacked by a swarm of killer bees in the woods. There's a house in the distance and a lake a few meters away.

3 You're doing parachute jump, but your parachute fails. If you stretch out, you could probably reach your friend.

B READ FOR GIST Complete the interview with the questions (a–d).

a Is that in your show this time?

b Can we expect any dangerous animals this year?

c Are you feeling excited about your new series starting next week?

d What can viewers expect from this series?

C READ FOR DETAIL Read again. Choose the correct options (a or b) to complete the sentences.

1 Chuck advises carrying a stick in the desert …

  a to move quicksand away from your body.

  b to stop yourself sinking into quicksand.

2 When you are in quicksand, Chuck suggests …

  a moving quickly to escape.

  b getting out carefully.

3 Chuck says that hitting killer bees …

  a is the first form of defence against them.

  b is likely to make the situation worse.

4 If you follow his advice, Chuck says you may break your arm when …

  a your friend's parachute opens.

  b your parachute opens.

D SPEAK Work in groups. Has anyone you know ever been in a life-threatening situation? How did they survive?

CHUCK ADAMS:

SURVIVE THE WILD

In the office of *Live, Play, Work Magazine*, we're all very excited to see the return to TV of Chuck Adams and his series *Survive the Wild*. Tom Wood caught up with Chuck to ask him about surviving in the desert, killer bees and why breaking your arm is sometimes the best thing to do …

Tom: **It's great to see you again, Chuck! 1___**

Chuck: I am. The first series was incredibly popular and we're taking viewers into some even more exciting situations in the new series.

Tom: **2___**

Chuck: Well, we look at how to survive dangerous situations in different locations. From mountains to deserts to the Arctic. For example, in the desert or along the coast, always carry a stick in case you need it. Quicksand is really dangerous! As soon as you start to sink, put the stick on the surface of the sand and lie on it. If you do this, it will stop you from sinking. Once you stop sinking, you need to crawl, climb and almost swim out. You'll be OK as long as you move slowly out of the sand. If you move too quickly, you'll sink.

Tom: **Sounds like hard work! Last series you looked at surviving crocodile attacks and shark attacks. 3___**

Chuck: Definitely! We have all sorts, including killer bees! People sometimes freeze when they see a bee, but this won't stop it from stinging you. And definitely don't try to hit them – this just makes them angrier. If bees fly around you, try to find shelter as quickly as possible. Provided you can get into a building, or shelter in long grass, you'll be fine. A lot of people jump into water to get away. Don't do this. The bees will just be waiting for you when you come up!

Tom: **That sounds horrible! What about surviving accidents? 4___**

Chuck: Of course! People usually do parachute jumps with other people. If your parachute doesn't open, grab the person near you, lock your arms together and hold onto each other. When your friend opens their parachute you will survive, but you will also probably break your arm – so be prepared for some pain!

Tom: **I feel a little sick at the thought of breaking my arm!**

Chuck: Maybe, but unless you lock arms, you won't survive!

Tom: Well we can't wait for the show to return next week! Thanks for speaking to us today.

GRAMMAR

Alternatives to *if* in conditionals

A Work in pairs. Read the extracts from the interview and choose the correct meaning.

1 … in the desert or along the coast, always carry a stick in case you need it.
   a Take a stick because you will definitely need it.
   b Take a stick because you might need it.
2 As soon as you start to sink, put the stick on the surface of the sand and lie on it.
   a When you start sinking, use the stick immediately.
   b When you start sinking, use the stick when you can.
3 You'll be OK as long as you move slowly out of the sand.
   a It's the only way to get out of the sand.
   b It's one way to get out of the sand.
4 Provided you can get into a building, or shelter in long grass, you'll be fine.
   a You will only be fine if you get into a building or shelter in long grass.
   b You will be fine whatever happens.
5 Maybe, but unless you lock arms, you won't survive!
   a Don't do this and you might survive.
   b Do this or you won't survive.

B WORK IT OUT Complete the rules with words and phrases in the box.

as long as | as soon as | in case | provided (that) | unless

Alternatives to *if* in conditionals

We use [1] ________________ to mean *if … not*.

We use [2] ________________ and [3] ________________ to mean *only if*.

We use [4] ________________ to talk about doing something now to prepare for a possible situation.

We use [5] ________________ to mean in the shortest time possible.

C Go to the **Grammar Hub** on **page 126**.

D SPEAK Work in pairs. Give advice about the following situations using conditional conjunctions.

1 You're in the middle of a field when a thunderstorm begins.
2 You're swimming in the ocean when you see a shark swim by.
3 You're lost in the country when your phone battery dies.
4 You're driving along when your car runs out of gas.

As long as you can walk to a gas station, you'll be able to buy gas.

PRONUNCIATION

Intonation in conditional sentences

3.4 **A** Listen to the conditional sentences. Draw arrows to mark rising (↗) or falling (↘) intonation.

1 Provided you don't run (__), the bull won't chase you (__).
2 Take a flashlight (__) in case it gets dark (__).
3 Unless you find a water source (__), you won't survive (__).

3.4 **B** Listen again and repeat the sentences.

SPEAKING

A PREPARE Read the scenario. Make a list of survival priorities.

> You are on a small plane that has crashed on a river in a jungle. You can swim to the side of the river, but you can only take a few things with you before the plane sinks. As far as you know, you're a long way from the nearest town and may have to spend a few nights in the jungle.

1 Make a shelter
2 …

B PLAN You have found the items below in the plane. Write notes on how you could use each item to help you achieve your priorities from Exercise A.

C DISCUSS Work in groups. Together you must decide on three survival priorities and how you will use the items from Exercise B.

A: I think we should use the rope to make a shelter.
B: That's fine by me, as long as we can save some of the rope for fishing.

LISTENING

A SPEAK Work in pairs. Look at the pictures and discuss the questions.

1 What fears are shown in the pictures?

2 Do you think these fears are rational (i.e. based on facts, not emotion) or irrational? Why?

3 What other common fears can you think of?

3.5 **B LISTEN FOR GIST** Listen to an extract from an audiobook about fear. Put the topics in the order they are discussed.

___ the influence of memory
___ potential dangers of the modern world
___ the physical effects of fear
___ how we assess a perceived threat
___ the brain's initial response

3.5 **C LISTEN FOR DEFINITIONS, EXAMPLES AND EXPLANATIONS** Listen to the extract again. Complete the notes below with no more than three words or a number. Use the information in the box to help you.

Listening for definitions, examples and explanations

Speakers usually use the following to make their ideas clearer:

Definitions

To explain topic-specific language, speakers usually provide definitions. These are usually clearly signaled by phrases such as *This is defined as …*, *This means …*, but can also be given mid-sentence (e.g. *Claustrophobia – a fear of being in a small or crowded place – is frequently …*).

Examples

To help clarify an idea, speakers use examples. These are signaled by phrases such as *For instance …*, *Such as …*, *An example of this is …*

Explanations

To make something easier to understand, speakers may also give explanations. These can be signaled by phrases such as *In other words …*, *That's to say …*, *Let me explain …*

Natural reactions

The amygdala is the section [1] ____________ *associated with our emotional responses.*

[2] ____________ *is the body's natural response to a perceived threat.*

The hippocampus and the prefrontal cortex help us to distinguish between a [3] ____________ *and a perceived threat. Our* [4] ____________ *influence this decision.*

We usually focus on dramatic or emotional events (e.g. although skin cancer causes over [5] ____________ *deaths a year, people worry more about plane crashes).*

Increased stress and anxiety can have a [6] ____________ *on our immune system > could lead to physical and mental health issues. Issue of the modern world?*

D SPEAK Work in pairs. Discuss the questions.

1 Do you think the 'fight or flight' response is useful in the modern world? Why/Why not?

2 Why do you think people frequently refuse to change their mind about something even when shown evidence against it?

3 What kinds of things do people fear now that they didn't fear 20 years ago?

VOCABULARY

Phrasal verbs to describe problems

A Match the phrasal verbs (1–7) to their definitions (a–g).

1 go through
2 sort out
3 put up with
4 talk over
5 deal with
6 work out
7 weigh out

a do what is necessary to solve a problem
b accept someone or something unpleasant in a patient way
c accept and control a difficult emotional situation so that you can start to live a normal life again despite it
d experience something difficult or unpleasant
e solve a problem by considering the facts
f discuss a problem or a plan
g consider the good and bad aspects of something in order to reach a decision about it

B Choose the correct verbs to complete the questions.

1 Do you think you are good at ***working out*** / ***dealing with*** how to solve problems?

2 Do you ***talk over*** / ***deal with*** your plans with the people around you?

3 What could you ***put up with*** / ***sort out*** more easily – a room full of spiders or snakes?

4 When was the last time you ***weighed out*** / ***put up with*** the risks and benefits before making a decision?

5 What scary situation have you recently had to ***go through*** / ***weigh out***? What happened?

6 How would you ***sort out*** / ***weigh out*** a situation where everyone was panicking?

7 In general, how well do you ***deal with*** / ***go through*** risky situations?

C SPEAK Work in pairs. Discuss the questions in Exercise B.

VOCABULARY

Dependent prepositions: adjectives

Dependent prepositions: adjectives

Some adjectives are usually followed by specific prepositions. These are called 'dependent prepositions' and they are followed by either a noun or *-ing*. For example:

My mother has always been terrified of spiders. NOT ~~*My mother has always been terrified about spiders.*~~

Choose the correct prepositions to complete the sentences.

1 I'm really anxious ***about*** / ***to*** speaking in public.

2 I feel a little ashamed ***of*** / ***for*** my fear of flying. I know it's not rational.

3 I'm sick ***about*** / ***of*** feeling this way – I really need to get some help.

4 I'm envious ***for*** / ***of*** people who can stay calm in dangerous situations.

5 They became suddenly aware ***of*** / ***from*** the danger around them.

6 I'm not really scared of anything, but I try to be sensitive ***toward*** / ***for*** people with a lot of phobias.

SPEAKING HUB

A PREPARE Read the scenarios (1–3). Write notes about what each person is afraid of and how it affects their life.

1 Emily Ronson is a 26-year-old graphic designer working in Seattle, Washington. She takes the subway to work every day but hates every minute of the 40-minute trip. Being in tight spaces with a lot of people makes her feel incredibly anxious. Sometimes, she feels so overwhelmed that she gets off the train and waits until it's less busy. Sometimes, this makes her late for work. She's ashamed of her fear so she hasn't told anyone about it.

2 Helen Masters is a retired police officer from Brazil. Several times over the past decade, she has had to cancel her vacation because she had a panic attack shortly after boarding the plane and demanded to get off. She knows this is an issue but has decided to live with it. Now she rarely travels out of the country and cannot see her grandchildren because they live in the UK.

3 Tom Hawksby is a 43-year-old accountant at a large computer software company in New York. Recently, the company hasn't been doing well and hundreds of people have lost their jobs. Tom is worried that he'll lose his job, too, and finds it difficult to sleep at night. This is making him tired and angry at work.

B DISCUSS Work in groups. Use your notes from Exercise A to discuss the questions.

1 Which of the fears do you think are irrational? Which are rational? Why?

2 How well do you think each person copes with their fear?

3 Do you think their fear is a big issue? Why/Why not?

4 What would you do in their position?

C PRESENT Choose one person from your group to present the main points of your discussion to the rest of the class.

- Discuss priorities in a survival situation
- Talk about fears and offer advice

Café Hub

3.3 Don't look down

A – shortened idioms S – backtracking

The great Tepui challenge

COMPREHENSION

A Work in groups. You are going to watch a video of people climbing Amaurai Tepui, a mountain in Venezuela. What do you think are the biggest challenges they will face?

B Watch the video. What makes the climbers think about giving up?

C Watch the video again. Are these sentences true (T) or false (F)? Correct the false sentences.

1. The team starts day five of the climb near the summit of the mountain. *T / F*
2. Presenter, Steve Backshall, hopes the improved weather indicates the end of the storm season. *T / F*
3. The team is attempting to become the first to climb this part of the mountain. *T / F*
4. One indication of the coming storm is the mass movement of birds. *T / F*
5. The team survives the storm by climbing back down the mountain. *T / F*
6. Steve thinks it would be a shame to give up having come so far. *T / F*

D Work in pairs. Read the extracts from the video. What do the words in bold refer to? Watch the video again to check your answers.

1. **It** would be nice after yesterday, wouldn't it?
2. There's a big storm coming and **they** know it.
3. **It** left us clinging to the cliff.
4. We've got to get off **this thing**; someone's going die.
5. … nothing is worth risking **this** for.

E Work in groups. Discuss the questions.

1. What do you think Steve means when he says, 'You could taste the fear'?
2. Would you like to take part in such an extreme challenge? Why/Why not?

AUTHENTIC ENGLISH

A Work in pairs. Read the extract from the video. What do you think *fingers crossed* means?

Steve: What do you reckon? Do you think our luck's changing?

Cameraman: Fingers crossed. It would be nice after yesterday, wouldn't it?

B *Fingers crossed* is actually part of a longer idiom. Which of the following do you think completes it?

a Have your … b Keep your … c Make your …

C Work in groups. Read the information in the box and guess the meaning of the shortened idioms in bold.

Shortened idioms

Some idioms are so common in informal spoken English that speakers don't need to say them in full for listeners to understand them.

*I've always been unhappy there but having my pay cut was **the last straw** [that broke the camel's back].*

*He called you a liar? Well, **if the shoe fits** [wear it].*

*I'm not surprised Max had a party while we were away. You know what they say – **when the cat's away** [the mice will play].*

*I was just thinking that, too. **Great minds** [think alike].*

D Work in pairs. Take turns reading the sentences and responding with an appropriate shortened idiom.

1. Why does my boss keep saying I'm lazy?
2. Nobody was doing any work when I got back.
3. Apparently we both bought him the same leaving gift.
4. Well, I worked pretty hard so hopefully I'll pass.
5. So, what made you fire her in the end?

SAM MALCOLM AMANDA HARRY EMILY

Snake Mountain

A Work in pairs. Why do you think people take part in extreme challenges (e.g. climbing mountains, sailing great distances, etc)?

B Watch the video. Write notes about Malcolm's story (e.g. where it happened, who he was with, etc).

C Work in pairs. Summarize Malcolm's story. Use your notes from Exercise B to help you.

SPEAKING SKILL

A Watch the video again and complete the extracts.

Sam: And I bet having all those snakes around doesn't make it any easier.
Malcolm: Eh? Snakes?
Sam: [1] ____________________, if it's called 'Snake Mountain', I assume there are a lot of snakes.

Malcolm: … we needed an adventure before we started trying to make our way in the world. Well, [2] ____________________, we were looking for an excuse to postpone looking for a job.

Malcolm: None of us knew what we were doing! Well, [3] ____________________, Peter was a pretty good climber, but the rest of us, well …

Malcolm: We couldn't see a thing. Well, [4] ____________________, but visibility was down to about a meter.

Malcolm: So we just carried on all the way to the summit. Though, [5] ____________________, I wasn't really thinking straight at the time!

B Work in pairs. What is the function of the phrases you wrote in Exercise A?

C Read the information in the box to check your answers to Exercise B.

Backtracking

Sometimes in conversation we need to correct a mistake in something we've said. This is called backtracking. To do this, we use phrases such as:

What I mean is … / What I meant was …, That is to say …, What I should say is … / What I should have said was …, That's not entirely true …, When I say … I really mean …

D Work in pairs. Student A – Talk about your trip to work or school today in great detail. When necessary, rephrase what you said to make your description clearer. Student B – Listen and ask questions, forcing Student A to backtrack. Then swap roles.

SPEAKING HUB

A **PREPARE** Brainstorm a list of interesting, dangerous or exciting trips or journeys you have been on.

B **PLAN** Choose a trip or journey from your list in Exercise A. Write notes about the following:

- Where were you and why?
- When did this happen?
- Who were you with?
- What were the key events?
- How did you feel before, during and after?

C **SPEAK** Work in groups. Take turns telling your stories. Listen and ask questions where appropriate. Reformulate and backtrack if you need to.

A: So I was all alone on the boat and I could see a storm coming. I kept saying to myself, 'Fingers crossed that I don't sink.'
B: Weren't you scared?
A: Well yeah, to be honest, I was terrified. But it was still an amazing moment.

D **REFLECT** Whose story was the most exciting? Was it the story itself or the way it was told that made it so exciting?

Describe a trip or journey

➤ Turn to page 156 to learn how to write a short story.

Unit 3 Review

VOCABULARY

A Choose the correct options (a, b or c) to complete sentences.

1 All I could hear was water _____ down the rock face.

a crunching b trickling c hissing

2 As he leaned forward, the branch _____, sending him falling toward the ground.

a snapped b rumbled c crunched

3 The old wooden bridge _____ under the weight of all of the cars.

a snapped b groaned c growled

4 Suddenly, a young child walked into the road. Slamming on the brakes, the car _____ to a halt.

a screeched b crunched c slammed

5 The gravel _____ under the car's tires as it slowly pulled away.

a hissed b snapped c crunched

6 In a rage, she stormed out of the room and _____ the door.

a smashed b creaked c slammed

B Complete the second sentence so it has a similar meaning to the first, using the words in bold.

1 It was a terrible experience for them to endure.
go through
They had to ________________________________.

2 Someone needs to organize the details of the party.
sort out
They need to ________________________________.

3 Try not to get so stressed at work.
stay calm
Try ________________________________.

4 I can't quit my job until I find a new one.
put up with
I'll have to ________________________________.

5 The management team is discussing the issues together before they make a decision.
talk over
Before making a decision, ________________________________.

6 The government must do something about the high level of unemployment.
deal with
The government ________________________________.

7 What's wrong with my computer?
work out
Can you ________________________________?

8 Let's look at the options and decide which one is best.
weigh out
To decide ________________________________.

C Complete the collocations with the adjectives in the box.

anxious	ashamed	aware	envious	sensitive	sick

1 You should be ______________ of your behavior! It's embarrassing!

2 I'm ______________ of having to clean up after you all the time.

3 I'm feeling a little ______________ about the job interview next week.

4 I think she's ______________ of your results – you're always at the top of the class.

5 Maybe you just need to be more ______________ toward other people's feelings.

6 You need to be more ______________ of how your actions affect the people around you.

GRAMMAR

A Choose the correct options to complete the sentences.

1 They ***left / were leaving*** the house and ***walked / were walking*** to the station.

2 I ***felt / was feeling*** pretty nervous until we ***scored / were scoring*** the second goal.

3 I ***hadn't taken / hadn't been taking*** my cell phone, so I ***had / was having*** no way of contacting them.

4 By the time I ***had gotten / got*** to the movie theater the movie ***started / had already started***.

5 ***I'd been waiting / I'd waited*** in line for 40 minutes before someone ***had served / served*** me.

6 I ***packed / was packing*** my suitcase when the phone ***rang / had rung***.

7 I ***was working / worked*** at my desk when a bird ***flew / was flying*** into the window.

8 He was exhausted because he ***had worked / had been working*** all night. He ***hadn't slept / hadn't been sleeping*** for 24 hours.

B Complete the sentences with *as long as, as soon as, in case, provided (that)* or *unless*. Sometimes more than one option is possible.

1 Call me ______________ you hear from him!

2 Don't disturb me ______________ it's really urgent.

3 You should bring a snack ______________ you get hungry.

4 ______________ you work hard, you'll get a pay raise this year.

5 I'm going to buy extra food ______________ more people come to the party.

6 ______________ you finish the swimming portion, you need to get right onto your bike.

7 I won't accept a contact request on LinkedIn ______________ I know them already.

8 It looks like we should get there on time ______________ the traffic isn't too bad.

4 THE FUTURE

The future belongs to those who believe in the beauty of dreams.

Eleanor Roosevelt

A father and daughter programming a VR simulator.

OBJECTIVES

- talk about future plans and goals
- make predictions about the future of work
- evaluate future predictions
- debate a range of transportation proposals
- give your opinion on automation in the workplace
- write a for and against blog post

Work with a partner. Discuss the questions.

1 Read the quote. What do you think Roosevelt means? Do you agree with her? Why/Why not?

2 What technological developments do you think will change the world in the future?

3 Are you generally optimistic or pessimistic about the future of the world? Why?

4.1 My future

- Talk about future plans and goals
- Make predictions about the future of work

G – future forms
S – identifying evidence
V – noun + preposition collocations; nouns and verbs with the same spelling
P – nouns and verbs with the same spelling

LISTENING

A Look at the pictures (a–e). Rank these life decisions from most to least important.

B SPEAK Work in pairs. Compare your ideas from Exercise A. Explain your reasoning. What do you agree about? What do you disagree about?

4.1 **C LISTEN FOR GIST** Listen to a podcast about turning points in people's lives. Match the speakers to the change they talk about.

1	Lucy	a	planning how to spend their retirement
2	Hadiyah	b	packing in preparation for a year of traveling
3	Frank	c	getting organized for a new arrival

4.1 **D LISTEN FOR DETAIL** Listen to the podcast again. Choose the correct option (a, b or c) to complete the sentences.

1 Lucy is planning to …
 a take a course in Spain
 b drive across Russia
 c work in the UK

2 Which country isn't Lucy going to?
 a Russia
 b China
 c Brazil

3 Hadiyah's husband …
 a thinks they are having a boy.
 b thinks they are having a girl.
 c is happy with a boy or a girl.

4 Who in Hadiyah's family are they thinking of naming the baby after?
 a one of the grandmothers
 b one of the aunts
 c one of her sisters

5 Frank has just bought …
 a a new car.
 b a new RV.
 c a fishing rod.

6 Frank is planning to …
 a go on a cruise.
 b retire in Florida.
 c take a road trip.

c where to live

4.1 **E LISTEN FOR KEY INFORMATION** Listen again. Use the table to write notes about each speaker

	Lucy	Hadiyah	Frank
What is each speaker excited about?			
What hasn't each speaker decided?			
What new skill does each speaker talk about?			

F IDENTIFY ASSUMPTIONS Work in groups. Read the extracts (1–2). Do you agree with the assumptions each speaker makes? Why/Why not?

1 Everyone there speaks some English, anyway.
2 Everyone wants to retire, don't they?

a whether to have a family

b what to wear

d what job to do

GRAMMAR

Future forms

.2 **A** Listen and complete the extracts with the correct future form of the verbs in parentheses.

1 I ______________________ (*fly*) to Paris because I have a friend there.

2 The classes ______________________ (*be*) three days a week from nine to four.

3 Then, I ______________________ (*visit*) as many countries as I can.

4 Parents are always really busy, so I ______________________ (*definitely / have*) to get better at managing my time.

5 Do you think you ______________________ (*miss*) work?

6 That's a good idea. I ______________________ (*add*) it to the list!

B WORK IT OUT Choose the correct tenses to complete the rules.

Future forms

We use the [1]***simple present / present progressive*** for definite future arrangements.

We use [2]***going to / will*** + base form to talk about general intentions.

We use [3] ***going to / will*** + base form for decisions made at the moment of speaking.

We use [4]***simple present / present progressive*** for timetabled events.

We use [5]***will + base form / present progressive*** for making predictions.

We use [6]***will / going to*** + base form for predictions based on something we know.

C Go to the **Grammar Hub** on **page 128**.

D PRACTICE Complete the sentences with the correct form of the verbs in the box.

break	come	fly	go	leave	miss	see	text

1 There's no milk left? OK, I ______________________ Bea and ask her to pick some up.

2 That chair doesn't look very strong – I think it ______________________!

3 We ______________________ with JetBlue on the way out, but haven't booked the return flight yet.

4 The next train to Cambridge ______________________ at 5:12 pm.

5 She probably ______________________ – she doesn't really like parties.

6 After college, I ______________________ traveling for a year. Not sure where though.

7 We're still miles away from the airport – we ______________________ our flight!

8 I ______________________ her on Friday, actually. We have a meeting at 2 pm.

VOCABULARY

Noun + preposition collocations

Noun + preposition collocations

Some nouns and prepositions are commonly used together. For example, we can say *the reason for* but not ~~*the reason of*~~.

Correct the prepositions in each sentence.

1 Congratulations for passing the exam!

2 I'm hoping to take a course for accounting.

3 I need to make more time of my family.

4 We're planning to visit a lot of places of Europe.

5 There's the possibility to changing jobs next summer.

6 I'm a little worried. There's the risk for not getting into college.

SPEAKING

A PREPARE You are going to interview your partner about their plans and goals for the future. Write questions about:

- home
- study
- work
- family
- travel
- achievements

1 What are you going to do after your course finishes?
2 Would you like to go traveling?

B SPEAK Interview your partner. Ask follow-up questions to find out more information.

A: When does your course finish?
B: At the end of July.
A: So, what are you going to do afterward?
B: Hmm ... I'm not sure. I'll probably try and find a job in a café or something.

READING

A SPEAK Work in groups. Which jobs do you think will be most affected by robots in the future? Why?

B SCAN Read *The future of work* quickly. Which of your ideas from Exercise A are mentioned?

THE FUTURE OF WORK

Few people would argue that society hasn't [1]**benefited** enormously from technological advancements. However, the future of many jobs may be hanging in the [2]**balance** due to the increased use of robotics in the workplace. According to Osbourne and Frey from Oxford University, almost 50% of jobs worldwide are at risk of being automated over the next 20 years. Taxi drivers could be replaced by driverless cars. In some warehouses, robots already move [3]**produce** around more efficiently than workers. Even the role of teachers could be dramatically affected as more and more of the learning process moves online. There's also a greater risk of change in certain countries where there are a high number of people employed in manufacturing. For example, the World Bank estimates that some countries risk up to 60% of jobs possibly being replaced by robots and automation, simply because technology is usually able to [4]**produce** more than human workers, with better accuracy and attention to detail. Yet many economists argue that despite the risks of increased automation, there are still many opportunities and [5]**benefits** ahead.

Although to many this may feel like a new problem, in reality it is a [6]**challenge** that has existed for years. Since the invention of the printing press, machines have continued to replace humans in the workplace. In fact, people have always worried about technology taking their jobs. During the Industrial Revolution in England, the Luddites – a group of clothes and textile makers – protested against new technology in factories by destroying machinery. They weren't against the technology, but they didn't like the [7]**control** and power it gave to factory owners to make working conditions worse. In the late 1950s, there were also widespread protests across the US in response to the [8]**influence** of automation on the shipping industry.

Although technological advances frequently [9]**challenge** society, overall levels of unemployment have never risen consistently. Periods of increased unemployment are usually temporary and associated with a recession. We don't run out of work – work simply changes and new jobs are created. People were once employed to open doors on trains and take people's tickets. Farmers, factory workers and elevator operators have all lost their jobs due to technological changes. People have simply moved on and found new types of employment.

Automation will no doubt [10]**influence** society greatly as it starts to [11]**control** more and more aspects of our lives. However, arguably, it won't change the total number of jobs in the economy. Studies into the impact of automation on employment focus only on which existing jobs could be replaced. They do not address the subject of which new jobs might be created. While planes and boats may not have a crew on board, they will still need to be operated by someone remotely. As more and more of life moves online, we may find we need fewer traditional police officers and that experts in preventing online crime will become increasingly important. Jobs that we cannot even imagine right now will become vital.

While many of our jobs are no doubt under threat, it is a dramatic exaggeration to present the idea that huge numbers of people will find themselves unemployed because of automation. Humans will always be vital in the workforce, just not necessarily in ways we are used to. Technology may even free up humans to work less and allow them more free time to [12]**balance** the pressures of work, family and other interests.

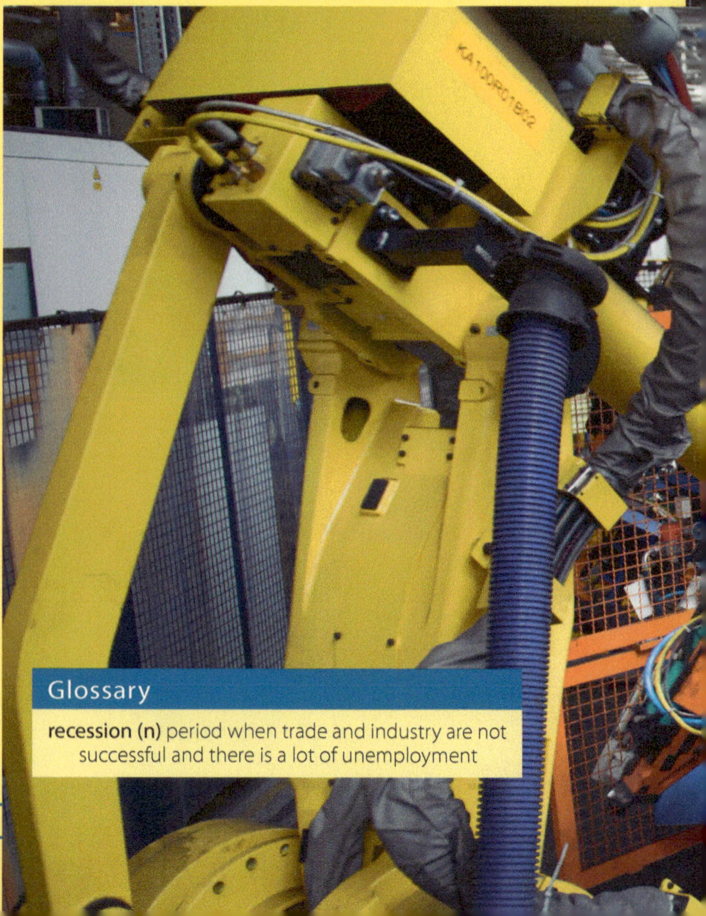

Glossary

recession (n) period when trade and industry are not successful and there is a lot of unemployment

C IDENTIFY EVIDENCE Read the article again. Underline the evidence used to support the arguments below. Use the information in the box to help you.

Identifying evidence

Good writers use evidence to support the argument or point they're trying to make. This can include references to specific studies, examples and statistics.

1 A large proportion of jobs are at risk from technological developments.
2 Some countries may suffer more than others due to automation.
3 Jobs have always been at risk from technological developments.
4 Many old jobs now no longer exist.
5 New jobs will be created that do not currently exist.

D SPEAK Work in pairs. Discuss the questions.

1 Do you think society needs to worry about automation affecting people's jobs? Why/Why not?
2 How might the increased use of robots and automation benefit society?
3 What skills do you think people need to develop to protect themselves from automation?

VOCABULARY

Nouns and verbs with the same spelling

A Scan the article again. Which of the words in bold (1–12) are nouns? Which are verbs?

B Complete the sentences with the correct form of the words in Exercise A.

1 One of the ________________ of robotics could be more free time for individuals.
2 We need to ________________ the convenience of automation with the need for employment.
3 We should constantly ________________ companies that get away with paying lower taxes.
4 There's no doubt that technology ________________ the way in which all industries work.
5 Some people think that automation gives companies more ________________ over workers.
6 Robots make it quicker and easier for companies ________________ their products.

PRONUNCIATION

Nouns and verbs with the same spelling

4.3 **A** Listen to the pairs of sentences. Are both forms of the words in bold pronounced the same way?

1 a The key **benefit** of increased automation is greater efficiency.
  b Technology should be used to **benefit** humans, not replace them.
2 a I think we'll all need to **upgrade** our skills.
  b This system is an **upgrade** to the previous one.

4.4 **B** Listen to the pairs of sentences. Underline the stressed syllable in each of the words in bold.

1 a An **increase** in automation will have a negative impact on jobs.
  b We need to **increase** the number of automated jobs in education.
2 a Robots are increasingly used to **produce** more and more products.
  b A lot of people are eating local **produce** to reduce their environmental impact.
3 a Many people would **reject** the idea of a machine being a doctor.
  b Products produced by machines usually lead to fewer **rejects** being made.

SPEAKING HUB

A PREPARE Would you be happy for a robot to do any of these jobs? Why/Why not? Write notes.

- a doctor
- a bus driver
- a waiter
- a sales clerk
- a teacher
- an accountant

B DISCUSS Work in groups. Discuss your ideas from Exercise A. Are there any other jobs that you think could or couldn't be automated?

C PRESENT Explain the main points of your discussion to the class. Which jobs do you think could be automated? Which couldn't? Why?

Talk about future plans and goals
Make predictions about the future of work

4.2 What will life be like?

- Evaluate future predictions
- Debate a range of transportation proposals

G – future perfect, future progressive and future perfect progressive
S – identifying agreement and disagreement   V – intensifiers   P – intonation with intensifiers

READING

A SPEAK Work in groups. Discuss which of the following will become common within the next decade.

- driverless cars
- virtual reality in the classroom
- space tourism
- 3D printing in the home

B PREDICT Work in pairs. Look at the subheadings in *When science fiction becomes science fact*. What predictions do you think each section will make about the future?

C READ FOR GIST Read the article quickly. Which of your ideas from Exercise B are mentioned?

D IDENITFY OPINION Read the article again. Write Y (Yes) if the statement agrees with the writer's opinion. Write N (No) if it contradicts the writer's opinion. Write NG (Not Given) if it is impossible to say what the writer thinks.

1 The author thinks pollution is the main threat to cities. ___
2 AI and robotics will dominate both our home and work lives. ___
3 Humans and robots will work side by side. ___
4 Social media will affect people's real-life status. ___
5 People will have little contact with each other. ___
6 We need laws to restrict the influence of social media. ___

WHEN SCIENCE FICTION BECOMES SCIENCE FACT

In 1989, the movie *Back to the Future 2* predicted that 26 years into the future, people would make video calls, use wearable technology and tablet computers, and play video games hands-free. While these predictions probably seemed pretty unrealistic at the time, all have come true in some form or another. Even the famous hoverboard could soon become a reality, as car giant Lexus has recently developed a working prototype. So, are predictions made in movies and TV always this accurate? Here we take a look at some of the key predictions made in science fiction over the past 30 years and assess which, if any, are likely to come true.

ENVIRONMENT

Many movies set in the future show changes to our environment. *Blade Runner* is set in the year 2049 and shows a dark future in which pollution levels in the city are shockingly high, and the sun is rarely seen. The natural environment has been almost completely destroyed and industrial cities dominate the landscape. While this movie focuses on the pollution and poor air quality in major cities, in reality the biggest environmental threat to cities is arguably rising sea levels. Recent estimates suggest that if we are unable to dramatically reduce the amount of carbon dioxide released into the atmosphere over the next few decades, [1]sea levels will have risen so much by 2050 that hundreds of millions of people will lose their homes. At present, the city most affected would be Shanghai. Projections show that the majority of the city will disappear under water if global temperatures increase by just three degrees.

TECHNOLOGY

Perhaps the most common types of predictions made in movies center around technology. According to Alex Proyas's movie *I, Robot*, by 2035 robots will have evolved to such a point that they will be able to carry out most human tasks.

[2]By 2035, we will have been living with computers for around 100 years, and while many predictions estimate that robots will be doing almost 50% of jobs worldwide within the next 20 years, a world like Proyas's is still a long way from reality. [3]It is much more likely robots will be working alongside humans, rather than replacing them.

E SPEAK Work in groups. Discuss the questions.

1 Which of the predictions in the article do you think will come true? Why?

2 What else do you think might happen in each of the categories over the next twenty years?

GRAMMAR

Future perfect, future progressive and future perfect progressive

A Scan the article again. Match the highlighted sentences (1–3) to the things they describe (a–c).

a an action or situation that will be finished before a specific time in the future ___

b an action or situation that will continue up to a specific time in the future ___

c an action or situation that will be in progress at a specific time in the future ___

COMMUNICATION

Movies are also full of predictions about the future of communication. The communicators in *Star Trek* are incredibly similar to modern cell phones, and the 1927 classic *Metropolis* showed video calls long before the creation of Skype. Our increased reliance on smartphones is taken a step further in the movie *Her*, where the main character has a relationship with a computer operating system that has a female voice.

If it's still popular in 2025, we will have been using Facebook for just over twenty years. The Netflix series *Black Mirror* shows a future where the 'like' feature of Facebook impacts on people's actual lives. The more likes someone gets, the higher their social status is in real life. As a result they can get better cars, houses and jobs. Although this is unlikely to happen, it does draw our attention to the worrying impact of social media on society.

B WORK IT OUT Scan the text again and complete the box with one more example of each tense.

Future perfect, future progressive and future perfect progressive

We use the **future perfect** to talk about something that will finish before a specific point of time in the future.

1 ______________________________

We use the **future progressive** to talk about an action or situation that will be in progress at a specific time in the future.

2 ______________________________

We use the **future perfect progressive** to talk about an action or situation that will continue up to a specific time in the future.

3 ______________________________

C Go to the **Grammar Hub** on **page 128**.

D PRACTICE Complete the predictions with the future perfect, future progressive or future perfect progressive form of the verbs in parentheses.

1 I ______________________ (*change*) jobs by the end of the year.

2 I ______________________ (*live*) in the same place in thirty years.

3 I ______________________ (*visit*) five new countries by the end of the decade.

4 By the end of the month, I ______________________ (*buy*) a new phone.

5 By the end of the decade, I ______________________ (*work*) for the same company for over twenty years.

6 In five years, I ______________________ (*still / study*) English.

E SPEAK Work in pairs. Which predictions in Exercise D do you think will become true for you? Why?

SPEAKING

A PREPARE Read the following predictions from different science fiction movies. Which do you think will become true? Write notes.

Police will be able to predict the future, preventing serious crimes before they happen. *Minority Report* (2002)

You will be able to pay to have your memory of a relationship that went wrong permanently erased. *Eternal Sunshine of a Spotless Mind* (2004)

Humans will learn how to communicate with aliens. *Arrival* (2016)

The Earth will be so damaged that humans will look for a new planet to call home. *Interstellar* (2014)

The rich will control cities from high-rise towers, while the poor will work machines underground. *Metropolis* (1927).

B SPEAK Work in pairs. Compare your ideas from Exercise A. Explain your reasoning.

1

2

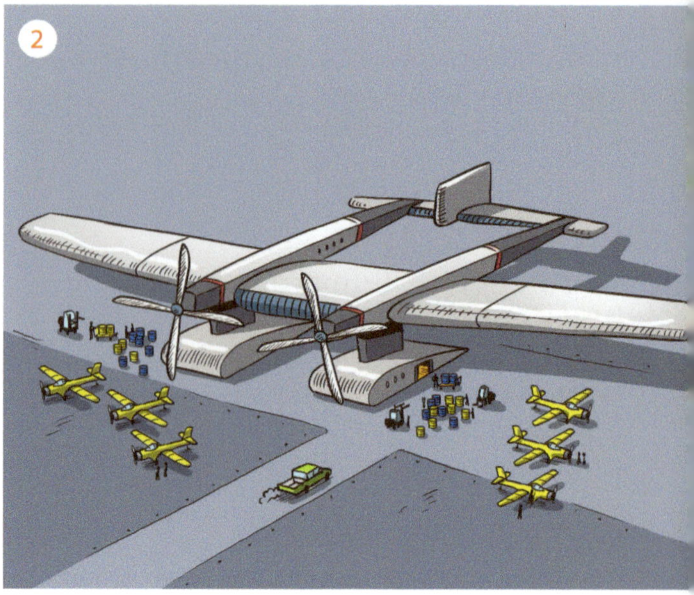

LISTENING

A SPEAK **Work in pairs. Look at the pictures (1–3) and discuss the questions.**

1 Which of the predictions about future transportation came true?

2 Which didn't come true and why do you think they failed?

3 How do you think transportation will change over the next ten years?

4.5 **B LISTEN FOR GIST** **Listen to a public debate about the future of transportation. Put the modes of transportation in the order they are discussed.**

___ hypersonic jets ___ driverless cars

___ hyperloop trains ___ flying bikes

4.5 **C IDENTIFY AGREEMENT AND DISAGREEMENT** **Listen again. Who makes the following points – Mark or Sarah? To what extent to they agree with each other? Use the information in the box to help you.**

Identifying agreement and disagreement

When arguing about a topic, speakers use expressions such as *I completely agree*, *I can't see …*, *Yes, but …*, etc to signal agreement or disagreement. These are typically followed by reasons and examples to counter or support the original point.

Speakers also highlight agreement or disagreement by responding with a single adverb (e.g. *Seriously?*, *Definitely!*, etc).

1 Driverless cars will soon become a common sight on our roads.

2 Driverless cars have better reactions than human drivers.

3 Hyperloops are safer than existing train systems.

4 Hyperloop train systems are unlikely to get the funding they need.

5 We're unlikely to develop flying cars within the next two decades.

6 There may be a market for space tourism in the future.

D SPEAK **Work in pairs. Read the driverless car scenario Sarah describes in the discussion. What do you think the car should do? Explain your reasoning.**

How can a car make a decision about what to do in a dangerous situation? Should it protect the driver at all costs? What if doing so might mean injuring somebody else? What does it do then? I just think it would be incredibly dangerous to have driverless cars on the road.

VOCABULARY

Intensifiers

A **Read the extracts from the discussion. Complete the definitions below with the words in bold.**

1 The way we get around is going to be **entirely** transformed.

2 I **firmly** believe there is no chance driverless cars will become popular.

3 It's **undoubtedly** true that driverless cars will have more consistent and quicker reactions than most drivers.

4 But it would **greatly** improve our lives!

5 Hyperloop train systems are **widely** expected to happen.

6 … **especially** things that save significant time, like the Hyperloop train…

7 … it will become **significantly** cheaper over time.

8 You seem **incredibly** focused on speed!

a ________________ completely, or in every way

b ________________ in a way that is relevant or that has an important effect on something

c ________________ used for saying that something is certainly true or is accepted by everyone

d ________________ very much

e ________________ extremely

f ________________ by a lot of people, or in a lot of places

g ________________ strongly

h ________________ used when mentioning conditions that make something more relevant, important or true

B Choose the correct intensifiers to complete the sentences.

1 Many of these inventions seem ***undoubtedly / incredibly*** unlikely to happen.
2 It's ***entirely / greatly*** possible that all cars will be driverless in the future.
3 There are ***significantly / firmly*** more passengers using the system than it was designed for originally.
4 Travel times would be ***greatly / entirely*** improved.
5 You are ***undoubtedly / especially*** right.
6 I ***firmly / widely*** believe that safety is more important than convenience.
7 That is ***especially / widely*** true when it comes to a company making a profit.
8 It is ***significantly / widely*** believed that commercial flights will eventually be powered by solar energy.

C Go to the Vocabulary Hub on page 145.

D SPEAK Work in pairs. Use intensifiers to give your opinions on the topics below.

- the likelihood of space tourism
- police traveling by hover bikes
- the widespread use of hyperloop trains

Space tourism in our lifetime seems incredibly unlikely.

PRONUNCIATION

Intonation with intensifiers

4.6 **A** Listen to the extract from the debate. What intonation does the speaker use on the intensifiers: rising (↗), falling (↘) or rise-fall (↗↘)? What effect does this have?

They're undoubtedly cheaper than building a normal high-speed train and travel times will be greatly reduced.

4.7 **B** Listen and repeat the sentences.

1 The city is incredibly congested!
2 The idea is entirely unrealistic. It will never happen.
3 Considering the environmental impact has become increasingly important.
4 Travel times will be greatly reduced.

SPEAKING HUB

A PLAN Read the information cards and write notes about the advantages and disadvantages of each form of transportation.

CITY TRAIN

Completion:	2030
Design:	Spacious and modern. Built-in wi-fi. First-class meeting tables
Cost:	$5 billion
Ticket cost:	$10 day ticket
Speed:	Much faster than road vehicles. Delays less likely

ECO BUS

Completion:	2022
Design:	Eco-friendly using renewable energy
Cost:	$300 million
Ticket cost:	$3 day ticket
Speed:	Faster than cars because it uses a designated bus lane. Delays possible

TROLLEY SYSTEM

Completion:	2025
Design:	A simple subway train. Many roads will need to be redesigned to fit trolleys
Cost:	$2 billion
Ticket cost:	$5 day ticket
Speed:	Relatively slow-moving. Delays possible

B PREPARE Work in three groups. You are going to propose a new transportation system for your city. Group A – City Train, Group B – Eco Bus, Group C – Trolley System. Prepare you arguments.

C DISCUSS Debate the best method as a class. Remember to question the weaknesses in the other methods.

- Evaluate future predictions
- Debate a range of transportation proposals

Flippy the robot

COMPREHENSION

A Work in pairs. You are going to watch a news report about a burger-flipping robot. What do you think the advantages and disadvantages of this kind of technology are?

B Watch the report. Which of your ideas from Exercise A are mentioned?

C Watch again. Complete the sentences with no more than three words from the report.

1 A combination of image recognition and ______________ ______________ tells Flippy which burgers need turning over.
2 The introduction of Flippy may lead to ______________ ______________ in the future.
3 CaliBurger will spend an estimated ______________ ______________ a year on maintenance.
4 Human employees frequently find the working conditions difficult and many leave after ______________ ______________.
5 Flippy isn't fully autonomous yet and regularly ______________ ______________ that a human employee wouldn't.
6 David Zito, the CEO of Miso Robotics, is confident that Flippy ______________ with time.
7 The presenter believes it won't be long before Flippy can both ______________ and serve customers.
8 Roboticists predict that new ______________ ______________ will emerge to replace those lost.

D Work in groups. Do you agree with the following predictions made in the report? Why/Why not?

1 It won't be long before the majority of unskilled jobs are automated.
2 In the future, it will be odd to go to a restaurant that isn't almost fully automated.

AUTHENTIC ENGLISH

A Read the extract from the report. Why do you think the speaker says *right*?

It's not a very fun job, **right**? Er, it's hot, it's greasy, it's dirty, erm, it hurts your wrist, **right**?

B Read the information in the box and check your answers to Exercise A.

> *right*
>
> In informal spoken English, speakers frequently use *right* in place of a question tag to check information or to ask if someone agrees with them.
>
> *You have tomorrow off,* ***right?***
> (= You have tomorrow off, don't you?)
>
> *You know where you're going,* ***right?***
> (= You know where you're going, don't you?)

C Read the extract in Exercise A again. Which regular question tags could be used instead of *right*?

D Work in pairs. Take turns using prompts (1–6) to make sentences with *right*.

1 You want to check that the movie starts at 9 pm.
2 You think your friend has met Yuki before.
3 You're not sure if a friend can speak Japanese.
4 You think a colleague is going to Seville next week.
5 You think a friend finishes early on Fridays.
6 You want to check if your friend knows how to get to the station.

So, the movie starts at 9 pm, right?

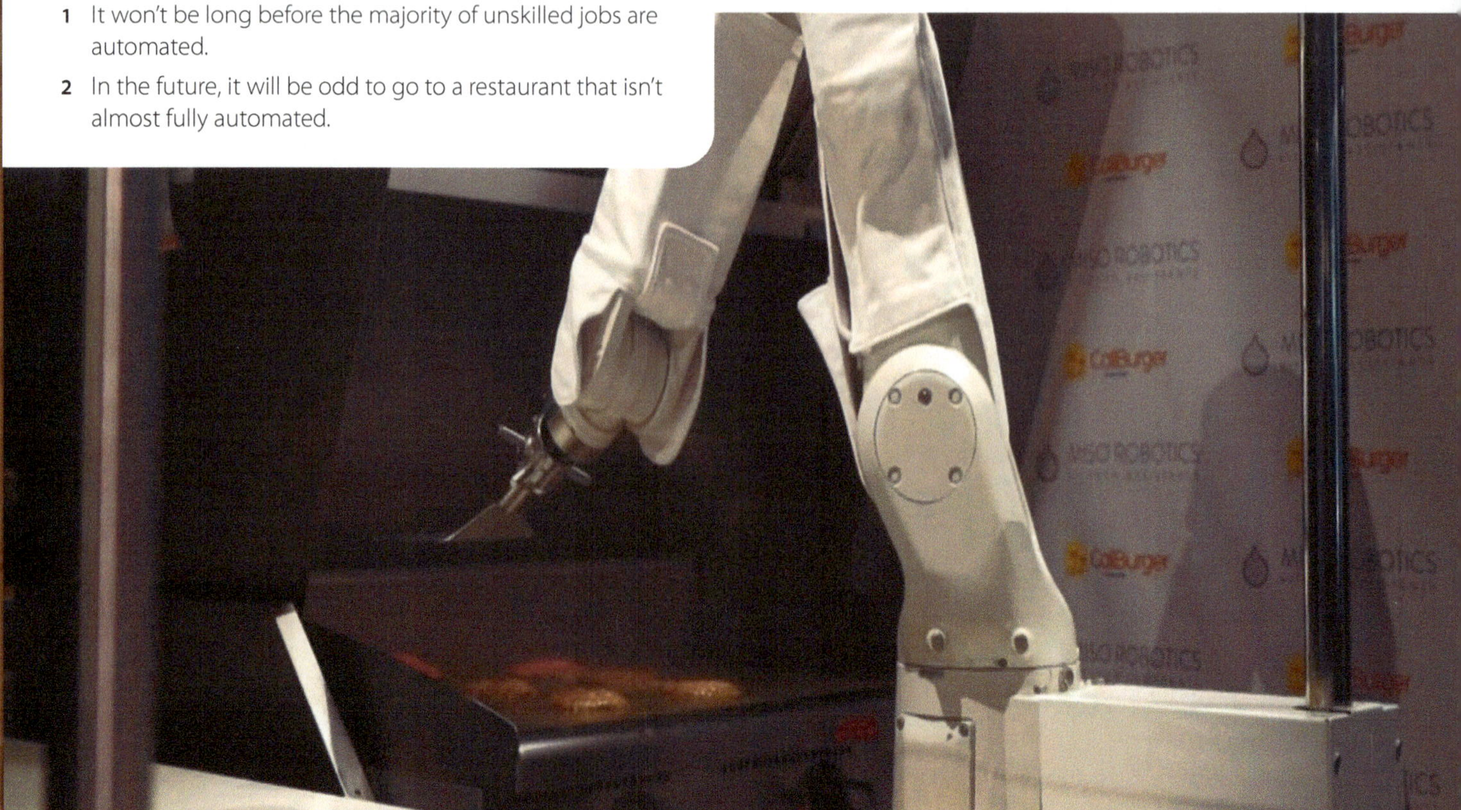

The perfect coffee

A Work in pairs. What's your favorite café? Why do you like it so much?

B Watch the video. Choose the best summary (1–3) of what Sam thinks customers want from an independent café.

1. They want to be served quickly and efficiently.
2. They want to make use of the latest technology.
3. They want to feel like a valued part of a community.

SPEAKING SKILL

A Watch the video again. Complete the box with examples from the conversation.

Asking for clarification

In conversation, we frequently need to check that we have understood something correctly. A common way to do this is to use a signaling phrase followed by an explanation of what we think the speaker meant.

Sam: I want the people who come to our café to feel that it is their space. So I often allow local clubs to hold meetings here or we host events like book signings or talks.

***Amanda: So you mean that** the café can be a hub for the local community?*

We use a number of other phrases for asking for clarification, some of which are more formal than others:

More formal

1 ____________________

2 ____________________

Less formal

3 ____________________

4 ____________________

B Work in pairs. Tell your partner about your job or a job you would like to have. Listen to your partner and ask for clarification of what they tell you. Then swap roles.

Talk about:

- what skills and knowledge you need
- who you work with
- what you like/dislike about the job
- what your responsibilities are
- what equipment you use

SPEAKING HUB

A PREPARE Work in pairs. You are going to conduct an interview about increased automation in the restaurant industry.

Student A – You are a journalist. Choose which questions to ask from the list below and add some of your own.

Student B – You are the interviewee. Write notes about your responses to the questions below.

- How might the industry benefit from increased automation?
- Which jobs do you think are most at risk from this trend?
- How do you think the public would react?

B SPEAK Conduct the interview. Ask each other for clarification if you need to.

Correct me if I'm wrong, but you seem to be saying that you'd be happy for robots to help prepare, but not serve your food. Is that right?

C DISCUSS As a class, discuss whether increased automation in the workplace is mainly positive or negative.

Give your opinion on automation in the workplace

➤ Turn to page 157 to learn how to write a for and against blog post.

Unit 4 Review

VOCABULARY

A Choose the correct prepositions to complete the sentences.

1. I want to take a course *in / on / for* accounting next year.
2. There's a risk *with / of / for* the company going out of business before the end of the year.
3. Do you have any knowledge *of / in / on* spreadsheets?
4. Congratulations *about / for / on* the birth of your new baby daughter!
5. There are a lot of historic places of interest *at / in / on* the northern part of the country.
6. Is there any possibility *for / of / about* getting a refund?

B Complete the sentences with words from the box.

balance	benefit	challenge
control	influence	produce

1. We are being expected ______________ far more than is humanly possible!
2. I'm so exhausted all the time. I think I just need a better work–life ______________.
3. Always ______________ yourself to try something new is extremely important.
4. The trend toward digital ______________ the new direction of the company.
5. If this deal goes through, XKOM ______________ 65% of the market.
6. One of the ______________ of exercise is that it lowers your stress levels.

C Choose the correct options (a, b or c) to complete the sentences.

1. He usually exaggerates so I'm not ___ sure I believe him.
   a entirely b firmly c widely
2. They've ___ improved the new model.
   a entirely b incredibly c significantly
3. ___, everyone survived the plane crash.
   a Undoubtedly b Incredibly c Widely
4. The price of tickets may vary ___ between distributors.
   a firmly b greatly c especially
5. I ___ believe that closing the company was the right decision to make.
   a firmly b widely c significantly
6. New England is usually pretty cold, ___ in the winter.
   a greatly b incredibly c especially
7. The population will ___ continue to rise as more people move there for work.
   a incredibly b undoubtedly c firmly
8. It is ___ believed that AI will place many jobs at risk.
   a widely b especially c entirely

GRAMMAR

A Complete the article with *will*, *going to* or the present progressive form of the verbs in parentheses. Sometimes more than one answer is possible.

Four changes to make to your life

At the start of every year, we all make promises to change certain aspects of our life. 'I [1] ______________ (*exercise*) more and 'I [2] ______________ (*eat*) more healthily' we say. But we typically fail to keep our promises. So what simple changes can we make that will make a big difference and be easy to achieve?

1. Get up and go to sleep at the same time. You [3] ______________ (*feel*) a lot more refreshed.
2. Be punctual. It reduces stress. If you start arriving early for things, you [4] ______________ (*find*) that life starts to feel less frantic.
3. Routine is good, but you should also be spontaneous occasionally. When a friend says, 'I [5] ______________ (*go*) the beach this weekend, do you want to come?' Say, 'Great! I [6] ______________ (*come*).'
4. Try to be optimistic. For example, if your company is struggling, don't think 'I [7] ______________ (*lose*) my job.' Be positive and think about the new good job you might get.

Make these simple changes in your life and I am sure you [8] ______________ (*be*) happier in the long run.

B Choose the correct options to complete the sentences.

1. Can we meet later? I *'ll be watching / 'll have watched* the World Cup final then.
2. At the end of this month, I *'ll be working / 'll have been working* at this company for 20 years!
3. Just think – this time next week, we *'ll be lying / 'll have been lying* on a beach in Hawaii.
4. I can't believe she's changing jobs again. She *'ll have had / 'll be having* three different jobs this year!
5. I *won't be finishing / won't have finished* this work by the deadline. I just don't have enough time.
6. *Will you be going / Will you have gone* to Sarah's party on Saturday?
7. In three years, I *'ll have completed / 'll be completing* college and I'll be starting to look for work.
8. This is ridiculous! In ten minutes time I *'ll have been waiting / 'll be waiting* for almost two hours!

5 CHANGE

> I cannot say whether things will get better if we change; what I can say is that they must change if they are to get better.
>
> Georg C. Lichtenberg

A traditional roof against a modern skyscraper in Seoul, South Korea.

OBJECTIVES

- summarize a sequence of past events
- evaluate a range of proposals
- talk about changes in your town or city
- evaluate candidates and put together a team
- discuss ways to help the environment
- write a problem solution article

Work with a partner. Discuss the questions.

1 Read the quote. What do you think Lichtenberg means? Do you agree with him? Why/Why not?

2 What are the biggest changes in the world that have happened in your lifetime?

3 What is the most positive change you have ever made?

5.1 Changing environment

- Summarize a sequence of past events
- Evaluate a range of proposals

S – identifying cause and effect
G – the passive voice; causative *have* and *get*
V – green vocabulary
P – glottal stops

READING

A SPEAK Work in pairs. Look at the food chain diagram and discuss the questions.

1 What does the diagram show?
2 In this diagram, the wolf is the top predator. What do you think that means?
3 What would happen if you removed the wolf from this food chain? Why?

B SCAN Read *How wolves change rivers* quickly and check your answers to Exercise A.

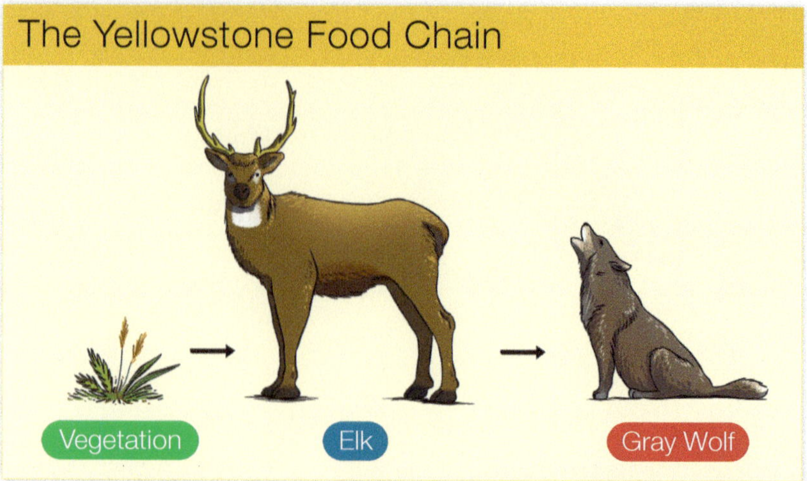

HOW WOLVES CHANGE RIVERS

Wolves are top predators and their beneficial effects on entire ecosystems are gradually being understood.

Wolves are crucial for maintaining a healthy ecosystem – a fact that many people overlooked when they were being hunted and killed in vast numbers across the United States at the start of the 20th century.

Meanwhile, the populations of other animals exploded. The entire ecosystem of the American countryside changed as a result of rapidly expanding populations of elk.

After years of political discussion, conservation biologists finally got their way and the gray wolf, *Canis lupus*, was reintroduced to several areas in the northern Rocky Mountains of the United States. One of those areas was Yellowstone National Park.

Although researchers only reintroduced a total of 41 wolves to the park, their beneficial influences soon became clear, and continue to be seen to this day. Since wolves are top predators that mainly hunt sick or aging elk, their reintroduction had two main effects. First, it slowed the expansion of the elk population, which had exploded without natural predators. Second, it actually improved the overall health of the elk population since only the strongest and fittest survived.

The presence of wolves even changed elk behaviors. For example, they stopped eating in valleys where they could easily be attacked by wolves. Because of this, native plants were able to regrow, increasing biodiversity by providing food and shelter to a growing variety of plants and animals.

Amazingly, the presence of wolves also changed many rivers in the park. After the reintroduction of the wolves, researchers noticed that riverbanks became stronger, the rivers became deeper and small pools formed. Why? Again, the plants that had been eaten by the elk had time to recover, strengthening the riverbanks and in turn, changing the geography of the park itself.

Basically, humans conducted a huge real-life experiment by removing and then reintroducing a top predator from a large area of land. Initially, the changes caused by the lack of wolves were too small to be noticed. But the results of their reintroduction clearly indicate that wolves are essential to restoring and maintaining the ecosystem of the entire region.

This type of relationship is known as a 'trophic cascade'. In Yellowstone National Park, researchers observed the effect when the removal of the top predator started a chain of effects that affected the entire web of life. Similar effects have been identified throughout the natural world, from the Amazon rainforest to the eastern Pacific Ocean.

As more species are reintroduced around the world, no doubt more will be learned about the impact each has not just on ecosystems, but also on the surrounding landscapes.

Glossary

biodiversity (n) the variety of different types of plant and animal life in a particular region
ecosystem (n) all the living things in an area and how they affect each other and the environment
predator (n) an animal that kills and eats other animals

C IDENTIFY CAUSE AND EFFECT Read the article again. Are the sentences true (T) or false (F)? Correct the false sentences. Use the information in the box to help you.

Identifying cause and effect

Texts frequently indicate a cause and effect relationship between different events. These relationships are usually signaled by fixed phrases such as *cause, bring about, lead to, as a result of, the main consequence was*, etc.

1. Wolves started to die out because there were not enough elk to eat. *T / F*
2. Growing elk numbers affected all the other plants and animals. *T / F*
3. Reintroducing wolves meant elk populations grew. *T / F*
4. Reintroducing wolves made elk populations healthier. *T / F*
5. A wider range of plants started to grow again as wolf numbers grew. *T / F*
6. The regrowth of plants meant that rivers became deeper. *T / F*

D SPEAK Work in groups. What animals are in danger of extinction in your country? What is being done about it?

GRAMMAR

The passive voice

A Scan the article again and underline ten examples of the passive voice. The first has been underlined for you.

B SPEAK Work in pairs. Discuss the questions.

1. What tenses are the examples in Exercise A?
2. Which include a modal verb?
3. Which are in the infinitive form?

C WORK IT OUT Choose the correct options to complete the rules.

The passive voice

We form the passive voice with *be* + [1]***simple past / past participle***.

The passive voice can be formed with [2]***all / some*** tenses – only the form of *be* changes.

We use the passive voice when:

- we [3]***know / don't know*** who or what caused an action
- it's [4]***important / not important*** who or what caused an action
- we want to focus on the person or thing that [5]***did the action / received the action***.

D PRACTICE Complete the sentences with the correct form of the verbs in parentheses.

1. As the population continues to grow, more and more land ________________ (*use*) for farming.
2. Very few fossil fuels ________________ (*burn*) before the Industrial Revolution.
3. Thousands of trees ________________ (*cut down*) every year before the government changed the law.
4. The future of humans ________________ (*could / threaten*) by further increases in temperature.
5. Many species ________________ (*affect*) by climate change over the decade.
6. Plastic bags ________________ (*ban*) recently in many countries.
7. Global temperatures ________________ (*rise*) for over a century.
8. Some people feel that the use of packaging needs ________________ (*control*).

E Go to the Grammar Hub on page 130.

SPEAKING

A PREPARE Go to the Communication Hub on page 151.

B DISCUSS Work in pairs. What are the main predators in your country? What other animals would be affected if they became extinct?

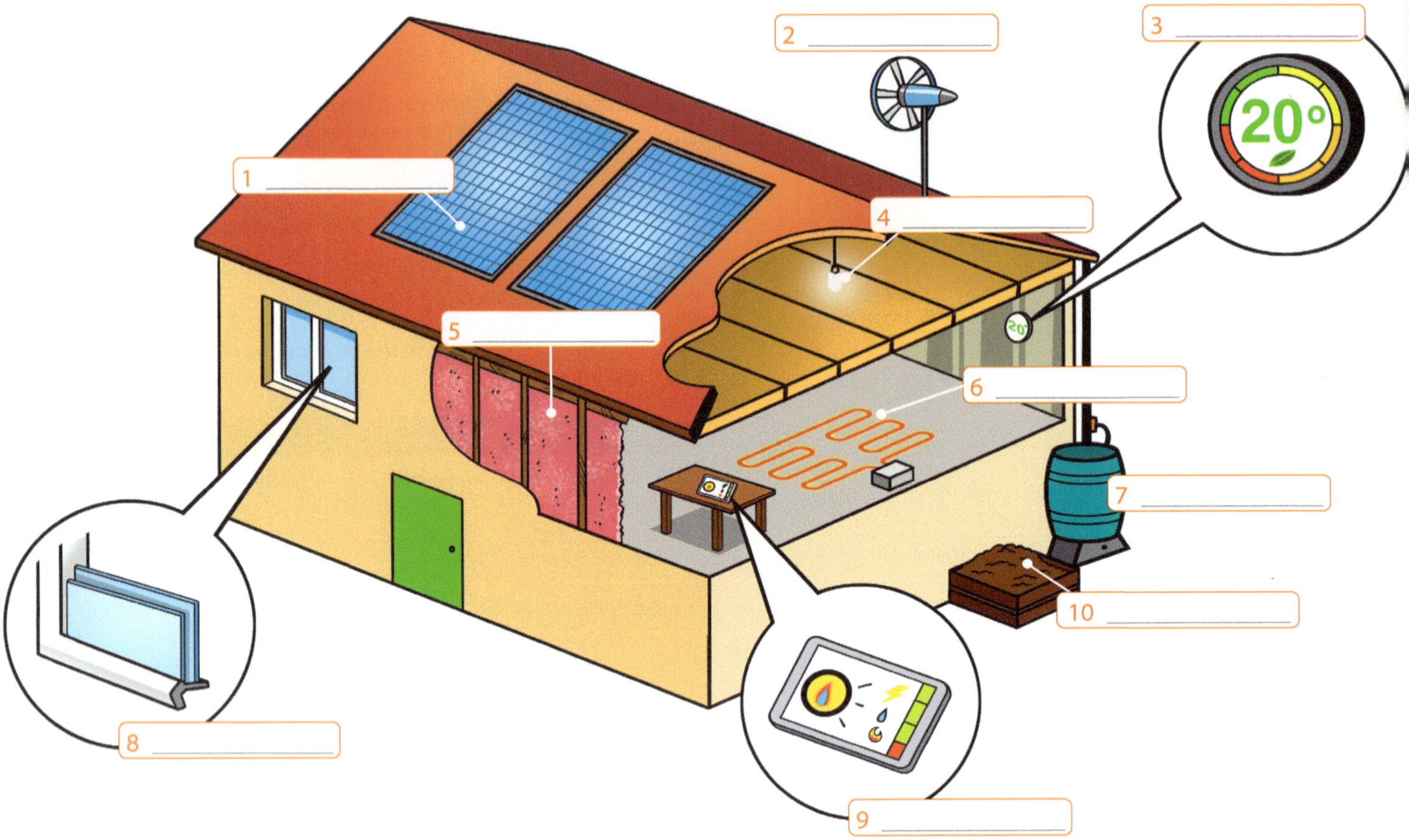

VOCABULARY

Green vocabulary

A Label the picture with words in the box.

compost heap double glazing energy-efficient lightbulb insulation smart meter solar panels thermostat underfloor heating rain barrel wind turbine

B Complete the sentences with words from Exercise A.

1 Turning down your ______ by just one degree can save money and energy.

2 Using ______ to produce energy from the sun can save you money.

3 ______ can be used to extract heat stored in the ground through the floor of the house.

4 ______ last much longer and use less energy than traditional ones.

5 Use a ______ to capture rain which can then be used in the garden and the toilet system.

6 Families frequently throw away a lot of food that could instead have been put in a ______.

7 Using a ______ can produce clean energy on windy days.

8 Installing a ______ helps keep track of energy use and may even save money.

9 Since warm air rises, it is important that you have ______ to keep the heat in.

10 ______ is much better at keeping heat in than traditional windows are.

C SPEAK Work in pairs. Which of these do you have in your home? Which would you install if you had the money?

LISTENING

A LISTEN FOR KEY WORDS Listen to a radio interview about an eco-friendly home. Which of the features in the vocabulary section are not mentioned?

5.1

B LISTEN FOR DETAIL Listen again. Complete the sentences with no more than four words from the interview.

5.1

1 Harry is making changes because he was surprised by his ______.

2 He made simple changes himself, such as putting ______ in each room and fitting ______.

3 The solar panels make ______ of the energy he needs.

4 The beehive means the roof is a source of ______ as well as energy.

5 The rain barrel now means the ______ uses rainwater.

6 The underfloor heating helps lower Harry's ______.

7 The smart fridge means they ______.

8 The new shower ______ to save water and energy.

GRAMMAR
Causative *have* and *get*

5.2 **A** Listen and complete the extracts from the interview.

1 Ah, I can see you're ________ solar panels ________.
2 We're ________ underfloor heating ________.
3 We need ________ the walls better ________.

B PRACTICE Complete the sentences using the prompts in parentheses. Use the information in the box to help you.

Causative *have* and *get*

We use the causative *have* and *get* (*have* / *get* + object + past participle) to say that someone does something for us – usually for tasks we can't or don't know how to do ourselves. Compare these sentences:

Camille is installing solar panels on her roof.
(= she is doing it herself.)

Camille is having solar panels installed on her roof.
(= someone is installing them for her.)

1 I ________ (*have / the car / repair*) at the garage last weekend.
2 We're ________ (*get / the house / paint*) right now.
3 We're also ________ (*have / a smart energy meter / fit*) to check how much energy we're using.
4 We ________ (*have / a roof garden / create*) last year to help keep heat in.
5 I'd like ________ (*get / new flooring / install*) in the living room.

C Go to the **Grammar Hub** on **page 130**.

PRONUNCIATION
Glottal stops

5.3 **A** Listen to the extract from the interview. Is the /t/ in the highlighted words pronounced or not pronounced?

We're also getting a **smart** meter installed. Hopefully, **it'll** help us keep an eye on how much – or how little – energy we're using!

5.4 **B** Listen and repeat the sentences.

1 It's a great way to save money on your bills.
2 We'd like to start growing our own food.
3 We should save about $100 a year.
4 We need to get quotes for the underfloor heating.

SPEAKING HUB

A PLAN A local school has $30,000 to spend to make the school more environmentally friendly. Write notes about the advantages and disadvantages of each idea.

ORGANIC GARDEN
Cost $500. The food grown could be served in the school cafeteria and save the school $300 a year. It would mean less playground space for the children.

DOUBLE GLAZING
Cost $25,000. This would save the school $2,000 a year in heating bills. The installation would take a long time and some classrooms couldn't be used for a while.

WIND TURBINES
Cost $10,000. There is the potential to save $1,000 per year but the school is not in a very windy location.

SOLAR PANELS
Cost $16,000. There is the potential to save $1,400 per year and the school is in a sunny location.

WATER SAVING TOILETS
Cost $3,000. This solution won't save the school any money, but it will reduce waste water a lot.

ENERGY SAVING BULBS
Cost $300. Saving the school $60 per year. This solution is quick and easy to implement.

B DISCUSS Work in groups. Discuss how to spend the $30,000. Explain your reasoning.

C PRESENT Explain which options you chose in Exercise B and why.

- Summarize a sequence of past events
- Evaluate a range of proposals

5.2 Changing places

- Talk about changes in your town or city
- Evaluate candidates and put together a team

V – describing areas of a city; prefixes
S – listening for rhetorical questions
P – words that lose a syllable
G – *-ing* and infinitive forms

READING

A PREDICT Work in pairs. Look at the pictures of Dubai. What do you think causes a city to grow so quickly? What do you think the effects of such quick growth are?

B SCAN Scan *Rise of the megacities* and check your predictions from Exercise A.

C READ FOR ORGANIZATION Read the article again. Fill in the blanks (1–6) with the sentences (a–f).

a Gyeonggi, on the southern outskirts of the city, has gained more than five million residents in the last 30 years.

b Today, it is a city of over a million but 60 years ago, its population was under 20,000.

c However, in recent years, rapid urbanization has been happening at a rate never seen before.

d Unfortunately, for many people, especially in poorer countries, this has not always been the case.

e At the heart of this rapid expansion in urban populations are the same factors that have been there for centuries.

f So, where and why is this happening at such an astounding rate?

D SPEAK Work in pairs. What are the main advantages and disadvantages of living in a major city?

Rise of the MEGACITIES

Large cities are not a new phenomenon. Attracted by work, better facilities and living standards, there have been cities with a population of over a million people for around 2,000 years. [1]___ This is particularly evident in the Middle East and across Asia, where many cities have swelled to populations in excess of ten million. Places that even just a few decades ago were nothing more than small farming towns or fishing villages now have millions of people living in them. [2]___

Seoul, in South Korea, is a prosperous **urban** area today, but in the 1950s it was a much poorer and smaller place. Once Seoul began to expand, much of the population growth was in the central **commercial** area. This has changed in the last 20 or 30 years, since much of the growth has been in the **suburbs**, where huge **residential** areas have been built on the edge of the city. [3]___ Overpopulation has meant redeveloping traditional **industrial** areas of the city, where vast **housing** projects have expanded the population greatly. Although the growth of Seoul has been extraordinary, it has been a large city for decades. Abu Dhabi, on the other hand, was once not much more than a small village, and has grown immensely in recent times. [4]___ It is not the only city to grow at this rapid rate, so what has led to this rapid expansion?

Population growth in general has come about due to falling death rates and improved life expectancy, but city populations are growing for numerous reasons. [5]___ High levels of unemployment and a lack of resources have always pushed people away from **rural** areas. There is a perception that life will be better in a city, as the future residents are attracted to the prospect of well-paid jobs, greater opportunities to find work, better health care and education. [6]___ All too many cities have illegal **slums** with poor living conditions, little or no electricity and limited access to clean drinking water. Yet this does not seem to deter new residents as both the central area and suburban populations continue to expand.

The trend of urbanization is unlikely to slow down any time soon, with millions of people expected to move to urban areas in the future, no doubt creating more megacities in the process. From Bogota to Chengdu, the march of the megacities shows no signs of stopping across the world.

VOCABULARY
Describing areas of a city

A **Scan the article again. Complete the definitions with the words in bold.**

1 ________________ (n) an area where people live that is outside the city
2 ________________ (adj) relating to industry
3 ________________ (adj) relating to towns and cities, or happening there
4 ________________ (n) a poor area of a town where the houses are in very bad condition
5 ________________ (adj) relating to where people live rather than work
6 ________________ (n) buildings for people to live in
7 ________________ (adj) relating to business
8 ________________ (adj) relating to or in the country

B **Choose the correct options (a, b or c) to complete the sentences.**

1 Over half of the world's population live in ___ areas and this is expected to grow.
a urban **b** commercial **c** slums
2 Depopulation in ___ areas has led to even less work and fewer facilities.
a commercial **b** suburb **c** rural
3 The ___ area is home to some of the largest banks and financial companies in the world.
a industrial **b** commercial **c** residential
4 When people have families, they frequently move to the ___ to have more space.
a suburbs **b** housing **c** residential
5 ___ areas with good transportation connections are usually more expensive to live in.
a Slum **b** Industrial **c** Residential
6 A lack of affordable ___ can lead to people living in poor conditions.
a suburbs **b** housing **c** slums
7 When traditionally ___ areas are in decline, many of the old factories are frequently converted to apartments.
a industrial **b** commercial **c** rural
8 The biggest ___ in the world has over half a million people living in poor quality housing.
a suburb **b** slum **c** urban

C **SPEAK** **Work in pairs. Use the words in Exercise A to describe your city or a city you know well.**

PRONUNCIATION
Words that lose a syllable

5.5 **A** **How many syllables are there in the underlined words? Write the number next to each sentence. Then listen and check.**

1 There are <u>reasonable</u> transportation connections in the area. ___
2 There has been a <u>considerable</u> rise in the cost of living. ___
3 <u>Traditionally</u>, industrial areas have been converted into housing. ___

5.6 **B** **Cross out the syllables that are not pronounced in the sentences below. Then listen and check.**

1 It's preferable to live in a central area since the shopping is better.
2 Much has changed, especially in terms of the transportation system.
3 My personal preference is to live near the transportation network.

VOCABULARY
Prefixes

Prefixes

Prefixes are added to the beginning of a word to change the meaning. For example, *mega-* is added to the beginning of a word to mean *very big or important* (e.g. *megacity*).

A **Complete the words in bold with a prefix from the box.**

extra- il- over- re- sub- un-

1 The cost of housing has led to some ______**legal** housing areas being built.
2 There have been some ______**ordinary** new buildings constructed in the center of the city.
3 ______**population** has become a problem in my city.
4 They have ______**developed** the old industrial area of the city.
5 The ______**urban** areas around the city have expanded rapidly.
6 Many were ______**happy** about the construction of a large grocery store on the site.

B Go to the **Vocabulary Hub** on **page 145**.

SPEAKING

A **PREPARE** **Write notes about important changes in your town or city over the past ten years. Think about:**

- transportation
- shopping
- the cost of living
- housing

B **SPEAK** **Work in pairs. Tell your partner about how your town or city has changed.**

C **DISCUSS** **Work in pairs. Discuss the questions.**

1 Do you think the changes in your city have been mostly positive or negative? Why?
2 What changes would you like to see in the future?

LISTENING

A SPEAK Work in pairs. Read the FAQs page and discuss the questions.

1 What is Mars One?
2 Would you qualify to be a Mars One astronaut?
3 Would you like to apply? Why/Why not?
4 What do you think you would find most difficult about being a Mars One astronaut?

5.7 **B LISTEN FOR MAIN IDEA** Listen to three radio interviews with Mars One candidates. Answer the questions with A (Agatha), T (Tim) or B (Bernie).

Who …

1 is confident about their physical ability? ____
2 would miss the city atmosphere? ____
3 thinks their attitude and work experience are important? ____
4 is going to have little contact with others to prepare for the mission? ____
5 would miss having a normal life? ____
6 is worried about losing part of their morning routine? ____

5.7 **C LISTEN FOR RHETORICAL QUESTIONS** Listen again. Check (✓) the questions that are used rhetorically. Use the information in the box to help you.

Listening for rhetorical questions

A rhetorical question is a question asked for effect, not because the speaker expects an answer. They are usually used to emphasize when the speaker thinks something is obvious, or to express surprise, doubt or agreement.

☐ Isn't that scary?
☐ Surely, being a scientist is the most important thing you bring to the team?
☐ Can you prepare yourself?
☐ Can anyone live without coffee?
☐ Can you take a short break?
☐ Who doesn't enjoy a challenge?
☐ Why would I be scared?

D INFER MEANING Work in groups. Tim says that 'everyone wants to leave their mark behind'. What do you think he means by this? How do you want to make your mark?

E SPEAK Work in small groups. Discuss which candidate you would choose for the mission and why.

HOME | NEWS | FAQS | MESSAGE BOARD

MISSION TO MARS

FAQS

What is the Mars One project?

The Mars One project was founded in 2011 with the goal of starting a human settlement on Mars.

How will candidates be selected?

Candidates will be selected through online applications, interviews, group challenges and simulations.

How old must candidates be?

The selection process is open to anyone over the age of 18.

What physical requirements are there?

Candidates must be healthy and have a good level of fitness. They must be between 157 and 190 cm tall.

What language(s) must you speak?

The official language of the project is English. However, you do not need to have a good level of English to take part in the selection process. You can apply in English, Spanish, Portuguese, French, German, Russian, Arabic, Mandarin Chinese, Korean, Indonesian or Japanese.

When will it happen and how long will it take?

Six teams of four will be chosen for training. They will train together until the launch in 2024. It takes seven months to get to Mars in an extremely challenging environment.

GRAMMAR

-*ing* and infinitive forms

5.8 **A** Complete the extracts with the correct form of the verbs in parentheses. Then listen and check.

1. For centuries, man has been obsessed with the idea of ______ (*go*) to Mars.
2. I think it's important ______ (*advance*) science whenever the opportunity presents itself.
3. ______ (*be*) a scientist isn't enough.
4. I really appreciate ______ (*drink*) a good cup of coffee every morning.
5. I'll never forget ______ (*run*) across the Sahara Desert for seven days.
6. I'm going to Mars ______ (*be*) a part of history.
7. We have to learn ______ (*live*) independently of planet Earth.
8. Some people get really stressed when they forget ______ (*take*) their phone with them.
9. In space, all you can ______ (*hear*) is endless silence.

B SPEAK Work in pairs. Look at sentences 5 and 8 in Exercise A. What's the difference in meaning of the word *forget* in each of these sentences?

C WORK IT OUT Match the examples in Exercise A to the rules in the box.

-*ing* and infinitive forms

We use verb + -*ing*:

a after prepositions ___

b as the subject of a sentence ___

c after some verbs (e.g. *admit, appreciate, avoid, finish, give up, mind, suggest*, etc) ___

We use the infinitive:

d after adjectives ___

e to talk about purpose ___

f after some verbs (e.g. *attempt, decide, expect, learn, manage, need, promise*, etc) ___

We use the base form:

g after modal verbs ___

Some verbs can be followed by either verb + -*ing* or the infinitive, but with a change of meaning (e.g. *forget, remember, try, go on*, etc)

h ___ / ___

D Go to the Grammar Hub on page 130.

E PRACTICE Complete the sentences with the correct form of the verbs in the box.

be do get have like plan produce work

1. ______ a positive attitude is the key to being a good team player.
2. It's important ______ everyone you work with.
3. One way of ______ more effective on a team is to become an active listener.
4. Never promise ______ more work than you can manage. You will let your team down.
5. Only teams with strong leaders can ______ good results.
6. Always remember ______ what you need to discuss in a team meeting, so you don't waste any time.
7. I'm worried about not ______ along with the other people on the team.
8. We need ______ together if we want to succeed.

F SPEAK Work in pairs. Do you agree with the sentences in Exercise E? Why/Why not?

SPEAKING HUB

A Go to the Communication Hub on page 147.

B PRESENT Tell the class which candidates you chose, which you rejected and why.

- Talk about changes in your town or city
- Evaluate candidates and put together a team

5.3 Getting into the habit

A– conditional counterarguments S– taking the floor

Reward or penalty?

COMPREHENSION

A Work in pairs. Look at the picture. Do you think cups like these are environmentally friendly? Why/Why not?

> **Glossary**
> **disposable (adj)** designed to be used once, then thrown away

B Watch a news report about an environmentally friendly scheme at a university. Choose the best summary (1 or 2).

1. The university found that a reward scheme had no meaningful effect on student behavior. By adopting a penalty scheme instead, they were able to reduce the number of disposable cups sold every year.
2. The university found that a penalty scheme had no meaningful effect on student behavior. By adopting a reward scheme instead, they were able to reduce the number of disposable cups sold every year.

C Watch the news report again and answer the questions.

1. How did the university originally try to encourage students to start using reusable cups?
2. What was the issue with the original scheme?
3. How did the university address this issue?
4. What else did the university do to encourage use of non-disposable cups?
5. Was the penalty scheme a success? Why/Why not?
6. How has the penalty scheme affected sales of hot drinks?

D Work in groups. Do you agree that you have to use penalties to meaningfully change behavior? Why/Why not?

> **Glossary**
> high street **(n) (British)** = main street **(n) (American)**
> a scheme **(n) (British)** = a plan or system **(n) (American)**

AUTHENTIC ENGLISH

A 01:33–01:41 Watch the last part of the report again and complete the extract.

Presenter: So this might work on a campus. That doesn't mean it's going to work on the high street, where people have a lot more choice.

Interviewee: ______________________ government were to legislate for it.

B Work in pairs. Read the extract again. Why does the speaker use a conditional? Which word does she stress? Why?

C Read the information in the box to check your answers to Exercise B.

> **Conditional counterarguments**
> In discussions, speakers sometimes use conditional structures to make a counterargument. These usually begin with conjunctions and use words, phrases or ideas from the original argument. The stress is usually put on the modal verb to emphasize the contrast between the two ideas.
> **A:** *It's a nice idea, but just doesn't work in practice. Nobody wants to carry around a reusable cup everywhere they go.*
> **B:** *But they might if coffee shops offered bigger discounts.*

D Work in pairs. Take turns reading the arguments (1–3) and responding with a conditional.

1. Sadly, most people like the convenience of disposable water bottles. This isn't going to change anytime soon.
2. Social media isn't dangerous. It's just a fun way to stay in touch with old friends.
3. Electric cars are a great idea, but will never replace gasoline-powered vehicles on our roads.

A green suggestion

A Work in groups. Do you think where you work or study does enough to protect the environment? Why/Why not?

B Watch the video and answer the questions.

1. What eco-friendly change does Harry suggest?
2. Why does Amanda support this idea?
3. What is Sam's criticism of the idea?

SPEAKING SKILL

A Read the extract from the conversation. Why do you think Amanda finishes Harry's sentence?

Harry: People respond better to a penalty than a ...
Amanda: ... reward. It's what we do at my office.

B Read the information in the box and check your answers to Exercise A.

Taking the floor

In discussions, one speaker will regularly interrupt another so they can start speaking. This is called taking the floor. In the video, Sam interrupts Harry by saying [1] ______________ and Malcolm interrupts Sam by saying [2] ______________.

To keep the floor, we need to avoid interruption. In the video, Harry stops Sam from interrupting him by saying [3] ______________.

We can also take the floor by agreeing or disagreeing with what someone has said.

Sam: Yes, well, I think we already do a fair bit to help the environment.

Harry: [4] ______________ we could do more?

Amanda: And it does seem to have changed how people behave.

Harry: [5] ______________. People begin to feel that it's normal to have their own cup. It's not something that deserves a special reward.

Sam: [6] ______________ we start penalizing them.

We can also show agreement or understanding by finishing someone's sentence, like Amanda does to Harry.

C Watch the video again. Complete the box with examples from the conversation.

SAM MALCOLM AMANDA HARRY EMILY

D Work in groups. Discuss one of the following topics using strategies from the box to take or keep the floor.

- recycling
- wind farms
- solar panels
- electric cars
- plastic packaging
- food waste

SPEAKING HUB

A PREPARE Work in groups. Write a list of five ways you could be more environmentally friendly in the following areas:

- travel and transportation
- recycling
- saving water
- eating smart
- reducing and reusing
- clothing

B PLAN Rank the points in Exercise A in order of importance. Try to reach an agreement in the group.

A: I really think recycling plastics is a top priority. We should all carry refillable water bottles with us.
B: Really? But surely people wouldn't want to carry a water bottle everywhere.
A: But they might if governments made plastic bottles expensive and provided a lot of places where we can refill our bottles.

C PRESENT Present your list to the class. Explain your reasoning.

Discuss ways to help the environment

➤ Turn to page 158 to learn how to write a problem solution article.

Unit 5 Review

VOCABULARY

A Complete the definitions with the words in the box.

insulation smart meter solar panel thermostat rain barrel wind turbine

1 _______________ a large container used to collect rain for watering plants
2 _______________ a large machine like a windmill used for producing electricity using the wind
3 _______________ material used to prevent heat, cold, noise, etc from passing through something
4 _______________ an electronic device used to record how much electricity is used
5 _______________ a piece of equipment that uses energy from the sun to create electricity
6 _______________ a piece of equipment that controls the temperature in a building

B Complete the sentences with the words in the box.

housing residential rural slums suburbs urban

1 They are building a new _______________ area near me with over 2,000 new homes.
2 The cost of _______________ has increased by almost 20% in the last year.
3 I don't really like living in the _______________. It's too far from the city and there isn't much to do.
4 In countries such as Germany and England, almost 80% of the population lives in _______________ areas.
5 Because of high unemployment, many people leave _______________ areas and move to cities to look for work.
6 In many _______________, many thousands of people have to share just one toilet.

C Complete the article with the correct form on the words in parentheses.

Simple ways to be more environmentally friendly

Climate change is a threat to all of us. You can help tackle this issue by making some of the following changes:

1 Buy a reusable bottle

Many plastics are used just once and can't be [1]_______________ (*recycle*). Many people believe single-use plastics are [2]_______________ (*necessary*) and should be banned. To help prevent plastic pollution, take a reusable water bottle with you instead of buying a plastic one.

2 Bike to work

Air pollution is also a major problem, particularly in [3]_______________ (*crowded*) cities. Campaigners would like heavily polluting vehicles to be made [4]_______________ (*legal*). In the past, a lot of bike paths were [5]_______________ (*standard*) but there has been a lot of recent investment in building new bike paths. Riding your bike to work is a great way to help reduce pollution while also getting some exercise!

GRAMMAR

A Complete the sentences with the correct passive form of the verbs in the box.

build film finish hold inform left

1 Parts of *Star Wars: The Last Jedi* _______________ in the salt plains of Bolivia.
2 An emergency meeting _______________ to discuss possible responses.
3 The public _______________ about the potential risk and is advised to avoid the area.
4 The house, which was the family home of the Harrogates, _______________ in 1858.
5 As they pulled into their drive, they noticed that the window _______________ open.
6 The new shopping mall was scheduled to be completed by now but it _______________ until next May.

B Complete the sentences with the correct form of the words in parentheses.

1 **A:** Can you give me a ride tonight?
B: No, sorry. I _______________________ (*my car / service*) right now.
2 **A:** _______________________ (*you / your shower / fix*)?
B: Not yet. Someone's coming to look at it tomorrow.
3 **A:** Have you seen Emily?
B: Yes, she's _______________________ (*nails / paint*).
4 **A:** Why are they eating out so much?
B: They are _______________________ (*kitchen / installed*) this week.
5 **A:** Everyone on TV has such white teeth!
B: I know. Actually, I'm thinking about _______________ _______________________ (*teeth / whiten*).

C Choose the correct options (a or b) to complete the sentences.

1 Chris has offered ___ me with the project I'm doing about homelessness.
a to help **b** helping
2 Mark has been in touch. Did you remember ___ him an email?
a to send **b** sending
3 I don't want ___ to work today, but I have so much to do.
a to go **b** going
4 Lucy texted. They're trying ___ to the party by eight.
a to get **b** getting
5 Our kids miss ___ in Madrid and wish we could move back.
a to live **b** living
6 These videos on YouTube are great to help you learn how ___ the guitar.
a to play **b** playing

6 COMING OF AGE

Anyone who stops learning is old, whether at 20 or 80. Anyone who keeps learning stays young.

Henry Ford

It's widely believed that our ability to learn new things declines with age.

OBJECTIVES

- discuss rules in education
- talk about changes to education in your country
- discuss age milestones in your country
- debate the best time to start college
- give your opinion on an aspect of education
- write a report

Work with a partner. Discuss the questions.

1 Read the quote. Do you agree with Ford? Why/Why not?

2 What are the most important birthdays in your country (e.g. 18, 21, 50, etc)? How are they celebrated?

3 If you could give your younger self one piece of advice, what would it be and why?

6.1 The right method?

- Discuss rules in education
- Talk about changes to education in your country

G – obligation, prohibition and permission
V – education
P – intonation to show interest
S – pronoun referencing

LISTENING

A SPEAK Work in groups. Look at the school rules (1–6). Which do you think are reasonable? Which do you think are unreasonable? Why?

6.1 **B LISTEN FOR GIST** Listen to a radio interview about different school systems. Choose the best summary (1–3).

1. Both guests had a similar school experience but disagree about which system to use today.
2. Both guests enjoyed their school experience but disagree about the best system to use today.
3. Both guests agree that students need rules, and that current systems should be stricter.

6.1 **C LISTEN FOR DETAIL** Listen again. Complete the sentences with no more than two words from the interview.

1. In Jessica's school, students and teachers could ________ on the rules.
2. Jessica thinks students behave better when they have the ________ to make decisions.
3. Jessica thinks teenagers want more ________ of their environment as they're becoming adults.
4. In Jessica's school, students got excellent ________ ________ and went on to further education and to have good jobs.
5. In Andrew's school, everyone had to have the ________ hair, bags and clothes.
6. Children who broke the rules in Andrew's school had to wear ________ around their necks.
7. Andrew thinks more ________ make things fairer because all teachers behave the same.
8. Jessica felt her experience at school made her more ________ when she left.

D SPEAK Work in pairs. Which school would you prefer to study at? Why?

SCHOOL RULES

1. Bathroom breaks during class limited to three times a week.
2. Students must not dye their hair.
3. Any student arriving more than five minutes late will be given cleaning duties.
4. Male students are strictly forbidden from having facial hair.
5. Shorts may not be worn between September 15th and May 15th.
6. No groups larger than five anywhere on school grounds.

GRAMMAR

Obligation, prohibition and permission

6.2 **A** Complete the extracts with the words in the box. Then listen and check your answers.

allowed needed obliged should required supposed

1 I'm not sure. In my school, students weren't ________ to attend classes.

2 I don't think students should be ________ to go to classes or to study certain subjects.

3 Well, in many cases people took subjects and exams earlier than they were ________ to.

4 We weren't ________ to have dirty shoes.

5 That's clearly unreasonable. The punishment ________ fit the crime.

6 You quickly learned what you ________ to do.

B **WORK IT OUT** Choose the correct options to complete the rules.

obligation, prohibition and permission

Strong obligation

We use *have to, must, need to, be obliged to, be required to* to talk about things that [1]***are necessary / aren't necessary***.

Lack of obligation

We use *don't have to, don't need to, be not obliged to, be not required to* to talk about things that [2]***are necessary / aren't necessary***.

Weak obligation

We use *should, be supposed to* to talk about things that [3]***are recommended / aren't recommended***.

Prohibition

We use *must not, can't, be not allowed to* to talk about things that [4]***are permitted / aren't permitted***.

Permission

We use *can, let* or *be allowed to* to talk about things that [5]***are permitted / aren't permitted***.

C Go to the Grammar Hub on page 132.

D **PRACTICE** Choose the correct options (a, b or c) to complete the sentences.

1 My parents didn't ___ me go out alone until I was 18.

a require b need c let

2 I'm going to ___ my children have a lot more freedom than I had.

a let b allow c need

3 I was ___ do a lot of housework, but usually I didn't bother.

a allowed to b need to c supposed to

4 I ___ practice the piano for an hour every day. I hated it!

a didn't have to b could c had to

5 I think people ___ be allowed to drive at 16. You can work then, so having a car would help.

a should b have to c must

6 We ___ study a foreign language. I think it was a mistake, because languages are important.

a had to b didn't have to c must not

E **SPEAK** Work in pairs. Change the sentences in Exercise D so they are true for you.

PRONUNCIATION

Intonation to show interest

6.3 **A** Listen to this exchange from the radio show. What kind of intonation does Jessica use to show interest: rise (↗), fall (↘) or rise-fall (↗↘)?

Andrew: We had to wear a tag around our neck with a message such as 'I have 24 hours to straighten up my uniform' if we looked sloppy. If we behaved badly in class, we had to study on our own. We were forced to do this for five classes. Hundreds of children had to do this. I have similar rules in my school.

Jessica: You're joking! How embarrassing!

6.4 **B** Listen to the same exclamations said in two different ways. For each exclamation, choose the speaker (a or b) that shows the most interest.

1 How embarrassing! a / b

2 Interesting! a / b

3 That's ridiculous! a / b

4 That's amazing! a / b

5 What a nightmare! a / b

C Write down three interesting facts about yourself.

D **SPEAK** Work in pairs. Take turns telling each other your facts from Exercise C. Use intonation to express interest. Then ask follow-up questions for more information.

SPEAKING

A **PREPARE** Work in pairs. Think about all of your previous schools. Discuss rules that you didn't like and why.

A: At my elementary school, anyone that forgot their uniform had to do the whole class in their underwear!

B: Really? How embarrassing!

B **PLAN** Work in pairs. Make a list of five rules for the perfect school, for both students and teachers. Use your ideas from Exercise A to help you.

C **PRESENT** Present your rules to the class. Explain your reasons for each.

Our first rule is simple – students must be given a say in the topics and subjects they cover. We think that ...

D **DISCUSS** As a class, discuss how to improve your language school. Would any of the rules from Exercise C improve your school experience?

VOCABULARY

Education

A Look at the infographic. Complete the definitions with the words in bold.

1 ________________ (n) a school that is free because it is funded by the government

2 ________________ (n) a school that you pay money to attend

3 ________________ (n) a school where students also live full-time

4 ________________ (adj) something that must be done because of rules or laws

5 ________________ (n) education at a university or at a college of a similar level

6 ________________ (n) the subjects studied in a school, college, etc.

EDUCATION

AROUND THE GLOBE

With fees of about $133,000 a year, *Le Rosey* in Switzerland is the world's most expensive **private school**.

Wearing a school uniform isn't **compulsory** in most high schools in the US, although there is usually a fairly strict dress code.

State schools in France have one of the shortest school years with nearly 4 months of vacation, but the longest school day in the world with up to 40 hours a week in the final years.

A lot of the **curriculum** in Canadian schools is taught in both English and French.

England is home to the world's oldest **boarding school**. Students have lived and studied in The King's School since 597 CE.

According to the Organization for Economic Co-operation and Development, 66% of students in Finland go into **higher education** to get a degree. This is the highest rate in Europe.

B Go the Vocabulary Hub on page 145.

C SPEAK Work in groups. Discuss the questions.

1 At what age do people start elementary school in your country? Do you think this is the right age? Why/Why not?

2 Would you send your children to private school if you could afford it? Why/Why not?

3 Which subjects are compulsory in your country?

4 Do you think higher education should be provided for free? Why/Why not?

5 Do you think lectures are an effective way to learn? Why/Why not?

READING

6.5 **A** Listen to an interview about a new movie. When is it set? Who does the actress play in the movie?

6.5 **B** Listen again. Complete the summary of school life in the period with no more than three words from the interview.

Most children used to [1]________________ and didn't go to school. Some [2]________________ boys could get scholarships but not girls. Girls from rich families sometimes went to boarding school, but most were taught at [3]________________ by a governess. A governess was a little like a [4]________________.

C PREDICT Work in pairs. You're going to read an adapted extract from Anne Brontë's novel *Agnes Grey*. What do you think might be hard for her as the governess of two young rich children?

D SCAN Read the extract and check your predictions from Exercise B.

Agnes Grey

Teaching and looking after the children became harder, rather than easier, as I got to know them. Master Tom not only refused to be controlled but tried to control me and his sister. He often refused to do his lessons. Sometimes I had to sit with my chair against the door in order to keep him in the schoolroom. At last, after trying to push me out of the way, and making faces at me, he would finally do his work.

Tom, however, was not as bad a pupil as Mary Ann. If I asked her to read a book or do some writing, she would drop to the floor and yell loudly. She was too heavy for me to pick her up and she would lie there until the lunch bell meant she could escape. Then she would jump up with a big smile on her face. She knew she had won.

In desperation, I decided that I should focus on two very important things in order to change their behaviour. I had to be patient and I had to be strict. So, I focused on doing this with all my strength over the coming weeks. However, it did not matter how hard I tried. Their behaviour did not get any better.

I will never forget one cold snowy January afternoon. The children had come into the schoolroom, shouting that they planned 'to be naughty,' and they had done exactly that. Mary Ann took my bag and started to look at what was inside it. When she saw that it only contained my work papers and books, she threw it on the fire! I ran to the other side of the room and pulled the bag out of the fire. Then Tom jumped up from his chair and yelled, 'Let's throw her desk out of the window!' He grabbed my desk, which contained my letters and what little money I owned. I quickly went to rescue it. Both children then ran away from me, out of the house and into the snow, where they rolled about shouting with happiness.

E PRONOUN REFERENCING Read the extract again. Match the pronouns (1–8) to the people or things they refer to. Use the information in the box to help you.

Pronoun referencing

Writers frequently use pronouns to refer backward and forward to different ideas in a text. These help to make the text more organized and the language more varied for the reader. Identifying what ideas these pronouns refer to will help you to understand a text better.

1 them (line 2) ________
2 him (line 6) ________
3 her (line 10) ________
4 she (line 10) ________
5 their (line 17) ________
6 this (line 19) ________
7 that (line 25) ________
8 it (line 26) ________

F SPEAK Work in groups. Discuss the questions.

1 In the first paragraph, Tom is described as 'making faces' at Agnes. What do you think this means?
2 What do you think Agnes could have done differently to control Tom and Mary Ann's behavior?
3 In the novel *Agnes Grey*, the children are allowed to choose when they study. Do you think this is a good idea? Why/Why not?

SPEAKING HUB

A PLAN Think about how education has changed in your country over the past 50 years. Write notes about:

- discipline
- subjects
- age of starting/leaving education
- college

B SPEAK Work in pairs. Use your notes to discuss changes in your country. What are the main differences between 50 years ago and now?

C DISCUSS Work in groups. Discuss the questions.

1 Has education in your country improved over the past 50 years? Why/Why not?
2 What would you change about the current education system in your country?
3 Is there anything from 50 years ago that you'd like to reintroduce to the current system?

- Discuss rules in education
- Talk about changes to education in your country

6.2 Traditions of youth

- Discuss age milestones in your country
- Debate the best time to start college

G – articles
V – compound adjectives; phrases with *make* and *do*
P – intrusive /j/ sounds
S – decoding: idioms

READING

A SPEAK Work in pairs. Discuss the questions.

1 At what age do you think someone becomes an adult? Why?
2 What events or celebrations happen in your country to show that someone is becoming an adult?

B SCAN Read *Coming of age* quickly. Match the ages (1–3) to the things they represent (a–c).

1 7 or 8 — a When you can learn to drive and leave school in the US.
2 20 — b When childhood is over in Vanuatu.
3 16 — c When someone becomes an adult in Japan.

C READ FOR DETAIL Read the article again and answer the questions. Underline the parts of the text that give you the answers.

1 In Vanuatu, what do mothers hold when their children complete their first jump? What happens to the item?
2 Which official venue do participants visit during the *Seijin-no-Hi* celebrations?
3 What traditions are associated with Sweet 16 celebrations?
4 What does giving a car to someone on their 16th birthday represent in the US and Canada?

D SPEAK Work in groups. What other coming-of-age ceremonies do you know of? What happens in them?

GRAMMAR
Articles

A Complete the extracts with *a, an, the* or – (no article). Then scan the article again to check your answers.

1 They traditionally signify a point in someone's life when ________ childhood is over.
2 In ________ Vanuatu, ________ small island in ________ Pacific Ocean, young boys jump from ________ 30-meter-high tower…
3 The vine is cut to a length that will just stop them from hitting ________ ground…
4 It is ________ ancient tradition that started almost 1,300 years ago.
5 In recent years, ________ popularity of ________ festival has declined…
6 Sweet 16 is the term given to ________ coming-of-age party to celebrate ________ teenager's 16th birthday.

COMING OF AGE

Coming-of-age events are important in many cultures. They traditionally signify a point in someone's life when childhood is over. Immediately afterward, the person is considered to have a different role within society. However, from shows of strength and bravery to simply having a big party, these life-changing events vary greatly throughout the world.

VANUATU LAND DIVE

Thrillseekers will love this high-risk ceremony! In Vanuatu, a small island in the Pacific Ocean, young boys jump from a 30-meter-high tower, with a bungee-like vine tied to their ankles. The vine is cut to a length that will just stop them from hitting the ground, but, unlike a bungee rope, it isn't elastic!

From the age of seven or eight boys are allowed to jump from a smaller tower. During their first few dives, their mothers hold an item which represents their childhood. Once they have completed the jump, the item is thrown away to symbolize that their childhood has ended.
As they grow older, boys jump from taller towers to show their manliness to their community.

SWEET 16

Sweet 16 is the name given to the coming-of-age party to celebrate a teenager's 16th birthday. It doesn't have a long history and there are no specific traditions to follow. However, it has grown in popularity in the US and Canada in recent years. The concept became well-known when MTV launched a show called *My Super Sweet Sixteen*, in which cameras followed parents spending hundreds of thousands of dollars on elaborate parties for their children, who wanted the biggest and best party in town.

In most states,16 is also the age when people can leave school and when they can start to drive. As a result, one tradition that has developed is the gift of a car. This symbolizes the person's increased freedom and responsibility as they become older.

SEIJIN-NO-HI

The coming-of-age festival called *Seijin-no-Hi* is held in Japan on the second Monday of January. It is an ancient tradition that started almost 1,300 years ago. The festival symbolizes the point at which the Japanese believe people become mature members of society – 20 years old. It is also the age at which they are permitted to vote.

During the day, 20-year-olds taking part dress up in their finest traditional clothes and attend a ceremony in local city offices. Government officials give speeches and small gifts are handed out. These young adults then go on to celebrate at parties in the evening. In recent years, the popularity of the festival has declined and many have stayed away from the celebrations.

B WORK IT OUT Complete the rules with the titles in the box.

definite article (*the*) indefinite article (*a/an*) zero article (-)

Articles

[1]We use the ______________________:

- when we talk about something for the first time
- when it's not clear or important which one of a group is being talked about

[2]We use the ______________________:

- when there's only one of something
- when it's clear which thing we're talking about (usually because we've mentioned it before)
- with superlatives
- with rivers, some mountains, oceans, seas, plural country names, groups of islands and deserts

[3]We use the ______________________:

- to talk about things in general
- with most towns, cities, countries, continents, states, lakes and mountains

C Go to the **Grammar Hub** on **page 132**.

D PRACTICE Work in pairs. Student A – Go to the **Communication Hub** on **page 151**. Student B – Go to the **Communication Hub** on **page 152**.

E SPEAK Work in pairs. Tell your partner about the coming-of-age ceremony you have just read about.

PRONUNCIATION

Intrusive /j/ sounds

6.6 **A** Listen to the sentence below. Notice the /j/ sound that appears between the words connected with a (‿).

The‿American legal system is complex, and laws vary from state to state. Depending on the state, the‿age you can get a full drivers licence is anywhere between 16 and 18 years old.

6.7 **B** Read the sentences below. Draw a (‿) between any words that you think are connected by a /j/ sound. Then listen and check.

1. The average age to drive a car in most countries is 18.
2. In Bangladesh, many children leave the education system at ten years old.
3. You can vote in Scotland from the age of 16.
4. In the UK, the older generation could leave school at 14.

VOCABULARY

Compound adjectives

Compound adjectives

Compound adjectives are single adjectives formed from two (or more) words. Many are joined with a hyphen (-), especially when they come before a noun.

Compound adjectives can:

- include numbers, e.g. *30-meter-high*
- use participles, e.g. *old-fashioned, well-known*
- have multiple parts, e.g. *coming-of-age*
- combine adjectives and nouns, e.g. *high-risk*

Do not add an *s* to compound adjectives with numbers, (e.g. *30-meter-high* not ~~*30-meters-high*~~).

Complete the sentences with the compound adjectives in the box.

coming-of-age last-minute old-fashioned seven-bedroom up-to-date well-known

1. For the most ______________ information on flights, please visit our website.
2. My parents have some pretty ______________ ideas about raising children.
3. Apparently, he just bought a huge ______________ house outside Houston.
4. It's a ______________ movie about three young friends growing up together.
5. I'm going to be late because there was a ______________ change to the schedule.
6. We've booked a ______________ author to speak at next month's event.

SPEAKING

A PLAN Write notes on the age people can do these things in your country. Do you think these are the right ages? Why/Why not?

- leave school
- start work
- drive a car
- retire

B DISCUSS Work in groups. What do you think is the best age for each of the things in Exercise A? Try to agree on one age for each.

C PRESENT Tell the class the ages you chose for each event and explain your reasons.

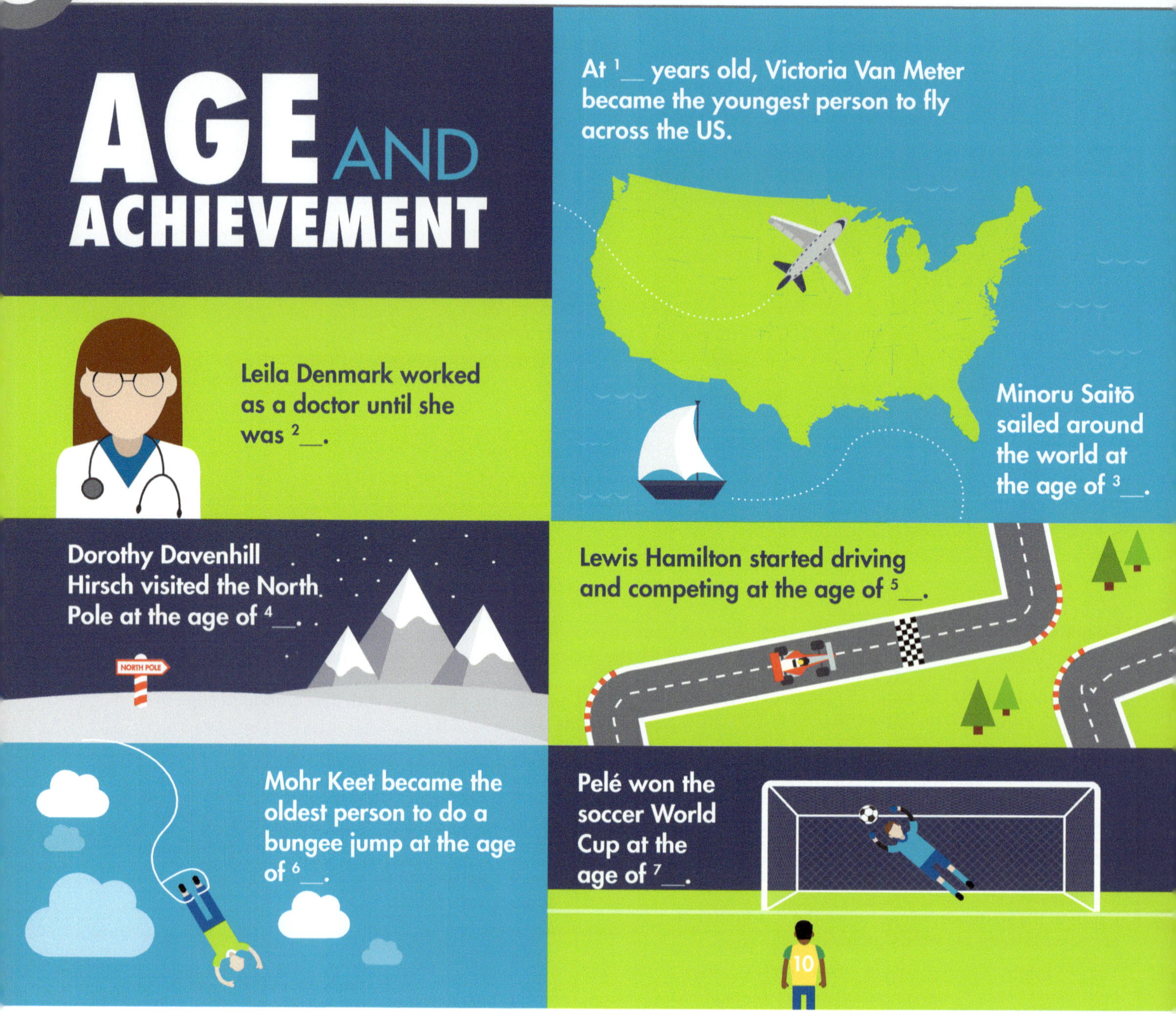

LISTENING

A PREDICT Predict when the achievements in the infographic were accomplished, using the ages in the box.

8	11	17	77	89	96	103

B COMPARE Work in pairs. Compare your predictions from Exercise A. Explain your reasoning.

C SPEAK Work in pairs. Discuss the questions.

1 What do you think motivated each person?
2 What difficulties do you think they might have faced?
3 What were you doing / What do you think you'll be doing at each age?

D DISCUSS Work in groups. Discuss the questions.

1 You are going to listen to three interviews from a TV show called *Age is just a number*. What do you think the title means? Do you agree with this idea?
2 The interviewees talk about achievements at the ages of 14, 28 and 70. What key events usually happen at these ages?

6.8 **E LISTEN FOR GIST** Listen and match the speakers (1–3) to an achievement (a–d). One achievement is not mentioned.

Speaker 1
Speaker 2
Speaker 3

a getting into college
b winning a competition
c starting their own company
d getting over a fear

6.8 **F LISTEN FOR DETAIL** **Listen to the interviews again and answer the questions. Use the information in the box to help you.**

Decoding: idioms

Idioms (e.g. *a blessing in disguise, blood is thicker than water*, etc) are frequently used in informal spoken English. They can be difficult to understand because their meaning is different from the meaning of the individual words. To help with this, listen for contextual clues before and after the idiom.

1 How did Janice feel about starting her business?
   - a She felt very confident.
   - b She was worried but pushed herself to do it.
   - c She started it without really thinking.

2 How successful is Janice's business?
   - a She's making a lot of money.
   - b She's making a reasonable amount of money.
   - c She's losing money.

3 What does Kayley say about school?
   - a It was challenging.
   - b It was boring.
   - c It was easy.

4 How did Robbie's wife feel about their honeymoon plans?
   - a She was fine because she understood his fears.
   - b She was angry because she thought his fear was irrational.
   - c She was fine because she wanted to stay in the US.

G SPEAK **Work in pairs. Look at the audio script on page 171 to find the idioms that gave you the answers in Exercise F. Do you have any similar idioms in your country?**

VOCABULARY

Phrases with *make* and *do*

6.9 **A** **Listen and complete the extracts from the interview. What do you think each phrase means?**

1 I used to ____________ and take care of the grandchildren a couple of mornings a week.

2 They ____________, they were just full of energy.

3 Well, you know… it's hard but I'm ____________ ____________.

4 I think schools should ____________ age restrictions for taking exams.

5 People are generally nice, and I think they'll ____________ ____________ for my age.

6 I hope I ____________, but I am a little worried.

7 She was trying to [a] ____________ the situation by [b] ____________ the exciting honeymoon…

B **Match the phrases in Exercise A (1–7) to their definitions (a–h).**

- a to be positive about a situation you don't like but can't change ____
- b to succeed in living or working without someone or something ____
- c something that you do for someone in order to help them ____
- d to get rid of something ____
- e try to make something work ____
- f causing no serious damage or injury ____
- g to consider the reasons for somebody's behavior and not judge them too severely ____
- h to make other people notice you in a positive way ____

C **Complete the questions with the correct form of the phrases in Exercise A.**

1 Do you ignore people's age, or do you think you ____________ for people because of their age?

2 When you ____________ for someone, do you expect them to do something in return?

3 Does eating junk food occasionally ____________?

4 Is there a time in your life when you had to ____________ a difficult situation?

5 Since my business is failing in its first year, should I keep ____________ to make it work or close it?

6 Should governments ____________ unemployment pay and benefits?

7 What's the best way to ____________ on others?

8 What would be the hardest thing to ____________ for a year?

D SPEAK **Work in pairs. Discuss the questions in Exercise C.**

SPEAKING HUB

A PLAN **Work in pairs. What are the advantages and disadvantages of going to college right after you leave high school?**

B PREPARE **Work in two groups. You are going to debate the following:**

Most teenagers don't know what career they want when they finish high school. Instead of making such a big decision at 18, they should work or travel for at least a year before going to college.

Group A – You agree with the idea above.

Group B – You disagree with the idea above.

Plan your arguments. Think about how to support your position, as well as what the other group might say.

C SPEAK **Hold your debate.**

– Discuss age milestones in your country

– Debate the best time to start college

A floating school

COMPREHENSION

A Work in pairs. Look at the picture and discuss the questions.

1 What kind of building do you think it is? Why?
2 Do you think it's temporary or permanent? Why?
3 Where do you think it is?

B Watch a news report about the building in Exercise A and check your answers.

C Watch the news report again. Choose the correct options (a, b or c) to answer the questions.

1 What does the reporter mean when he says that 'water is in the blood' of these children?
  a They are used to living and working on the water.
  b Their parents expect them to become fishermen.
  c They never travel to the mainland.
2 What does the reporter mean when he says the school is 'widening horizons' for the children?
  a It provides them with the chance to travel.
  b It provides them with a unique view of their community.
  c It provides them with more opportunities in life.
3 Which of the following doesn't the reporter describe on his tour of the school?
  a the number of students
  b the conditions in the classroom
  c the view from the classroom
4 Which sentence best describes the school's founder?
  a His father was the oldest of 22 children and the first to get an education.
  b He is the youngest of 22 children and the first to get an education.
  c He is the father of 22 children and the first to get an education.

D Work in groups. Discuss the questions.

1 What do you think the reporter means when he says, 'What the community lacks in glamour, it makes up for in grit'?
2 What do you think the reporter means when he says, 'the school has given students the opportunity to think big'?

AUTHENTIC ENGLISH

A Work in pairs. Read the extract from the video. What type of clause is used at the beginning of the sentence? How does this affect the emphasis?

What's unique about this classroom is that it's open air.

B Read the information in the box and check your answers to Exercise A.

Emphatic structures

Speakers frequently emphasize a specific part of a sentence by building up to it with an essential adjective clause. Beginning the clause with *What* puts the emphasis on the information after *be*.

What's really interesting about the school is the location. (= the emphasis is on *the location*)

We can also use *the thing that, the* + adj + *thing* and *all I* + verb to achieve the same effect.

The most impressive thing at my school was the main hall.

All I wanted to do was play soccer, not study!

C Work in pairs. Take turns completing the sentences (1–5) with your own ideas.

1 What's unique about my hometown is …
2 What I don't miss about school is …
3 The thing that I worry about most is …
4 The interesting thing about my country is …
5 All I want for my birthday this year is …

Who are you talking to?

SAM MALCOLM AMANDA HARRY EMILY

A Work in pairs. Discuss what you think makes a good presentation. Explain your reasoning.

B Watch the video and answer the questions.

1 What has Malcolm agreed to help Harry with?
2 Why is he qualified to do this?
3 Does Harry improve with Malcolm's help?

SPEAKING SKILL

A Watch the video again. What does Malcolm think is the main issue with Harry's presentation?

B Look at the two different versions of Harry's introduction. Identify the informal and formal features. Use the information in the box to help you.

1 Hey guys! How's things? So glad you were able to drop by for my little chat today. I'm gonna be talking 'bout some of the cool ideas that people have come up with for teaching kids in developing countries. I'll be letting you know if I think they're any good and …

2 Thank you for coming to my presentation today. I am going to be talking about some of the educational innovations that governments and individuals have devised for teaching children in developing countries. I will be assessing these on their effectiveness and …

Using correct register

Informal register

We generally use an informal register when we are talking to our friends and family. Some common features of an informal register are:

- Shortened sentences – ~~(I'm)~~ *so glad you were able to …*
- Phrasal verbs – *OK if we quickly run through this presentation now?*
- Slang – *Cheers, dude.*
- Idioms – *… he'll give me a hand …, OK if I take five?*
- Abbreviations – *… I've seen it on TV.*

Formal register

In addition to avoiding the features listed above, we frequently use less direct language when we are being formal, such as *I would be grateful if you could …, I was wondering if I might …, I'm sorry, but I'm afraid …*

C Work in pairs. Why is it important to adapt your register to your audience?

D Work in pairs. Student A – Do one of the following in an informal register. Student B – Say the same thing in a formal register. Then swap.

- Ask your partner if you can do something.
- Offer something to your partner.
- Refuse an invitation from your partner.
- Apologize to your partner for something.

A: Shut the window, will you?
B: Excuse me, I was just wondering if I could ask you to close the window?

SPEAKING HUB

A PREPARE Work in pairs. Choose one of the topics to give a presentation about. Write notes.

- the right time to go to college
- school rules and discipline
- different school systems

B PLAN Organize your notes from Exercise A into a plan for a formal presentation.

C PRESENT Work in groups. Give your presentation and answer any questions.

D DISCUSS Work in new pairs. Tell your partner what you learned in the presentations using an informal register.

Give your opinion on an aspect of education

➤ Turn to page 159 to learn how to write a report.

Unit 6 Review

VOCABULARY

A Choose the correct options (a, b or c) to complete the sentences.

1 The fees for my ___ are $20,000 a year.
  a state school
  b private school
  c higher education

2 More and more people are staying in ___ until they complete a master's degree.
  a higher education
  b graduate
  c campus

3 There were over 500 students in my ___ on International Management today because we had an exam.
  a curriculum
  b seminar
  c lecture

4 The university has its own ___ that you need to pass to get in.
  a entrance exam
  b scholarship
  c seminar

5 My sister has won a ___ to a top college.
  a scholarship
  b seminar
  c graduate

6 I'd like to do a ___ course in something like electronics.
  a compulsory
  b curriculum
  c vocational

B Work in groups. Discuss the questions.

1 Would you rather stay on campus while in college or commute from home? Why?
2 Which subjects do you think should be added/removed from the school curriculum in your country? Why?

C Complete the second sentence so it has a similar meaning to the first, using the words in bold.

1 They've just moved into a house with three bedrooms.
  three-bedroom
  They've just moved ______________________.

2 The décor in this restaurant isn't very modern.
  old-fashioned
  The décor ______________________.

3 The author Haruki Murakami is well known in Japan.
  well-known
  Haruki Murakami is a ______________________.

4 Isaac's commute takes two hours!
  two-hour
  Isaac has ______________________.

D Match the numbers (1–8) to the letters (a–h) to form full sentences.

1 I'm not happy with my apartment but I'm trying to …
2 We've been trying …
3 Can you …
4 I think you need to make …
5 Just one soda a day isn't going to …
6 What do you think of this suit? I want to …
7 It's hard living in a new city but I'm …
8 This new system will allow us …

a do me a favor?
b do any harm.
c make the best of it.
d doing my best.
e make a good impression.
f allowances for his lack of experience.
g to do without a car for the last month.
h to do away with a lot of paperwork.

GRAMMAR

A Choose the correct options to complete the sentences.

1 I was ***supposed to*** / ***required to*** finish it by five but I can't be bothered.
2 You ***don't need to*** / ***must not*** bring anything to the party but you can if you want to.
3 I think you ***'re required to*** / ***should*** complain to the manager. You might get a refund.
4 We ***must not*** / ***needn't*** leave any garbage or we'll get fined.
5 You ***are required to*** / ***should*** show ID or they won't let you in.
6 We ***aren't allowed to*** / ***should*** accept gifts from our clients or we could get in trouble.
7 You really ***are required to*** / ***need to*** drink more water when it's this hot!
8 You ***aren't supposed to*** / ***can't*** smoke in public buildings. It's against the law.

B Work in pairs. Discuss any rules or obligations in your school or work that you'd like to change and why.

C Complete the sentences with *a, an, the* or – (no article).

1 _______ education should be free for everyone.
2 Did you go to _______ movies last night?
3 He ran seven marathons through _______ Sahara Desert.
4 I'll meet you on _______ Main Street at seven.
5 Do you have _______ address for the apartment?
6 Do you have _______ signal on your phone?
7 We're having _______ party to celebrate his 21st birthday.
8 _______ Germany went out of the World Cup in the group stages.

7 COMMUNITY

A group of young community farmers displaying the produce of their shared allotment.

OBJECTIVES

- discuss community development projects
- discuss responses to hypothetical situations
- talk about wishes and regrets
- design and present a community project
- give your opinion on a social initiative
- write a formal letter of complaint

Work with a partner. Discuss these questions.

1 Read the quote. What do you think Ibsen means? Do you agree with him? Why/Why not?

2 What do you do to help people in your local community?

3 What do you like most about where you live?

7.1 Open spaces

- Discuss community development projects
- Discuss responses to hypothetical situations

G – first conditional with different future forms; unreal conditionals
S – identifying speculation
V – verbs to describe change
P – connected speech in conditionals

LISTENING

A SPEAK Work in groups. Look at the picture and discuss the questions.

1 Are there any buildings like this in your town or city?
2 What were they originally used for? What are they used for now?
3 What do you think would be a better use of the space?
4 Is it better to repurpose them or knock them down? Why?

7.1 **B LISTEN FOR MAIN IDEA** Listen to the talk. Match the original spaces to what they are used for now and the main reason for the change.

	Original space	New use	Main reason for the change
1	industrial estate	art gallery	to inspire local children
2	warehouse	community garden	to educate local children
3	wasteland	community park	to tackle obesity

C SPEAK Work in pairs. Summarize what you remember about each of the projects. Use the information in Exercise B to help you.

7.1 **D LISTEN FOR DETAIL** Listen to the talk again. Are these sentences true (T) or false (F)? Correct the false sentences.

1 Originally, the industrial estate was going to be used for offices. *T / F*
2 The park gives many urban children their first taste of nature. *T / F*
3 The gallery exhibits artwork inspired by the city. *T / F*
4 Local schools can exhibit work twice a year. *T / F*
5 Many people don't eat fresh produce because of the expense. *T / F*
6 All the food from the garden is given to homeless people. *T / F*

E SPEAK Work in groups. Would any of the regeneration projects described in the talk work well in your town or city? Why/Why not?

GRAMMAR

First conditional with different future forms

7.2 **A** Listen and complete the extracts with the correct form of the verbs in parentheses.

1 In fact, if we ____________ (*maintain*) our current numbers, we ____________ (*have*) 15,000 visitors in our first year.
2 If we ____________ (*give*) kids opportunities like this, what ____________ (*they / achieve*) in the future?
3 If you ____________ (*think*) about starting a garden, ____________ (*speak*) to me later.
4 If we ____________ (*not come*) together as a community, neighborhoods like mine ____________ (*fall*) apart.
5 If you ____________ (*care*) about your community, ____________ (*do*) something to improve it.

B WORK IT OUT Choose the correct options to complete the rules.

First conditional with different future forms

We use the first conditional to talk about something that is possible in the [1]*past / future*.

We can use any [2]*present / future* tense in the *if*-clause and any [3]*present / future* tense or an imperative in the main clause.

C Go to the **Grammar Hub** on **page 134**.

D PRACTICE Choose the correct options to complete the sentences.

1 If everything goes according to plan, *we'll have opened / we'll open* a total of 20 community gardens in the city by 2020.
2 We're going to convert this old factory into a skate park if *we get / we'll get* the funding.
3 If they don't hurry up, the project *isn't / won't be* finished on time.
4 *We'll be looking / We'll have looked* at the plans tomorrow if you want to come along.
5 If you go to the meeting, *ask / to ask* the residents how they feel.
6 If *they're growing / they'll be growing* their own vegetables, they should sell them, too.

VOCABULARY
Verbs to describe change

A Read *Transforming Main Street*. Complete the definitions with the words in bold.

1 ______________ to make longer or bigger
2 ______________ to move to another place
3 ______________ to change the use of something
4 ______________ to knock down or destroy
5 ______________ to repair something so that it looks the same as it did originally
6 ______________ to build or make something like a building, road or machine
7 ______________ to change something completely

Home News Contact

Transforming Main Street

Our main priority is to **transform** the public spaces in the city center.

We need to encourage large chains to **relocate** to the city center to make Main Street a thriving shopping area again.

The next most important thing is to deal with the former industrial area. There is the potential to **convert** this into residential properties, stores, cafés and restaurants. We should **demolish** some of the worst buildings but **restore** any of historical interest.

To make this development a success, we will need to **extend** the blue subway line into the area and **construct** new schools for the residents' children.

B Complete the questions with the correct form of the verbs in Exercise A.

1 Do you think it's better to ______________ old buildings or ______________ them to make way for new ones? Why?
2 What is one change that would completely ______________ your hometown for the better?
3 Your hometown wants to ______________ a new road through a local park. How would you feel?
4 What could old unused Main Street stores be ______________ into now that most people shop online?
5 Why do you think so many stores ______________ from the main street to out-of-town shopping malls?
6 Do you think it is better to ______________ public transportation to all parts of a city or to encourage more bike riding? Why?

C Work in pairs. Discuss the questions in Exercise B.

SPEAKING

A PREPARE Work in pairs. Look at the map of an abandoned area and discuss the main issues.

B PLAN Work in groups. Discuss how the area could be improved for the local community. Agree on three changes to make and rank them in order of importance.

I think the easiest area to address is the park. If we clean up the garbage, children will have somewhere to play soccer.

C PRESENT Present your ideas to the class. Explain your reasoning.

READING

A SPEAK Work in pairs. Discuss the questions.

1 What are the most important elements of a successful restaurant?
2 Why do you think so many restaurants close within their first year?

B SCAN Scan *It could have been so much better …* quickly. What is it about?

1 The rise and fall of China Garden.
2 Why you shouldn't start a business.
3 Why China Garden is failing.

C IDENTIFY SPECULATION Read the article again and answer the questions. Underline the parts of the text that gives you the answers. Use the information in the box to help you.

Identifying speculation

Speculation is when someone guesses reasons behind something without necessarily having all the facts, e.g. *I don't know … maybe it's the right restaurant, but just the wrong location.*

1 Why does Mei Lù think the business is failing?
2 What does Mario Coniglio believe makes the chefs' standard of cooking lower?
3 What does he feel creates a bad atmosphere for the customers?
4 What would encourage Nicki Wright to eat at China Garden more frequently?
5 What does Alex Mullins feel would have attracted more customers when the restaurant first opened?
6 What does he think the problem is with the restaurant's ingredients?

D SPEAK Work in pairs. What are the top three issues you think the owner needs to address?

GRAMMAR

Unreal conditionals

A Work in pairs. Read the following sentences from the article. Do they describe things that actually happened or imaginary situations? Do they describe possible results in the past, present or future?

1 If I hadn't set up China Garden, I would have continued working in an office job that I hated for the rest of my life.
2 If there was less competition in the area, I think the business would be much more successful.
3 If they'd spent more money on promotion in the area, more people would know about the restaurant.

B WORK IT OUT Match the sentences (1–3) in Exercise A to the rules (a–c).

Unreal conditionals

a Second conditional ___

We use *if* + simple past + *would/might/could* + base form to talk about the consequences of an imagined present or future.

b Third conditional ___

We use *if* + past perfect and *would/might/could* + *have* + past participle to talk about the past consequences of a hypothetical, different past.

c Mixed conditionals ___

We can use a mixture of the second and third conditional by using *if* + past perfect + *would/might/could* + base form. This is used to imagine the present consequences of a hypothetical, different past.

C Go to the Grammar Hub on page 134.

IT COULD HAVE BEEN SO MUCH BETTER …

In New York, there are hundreds of good Chinese restaurants already in existence, so establishing a new one is always going to be extremely challenging. China Garden is a family-run restaurant selling Chinese and Asian fusion food in New York's Chinatown. However, the restaurant is in trouble. Last year it lost almost $300,000. If things continue in the same way, the restaurant won't be there in six months.

When we met with the owner, Mei Lù, she was understandably not in a very positive mood. 'I always wanted to run my own restaurant. If I hadn't set up China Garden, I would have continued working in an office job that I hated for the rest of my life. But now I'm really starting to regret the decision. If there was less competition in the area, I think the business would be much more successful. I don't know … Maybe it's the right restaurant, but just the wrong location.' So, is Mei right? Did she just set up business in the wrong part of the city or are there other reasons behind the restaurant's poor performance? We spoke to the staff, locals and critics to dig a little deeper.

Mario Coniglio has been the head waiter at China Garden since it opened last July. Despite the competition, he thinks the location is fine, but the number of items on the menu is having a negative effect on the business. 'The menu is enormous, and a lot of customers seem to find it difficult to know where to start. If we had fewer options, customers could choose more easily. Also, our chefs could probably

D PRACTICE Complete the sentences with the correct form of the verbs in parentheses. Use contractions where possible.

1 If I started a business, it __________ (*be*) in IT because I have a lot of ideas in that area.

2 If I saw someone committing a crime, I __________ (*stop*) it myself because it's too dangerous. I __________ (*call*) the police.

3 If I had a lot of money, I __________ (*buy*) a sports car.

4 I __________ (*be*) a lot happier now if I hadn't dropped out of college.

5 I __________ (*work*) much harder if I was paid more.

6 If I hadn't taken my current job, I __________ (*meet*) my husband.

E SPEAK Work in pairs. Change the sentences in Exercise D so they are true for you. Ask follow-up questions for more information.

A: I'd be a lot happier if I hadn't failed my exams.
B: Which exams did you fail?

PRONUNCIATION

Connected speech in conditionals

7.3 **A** Listen and repeat the clauses. Is there a pause between the words in bold? Is the pronunciation of *have* strong or weak?

1 Customers **would have** paid more if …

2 Customers **might have** preferred it if …

3 The staff **couldn't have** been friendlier if …

7.4 **B** Draw a (‿) to show connected speech in the following sentences. Then listen, check and repeat.

1 I wouldn't have spent the money if I'd known it was such a risk.

2 If the restaurant had been busier, it would have survived longer.

3 If the menu had been simpler, it might have been easier to choose.

4 I think it could have worked if they'd focused more on advertising.

SPEAKING HUB

A PREPARE Read the situations (1–4) and write notes about what you would do in each.

1 Your dream business is failing. You spent too much money, employed too many friends and borrowed too much from the bank. In order to continue, you need to sell the family home and move into a rented apartment.

2 When you chose your degree in architecture there were a lot of construction jobs in the country. Now the property market has crashed. You have been offered a job as a math teacher.

3 $50,000 was transferred into your bank account by accident. You spent half of the money and the police have arrested you.

4 You left your passwords written in a book in a drawer. Your roommates found it and started posting on your social media for fun. Some of your friends have now unfriended you.

B PLAN Work in pairs. Discuss your ideas from Exercise A. Try to agree on the best solution for each situation.

A: If someone posted things through any of my social media accounts, I would shut them all down.
B: Ha ha! Really? I'd just share something embarrassing about them!

C SPEAK Work with another pair. Explain what you decided in Exercise B and why. Did you agree?

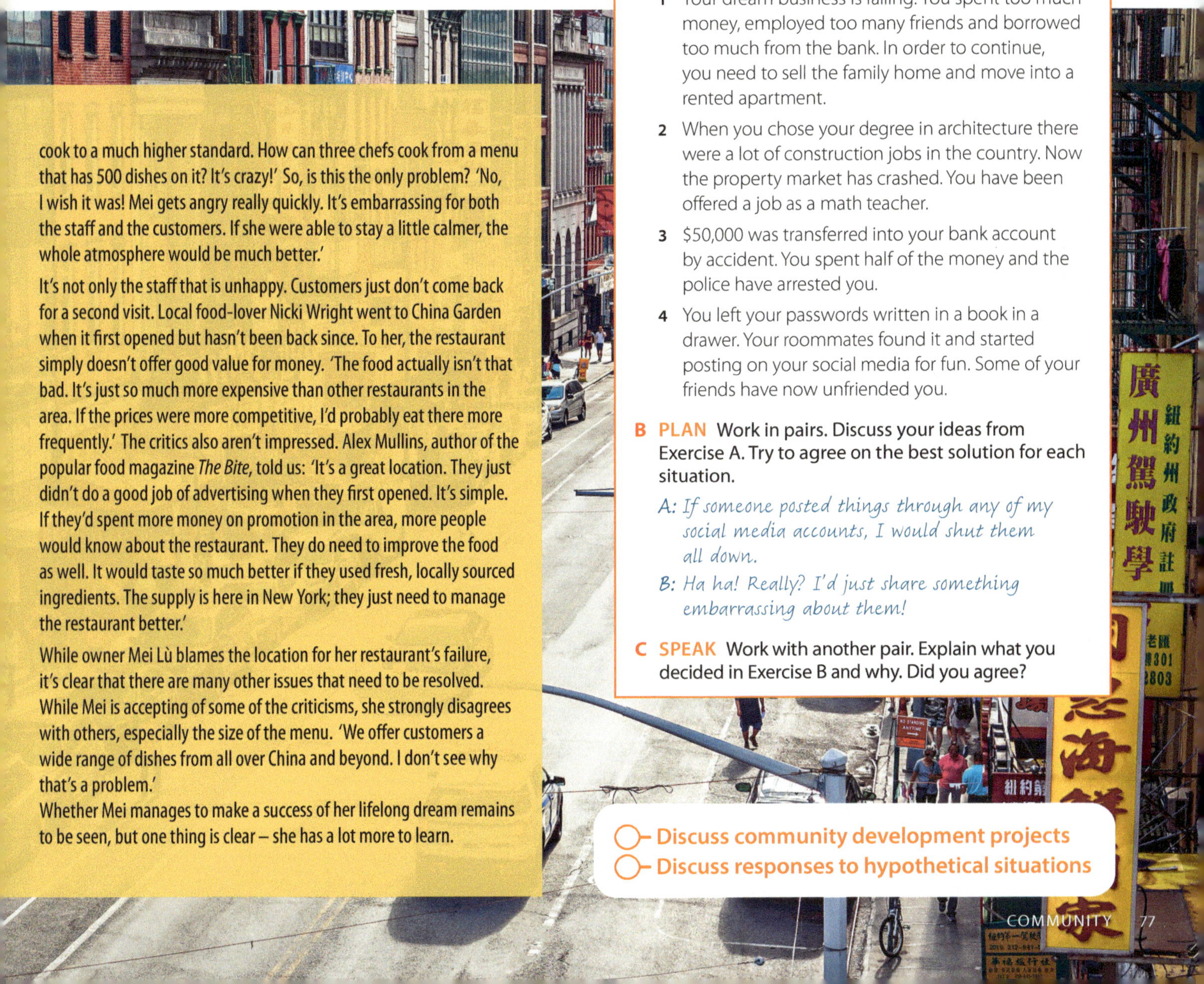

cook to a much higher standard. How can three chefs cook from a menu that has 500 dishes on it? It's crazy!' So, is this the only problem? 'No, I wish it was! Mei gets angry really quickly. It's embarrassing for both the staff and the customers. If she were able to stay a little calmer, the whole atmosphere would be much better.'

It's not only the staff that is unhappy. Customers just don't come back for a second visit. Local food-lover Nicki Wright went to China Garden when it first opened but hasn't been back since. To her, the restaurant simply doesn't offer good value for money. 'The food actually isn't that bad. It's just so much more expensive than other restaurants in the area. If the prices were more competitive, I'd probably eat there more frequently.' The critics also aren't impressed. Alex Mullins, author of the popular food magazine *The Bite*, told us: 'It's a great location. They just didn't do a good job of advertising when they first opened. It's simple. If they'd spent more money on promotion in the area, more people would know about the restaurant. They do need to improve the food as well. It would taste so much better if they used fresh, locally sourced ingredients. The supply is here in New York; they just need to manage the restaurant better.'

While owner Mei Lù blames the location for her restaurant's failure, it's clear that there are many other issues that need to be resolved. While Mei is accepting of some of the criticisms, she strongly disagrees with others, especially the size of the menu. 'We offer customers a wide range of dishes from all over China and beyond. I don't see why that's a problem.'

Whether Mei manages to make a success of her lifelong dream remains to be seen, but one thing is clear – she has a lot more to learn.

- Discuss community development projects
- Discuss responses to hypothetical situations

7.2 Make a change

- Talk about wishes and regrets
- Design and present a community project

S – inferring meaning
V – three-part phrasal verbs; compound nouns
G – *wish* and *if only*
P – two-stress phrasal verbs

READING

A SPEAK Work in pairs. Look at the infographic. What regrets do you think people might have in each of these categories?

B SCAN Read the comments. Match each regret to a category in the infographic. Were any of your ideas from Exercise A mentioned?

TOP FIVE REGRETS IN LIFE

We all have regrets. That job we didn't take. That house we should have bought. However, according to a recent survey by Pulse Media, most people's biggest regrets are connected to – you guessed it – romance, with family coming in a close second. Here are some other interesting results of the survey.

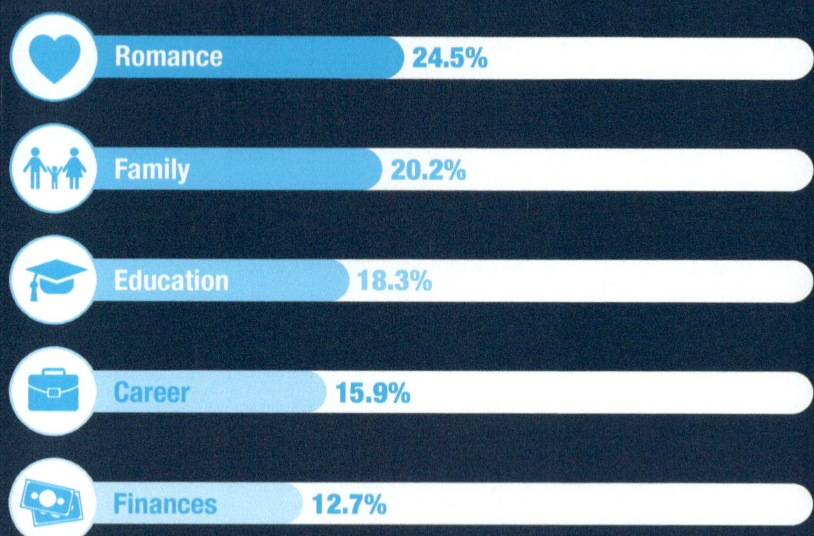

Hayley • 1 hr ago
[1]I wish I hadn't spent so much time worrying about what others thought of me when I was a child. It meant that I forgot to focus on the important issues. If only I'd spent more time studying. [2]I should have gone to a top college, but my grades just weren't good enough. I really feel like I missed out on a massive opportunity.
Reply 5 0

Chris • 1 hr 30 min ago
I'm starting to regret my career choice. I chose a career in finance because I knew I could make a lot of money, but I wish I had chosen a career I enjoyed more. I spend all of Sunday night in a bad mood.
Reply 2 0

Nick • 1 hr 38 min ago
We've recently moved to another town because my dad thinks his career is more important than his family. My mom was happy to move but [3]I wish we still lived in our old town. [4]I wish people wouldn't think only of themselves.
Reply 9 0

Sam • 1 hr 42 min ago
I really wanted to ask out a girl named Maria when I was 16! 🙂 I just used to blush and had no idea what to say to her! I was soooo painfully shy … I wish I had her number now!
Reply 4 0

Christina • 2 hrs ago
My sister and I haven't spoken for two years now. I miss her so much! I'd take back everything I said if I could. I wish she would just pick up the phone and call me.
Reply 1 0

Kelly • 2 hrs 3 mins ago
The last summer of college was one of the happiest times of my life. We traveled so much back then. [5]I wish we could all go back to that beach in Thailand, but everyone's so busy now with work and family. Maybe I wouldn't eat the seafood this time, though!
Reply 3 0

C INFER MEANING Read the comments again and answer the questions. Use the information in the box to help you.

Inferring meaning

Writers do not always say directly what they mean. We usually have to use context and our general knowledge to infer meaning.

I chose a career in finance because I knew I could make a lot of money, but I wish I had chosen a career I enjoy more. I spend all of Sunday night in a bad mood.

Here we can infer that the writer spends Sunday night in a bad mood because he doesn't want to go to work the next day.

1 What does Hayley mean by 'the important issues'?
 a being popular
 b getting good grades
 c other people's opinions
2 What massive opportunity did Hayley miss out on?
 a having good friends
 b going to a top college
 c doing well at school
3 Why did Nick's family move?
 a His parents didn't like the old town.
 b His dad got a new job.
 c His mom wanted to move.
4 What happened between Christina and her sister?
 a They never got along.
 b Their parents preferred Christina.
 c They had an argument.
5 What didn't Kelly like about the trip?
 a She got food poisoning.
 b She was on her own.
 c She couldn't find her friends.

D SPEAK Work in groups. Do you think regrets can ever be beneficial? Why/Why not?

GRAMMAR

Wish and *if only*

A SPEAK Work in pairs. Read the comments again. Look at the underlined sentences and answer the questions.

1 Which sentence describes things that annoy us about other people or things?
2 Which sentences describe regrets about the past?
3 Which sentences describe things we would like to be different in the present or future?

B WORK IT OUT Complete the box with other examples from the comments.

wish* and *if only

We use *wish* + simple past to talk about how we would like the present to be different.

a ________________

We use *wish* + past perfect to talk about things we regret in the past.

b ________________

We use *wish* + object + *would* + base form to talk about something we want others to do or stop doing because it annoys us.

c ________________

We can use *if only* instead of *wish* in all of these structures to sound more dramatic or emphatic.

d ________________

C Go to the Grammar Hub on page 134.

D PRACTICE Rewrite the sentences using the words in bold.

1 It annoys me when people throw garbage on the street.
 wish
 ________________.
2 I regret moving to the country.
 wish
 ________________.
3 I don't want to work evenings and weekends.
 If only
 ________________.
4 I forgot my passport and couldn't go on vacation.
 If only
 ________________.
5 It annoys me when people are so rude online.
 wish
 ________________.

E SPEAK Work in pairs. Complete the sentences with your own ideas. Tell your partner. Ask follow-up questions for more information.

I wish people wouldn't … If only I'd bought …
If I hadn't studied … I wish I were …

SPEAKING

A PREPARE Write notes about any wishes or regrets you have about the following areas:

career education family finances romance

B PLAN Work in pairs. Discuss your wishes and regrets from Exercise A. Which is your biggest regret?

C DISCUSS Work in groups. Explain your biggest regrets. What can you learn from them? How could you avoid making the same mistakes in the future?

LISTENING

A Read the article and answer the questions. Underline the parts of the text that gives you the answers.

1. What is the Freeconomy Community?
2. Why is Mark Boyle called 'the moneyless man'?
3. How did he pay for the farm in Ireland?
4. What system is used on the farm?

7.5 **B LISTEN FOR ORGANIZATION** Listen to an interview with someone who started their own Freeconomy Community. Put the topics in the order they are discussed.

___ starting networking events and workshops to share skills

___ holding community barbecues and street parties

___ starting a website to share goods and skills

___ finding a community site where people can meet

___ finding building materials and people to help

7.5 **C LISTEN FOR DETAIL** Listen again. Complete the sentences with no more than three words from the interview.

1. Callum's experience with one of his ________________ inspired him to set up the Facebook group.
2. They only have a few users but everyone is pretty ________________.
3. They use an old ________________ for their community building.
4. A ________________ gave them their old kitchen equipment to set up a café.
5. They run ________________ events twice a week for people to share their skills.
6. All the food in the café comes from the garden or ________________.

D SPEAK Work in groups. Discuss the questions.

1. How well do you know your neighbors?
2. What kind of community events are there in your area?
3. Would you like to be part of a moneyless community? Why/ Why not?

How We Live

returns for a second series

The popular documentary series *How We Live* returns this month, covering a diverse range of topics from ice fishing in Canada to surfing in Iran.

Episode one focuses on the Irish activist and writer Mark Boyle, best known for establishing the Freeconomy Community – an online network that encourages its members to share skills, tools and land for free. Boyle is commonly referred to as 'the moneyless man', a name he earned by living without money for almost two and a half years. Back in 2008, Boyle quit his job with an organic food company and set up home in a camper he got for free online. Generating electricity via a solar panel he bought for $360, Boyle spent the next few years growing his own food and volunteering on a local farm. In 2010, he published an account of his experience – *The Moneyless Man* – before returning to the monetary world in 2011.

Boyle uses proceeds from the book to purchase land for the Freeconomy Community, including the small farm in County Galway, Ireland, where he currently lives with his partner. The farm, which houses up to 30 volunteers rent free, is based around the idea of 'paying it forward', a system in which one member helps another with the understanding that they will go on to help someone else.

Episode one of How We Live *is available on August 31st.*

VOCABULARY

Three-part phrasal verbs

7.6 **A** Complete the sentences with the correct form of the phrasal verbs in the box. Use the definitions in parentheses to help you. Then listen and check.

come up with	come up against	cut down on
get around to	get along with	look up to

1. Well, obviously I ________________ (*respect and admire*) people like Mark Boyle. He's achieved amazing things.
2. Anyway, luckily, I ________________ (*have a good relationship with someone*) my neighbors and one of them is a professional decorator.
3. Anyway, it turned out he was looking for an accountant, so we ________________ (*think of*) a plan to help us both.
4. So, I set up the Facebook group to give people somewhere to share their skills or give away things they don't want anymore. It actually helps ________________ (*reduce*) waste as well.
5. We had a lot of great ideas that we'd never ________________ (*to finally do something*) working on because we rarely met.
6. It's great because if you ________________ (*to have to deal with something difficult*) a problem, then you can usually find someone here to help.

B Go to the Vocabulary Hub on page 146.

C Complete the questions with the correct form of the phrasal verbs in the box.

come up against get along with get around to keep up with look up to run out of

1 What things do you regularly want to do but never ______________ doing?

2 Do you think it's important to ______________ your neighbors?

3 Do you have a hero that you ______________?

4 How do you ______________ local news and community events?

5 If you ______________ gas when driving, what would you do?

6 If you ______________ a difficult situation, who do you turn to for help?

D SPEAK Work in pairs. Discuss the questions in Exercise C.

PRONUNCIATION

Two-stress phrasal verbs

7.7 **A** Listen to the sentences. Which parts of the phrasal verbs are stressed? Circle the main stress. Underline the secondary stress.

1 We need to **come up with** a new way to use the space.

2 People create so much waste trying to **keep up with** the latest trends.

3 We **came up against** many challenges during the project.

7.8 **B** Listen to each sentence said in two different ways. Choose the sentence that is said with the correct stress on the phrasal verb (a or b).

1 Many old people don't have anyone to **take care of** them. a / b

2 We **teamed up with** the local government and worked on it together. a / b

3 It's a great way to **catch up with** friends. a / b

VOCABULARY

Compound nouns

Compound nouns

A compound noun is a single noun formed from two or more words. The most common type is formed by joining two nouns. For example, *community center*, *project leader*, *skill shortage*, etc.

Match the numbers (1–5) to the letters (a–e) to form compound nouns.

1 We need more **volunteer** ...

2 I want to improve my Spanish, so I've joined a **language** ...

3 We set up a **car-sharing** ...

4 We have opened a **food** ...

5 Next week we have organized a **street** ...

a **exchange** group.

b **bank** to distribute food to the poor.

c **workers** to help run the youth club.

d **party** in our neighborhood.

e **system** to help reduce pollution and congestion.

SPEAKING HUB

A PREPARE Create a list of skills you could use to help other people. For example, languages, accountancy, design, technology, etc.

B PLAN Work in groups. Discuss your individual skills and decide on a community project you could start together. Write notes about:

- who it will help
- how you will set it up and advertise it
- where it will be based
- what activities you will offer to engage people

C PRESENT Present your project to the class, explaining how it would help the community. Answer their follow-up questions.

Talk about wishes and regrets

Design and present a community project

Café Hub

7.3 A shared vision

Ⓐ– *you know* Ⓢ– talking on the telephone

An innovative solution

COMPREHENSION

A Rank the following issues according to how big of a problem they are in your country.

___ house prices
___ cost of living
___ job opportunities
___ street crime
___ corruption
___ access to health care

B Work in pairs. Compare your lists from Exercise A.

Glossary

freehold (n) the legal right to own a building or piece of land for an unlimited period of time

leasehold (n) the legal right to use a building or piece of land for a limited time (as agreed upon in a property contract)

C Watch a news report about a housing project in London and answer the questions.

1 How did the families address the issue of rising house prices?
2 Why is this a cheaper option for them?
3 What other benefits do the residents gain?

D Watch the report again. Are these sentences true (T) or false (F)? Correct the false sentences.

1 The project was part of a housing scheme offered by the local council. T / F
2 The houses have turned out to be approximately a fifth cheaper this way. T / F
3 The expert believes that properties which share facilities are a better use of land. T / F
4 Cressida says she likes how easy it is to socialize with other residents. T / F
5 Projects like this could help address housing issues because there is a lot of unused land in the capital. T / F

E Work in groups. Do you think community housing projects like this would be effective in your area? Why/Why not?

AUTHENTIC ENGLISH

A Work in pairs. Read the extract from the video. Why do you think the speaker says *you know*?

So you can actually put what are, **you know**, fairly generous houses on quite a small plot of land.

B Read the information in the box and check your answers to Exercise A.

you know

In informal spoken English, we use *you know* for three main reasons:

a To show that what you are referring to is known or understood by the listener.
Guess who I saw the other day? Juan! ***You know****, the guy who used to work on the IT team.*

b To give yourself time to think about what to say next.
Well, maybe it's time to, ***you know****, move on with your life.*

c To emphasize what you're saying.
It's just so different now, ***you know****?*

C Match the sentences (1–3) with the uses in the box (a–c).

1 I was wondering if you'd like to, you know, go and see a movie or something.
2 It's not easy being the only 50-year-old here, you know.
3 What's the name of that movie – you know, the one with Emily Blunt in it?

D Work in pairs. Take turns finishing the sentences with your own ideas.

1 What's the name of that guy in our class? You know, …
2 You know, you really should …
3 We're just going to go shopping and, you know, …

Living together

A Work in pairs. Discuss the questions.

1. Who is the first person you tell when you have big news? Why?
2. Would you ever tell someone something important over the phone or on Skype? Why/Why not?

B Watch the video and answer the questions.

1. Why do you think Amanda's mom mentions Mabel Sanderson at the beginning of the conversation?
2. Why doesn't Amanda's mom like the idea of a shared housing project?
3. What do you think Amanda is thinking when she says, 'you might just be right'?

SPEAKING SKILL

A Complete the box using the phrases below. Then watch the video again to check your answers.

Got to go. I'd better be going … I need to go
Is it a good time? is that you? I didn't catch that.
that brings me to what I was calling about.
What are you up to? What was that Yes, it's me
You're breaking up.

Talking on the telephone

Phone conversations generally follow a set routine. At the beginning of the conversation, we usually …

- confirm we're talking to the right person:
  Mom: Oh, Mandy, [1] ________________
  Amanda: [2] ________________ *, Mom.*
- find out what the person is doing:
  Amanda: [3] ________________
- ask if they are free to talk:
  Amanda: [4] ________________

After exchanging greetings, we usually give a reason for calling:

Amanda: Actually, [5] ________________

Having discussed the reason for calling, we try to bring the conversation to an end:

Amanda: [6] ________________
Amanda: So, [7] ________________ *, Mom …*
Amanda: [8] ________________

We also might need to let the other person know that we didn't hear what they said:

Mom: [9] ________________
Mom: [10] ________________ *, darling?*
Amanda: [11] ________________

B Work in pairs. You are going to role-play a telephone conversation.

Student A – Call your partner to discuss one of the topics from the list below.

Student B – Listen to your partner. Make helpful suggestions before trying to bring the conversation to an end.

Then, swap roles.

- discuss a problem at work
- ask for a restaurant recommendation
- try to sell a new product
- ask to borrow some money

SPEAKING HUB

A PREPARE Work in pairs. Brainstorm the advantages and disadvantages of shared housing.

B PLAN Role-play a telephone conversation. Student A – Plan how to convince your partner not to move into a shared housing project. Student B – Plan how to convince your partner that moving into a shared housing project is a good idea.

C SPEAK Role-play the telephone call.

A: Yes, but if a lot of people are using the same facilities, they will break down sooner, so you might not be saving as much money as you think.
B: But houses are so expensive that we have to save money somehow.

Give your opinion on a social initiative

➤ Turn to page 160 to learn how to write a formal letter of complaint.

VOCABULARY

A Choose the correct verbs to complete the sentences.

1 They plan to ***extend / construct*** the vacation resort by two square kilometers.
2 The local council are going to ***convert / relocate*** the hospital to a new site on the edge of town.
3 Almost all of the old factories in the city center have been ***restored / converted*** into apartments.
4 The old power station is going to be ***demolished / constructed*** to make way for a new shopping mall.
5 There are some beautiful old buildings in the city, but it would be expensive to ***restore / transform*** them.
6 After spending millions of dollars, the old docks have been ***transformed / extended*** into a vibrant area.
7 Plans to ***construct / relocate*** a new hospital have been put on hold due to financial constraints.

B Work in pairs. Discuss what changes you think should be made to your neighborhood and why.

C Match the numbers (1–8) with the letters (a–h) to form full sentences.

1 The city needs to come …
2 New recycling bins have been installed in order to cut …
3 The local government has teamed …
4 While building the new road, the government ran …
5 Facilities such as schools and hospitals can't keep …
6 The country has spent a lot of money trying to catch …
7 It's important to take care …
8 I don't really get along …

a up with local businesses to renovate the area.
b up with development in neighboring countries.
c of less fortunate people in society.
d up with a solution to the overcrowding.
e out of funding.
f up with the population growth in the area.
g with many of my neighbors.
h down on waste.

D Complete the compound nouns with the nouns in the box.

car food language street volunteer

1 A __________ party was organized to celebrate the royal wedding.
2 Since the introduction of a __________-sharing system, traffic levels have reduced almost by half.
3 For some people, access to a __________ bank is vital in order to feed their families.
4 I've really improved my level of English since I joined a __________ exchange.
5 After the floods, hundreds of __________ workers helped to clear up the area.

GRAMMAR

A Complete the first conditional sentences with the correct form of the verbs in the box.

call do finish reach sit work

1 If the city continues to grow, the population __________ ten million inhabitants soon.
2 If you get lost, __________ me.
3 What __________ if it rains?
4 If they meet the deadline, the new stadium __________ by the start of the season.
5 If you arrive late, we __________ on the beach.
6 You're not going to get promoted if you __________ harder.

B Choose the correct options to complete the sentences.

1 I wish you ***'d hurried up / 'd hurry up***. We're going to be late.
2 If only we ***left / 'd left*** earlier! I was so annoyed that we missed the beginning of the concert.
3 There's so much more I want to see here in Rome. If only we ***'d had / had*** more time.
4 I wish you ***could have come / could come***. It was so much fun.
5 I wish it ***hadn't rained / wasn't raining***. I'm so wet!
6 I wish my roommate ***would do / would have done*** the dishes more often. He never does it!
7 I think we're lost. If only I ***listened / 'd listened*** to the directions more carefully.
8 If only I ***'d had / had*** more money. I definitely won't be going on vacation this year.

C What might you say in these situations? Write sentences with unreal conditional structures.

1 You would like to get a taxi but you have no reception on your phone.
__________________________________.
2 The map on your phone isn't working so you got lost.
__________________________________.
3 You would like to play soccer but your foot hurts.
__________________________________.
4 You should have started the essay sooner. You missed the deadline.
__________________________________.
5 I stayed out in the sun too long yesterday and got sunburned.
__________________________________.
6 Look at the weather in Lisbon this week! It's much better than last week when we were there.
__________________________________.

D Work in pairs. Compare your ideas from Exercise C.

8 MYSTERY

An ancient sequoia forest in Mendocino County, California.

OBJECTIVES

- speculate about past events
- summarize a cultural story
- write and perform a short scene
- speculate about the causes and consequences of a crime
- discuss how to test an idea
- write a complex essay

Work with a partner. Discuss the questions.

1 Read the quote. What do you think Wilde means? Do you agree with him? Why/Why not?

2 What crime novels or TV shows do you enjoy watching? Tell your partner about one of them.

3 What crimes are the biggest problem in your society? What do you think can be done to deal with them?

8.1 Myths and legends

- Speculate about past events
- Summarize a cultural story

S – decoding: similes and metaphors
V – word families
G – past modals of deduction
P – thought groups

READING

A Do you believe that ghosts, aliens or monsters exist? How certain are you on a scale of 1–5 (1 = I'm sure they don't exist, 5 = I'm sure they do exist)? Write notes.

B **SPEAK** Work in groups. Compare your answers from Exercise A. Explain your ideas, giving examples where appropriate.

HOW DO YOU EXPLAIN THAT?

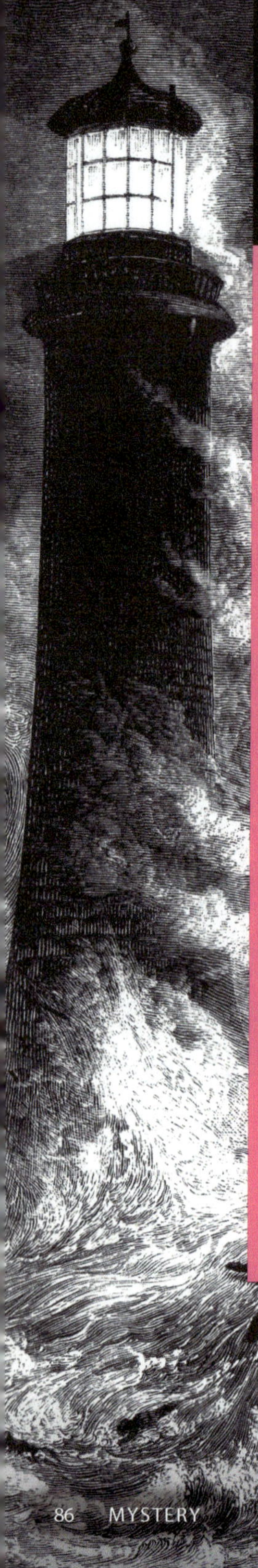

There is nothing like an unexplained mystery to capture the public imagination. We seem drawn to violent or supernatural causes, yet the real explanation is usually far less dramatic. Here we explore two unusual incidents with obvious explanations.

THE FLANNAN ISLES LIGHTHOUSE

On December 15,1900, a passing ship noticed that the lighthouse on Flannan Island, off the coast of Scotland, wasn't working. Bad weather made it impossible for a ship to reach the island before December 26th, when the Eilean Mòr docked to deliver supplies to the three men that were living there – Thomas Marshall, James Ducat and Donald MacArthur. Strangely, the lighthouse was like a ghost town, with no one in sight and an uneaten meal on the table. Stranger still, despite the bad weather, one of the men had left his waterproof clothing behind, a chair had been knocked over and all of the clocks had stopped. An extensive search of the island was conducted but none of the men were ever found.

Once the unusual events had been reported, the public immediately began to speculate about what had happened. [a]Many believed that the men must have been murdered. [b]Others suggested they might have been eaten by a sea monster or could even have been carried away by a ghost ship in the night.

Although the speculation continued for years, the most likely explanation is the terrible weather. Since their bodies have never been found, [c]the three men must have been blown into the sea and drowned. [d]Two of them may have been working outside when the other noticed a huge wave approaching. As quick as a flash, he must have rushed outside to warn his friends, leaving his waterproof clothing behind and knocking over the chair. Some of the more unusual clues, such as the untouched meal, are thought to have been made up because they certainly weren't included in the original report.

THE DYATLOV PASS INCIDENT

On February 2, 1959, nine hikers set out to climb Kholat Syakhl ('Mountain of the Dead') in Russia but never returned. Three weeks later, a search party found the group's badly damaged tent abandoned and half covered in snow. Footprints left by people who were either barefoot or wearing little on their feet led rescuers to the edge of a forest where they found five bodies, each with missing or ripped clothing. Although the hikers had sustained few external injuries, their skin had turned a strange shade of orange and investigators found high levels of radiation on their clothing. The other four bodies were found on May 4th, almost 100 meters away. Although better dressed than the first group, they had major injuries, including broken ribs and a fractured skull. Rescuers must have turned white as a sheet when they discovered that one of the female hikers was missing her tongue.

Theories of what had happened soon began to circulate. [e]Some thought the group might have been murdered by the indigenous Mansi people. Others suggested they had been attacked by wild animals or even a yeti. [f]However, the hikers can't have been murdered or attacked by animals because there were no signs of a fight. It is far more likely that the destruction of the tent and the second group's physical injuries were caused by an avalanche, while the missing tongue was probably eaten by a wild animal. The first group's lack of clothing can be explained by something called 'paradoxical undressing' – a phenomenon in which people in the final stages of hypothermia start to feel incredibly hot and take off their clothes in an attempt to cool down. Their orange skin and the radiation levels on their clothing are thought to have been caused by overexposure to the sun.

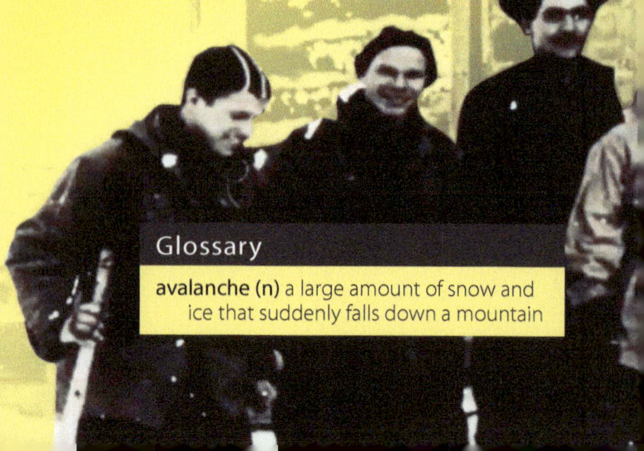

Glossary

avalanche (n) a large amount of snow and ice that suddenly falls down a mountain

C SCAN Scan *How do you explain that?* What explanations were originally given for each mystery?

D READ FOR DETAIL Read the stories again and answer the questions.

1 What had been left in the lighthouse?
2 What does the writer say happened to the men?
3 What does the writer think caused the chair to fall over?
4 Where were the two groups of bodies found?
5 What physical injuries had the hikers sustained?
6 What explanation is given for the missing tongue?

E DECODE: SIMILES AND METAPHORS Read the stories again. Answer the questions by identifying similes and metaphors in the text. Use the information in the box to help you.

Decoding: similes and metaphors

In articles describing dramatic events, writers frequently use descriptive language to make the story more engaging. Two common techniques used are:

a **Similes** – comparing one thing to another using *as* or *like*.
He may look small, but he's ***as brave as a lion***.

b **Metaphors** – describing something as if it were something else.
The snow ***was a white blanket***. (= *It wasn't actually a blanket; it just looked like one.*)

1 What was the lighthouse like when the ship arrived?
a like a small town b empty
2 How does the writer think the third man left the kitchen?
a slowly b quickly
3 How does the writer think the rescuers felt when they discovered the female hiker?
a frightened b angry

F SPEAK Work in groups. Why do you think people look for unusual explanations to mysteries, when there are frequently more obvious solutions?

GRAMMAR
Past modals of deduction

A Work in pairs. Look at the highlighted sentences in the article. Which sentence(s) mean …

1 it's almost certain that something happened or is true.
2 it's possible that something happened or is true.
3 it's impossible that something happened or is true.

B WORK IT OUT Complete the structures in the box.

Past modals of deduction

We use modals of deduction to make guesses about what happened in the past.

a We use ________ + *have* + past participle to say we're sure something happened because there's strong evidence.

b We use ________ / ________ / ________ + *have* + past participle to say we think something is possible, but we aren't sure.

c We use ________ + *have* + past participle to say we're sure something didn't happen because there's strong evidence.

C Work in pairs. Go to the Grammar Hub on page 136.

D SPEAK Work in pairs. Read the situations (1–3) and discuss what you think happened using past modals of deduction.

1 Hundreds of children got sick at a school in New York. Children who brought in their own lunch were unaffected.
2 Tasmin took the train to work as normal and went to buy coffee from a café nearby. However, when she went to pay, she discovered her wallet was missing.
3 A math teacher was amazed when one of his students finished their exam in 20 minutes. The exam has 100 questions and usually takes an hour and a half.

SPEAKING

A DISCUSS Work in groups. Read *The Hopkinsville goblin case* and discuss what you think happened.

The Hopkinsville Goblin Case

In 1955, the Sutton family and their friend Billy Ray Taylor were relaxing on their porch. Suddenly, Billy Ray saw lights in the sky and shouted for everyone to come and take a look. They saw what they thought was an alien with glowing eyes, a large head, pointed ears and claws. The family and their friend grabbed their guns and started shooting. They heard their bullets hitting something metal, which they thought must have been the alien's spaceship.

B Go to the Communication Hub on page 151 and compare your ideas from Exercise A with the likely solution.

LISTENING

A SPEAK Work in pairs. Look at the illustrations of three famous myths from around the world. What do you think happens in each story? Where do you think these stories are from?

8.1 **B LISTEN FOR GIST** Listen to an interview with an expert on myths and legends. Check your ideas from Exercise A.

8.1 **C LISTEN FOR DETAIL** Listen again. Choose the correct options (a, b or c) to complete the sentences.

1 According to Phillip Norris, myths and legends …
  a usually have the same origin.
  b are similar in neighboring countries.
  c have similar themes across cultures.

2 The tales of Sinbad the Sailor are given as an example of …
  a a hero myth.
  b a monster myth.
  c an urban legend.

3 Sinbad and his crew go to the castle on the island …
  a to look for food.
  b to escape from their attackers.
  c to shelter from the storm.

4 Anyone who looks directly at Medusa …
  a is bitten by the snakes in her hair.
  b is turned to stone.
  c is killed by Perseus.

5 The Yeti and Bigfoot are given as examples of …
  a stories inspired by wild animals.
  b ancient legends.
  c modern monster myths.

6 To call Hanako-San, you have to …
  a knock on the bathroom mirror three times.
  b say her name three times.
  c knock on the bathroom door three times and say her name.

7 According to Phillip Norris, myths like Hanako-San are …
  a unique to Japan.
  b surprisingly different across cultures.
  c popular with young children.

D SPEAK Work in groups. Why do you think myths and legends are still told today? Why do you think new ones are still created? Explain your reasoning.

1

2

VOCABULARY

Word families

A Complete the word families in the table. Use the information in the box to help you.

Word families

A word family is a group of words with the same root. Learning the associated words (e.g. the verb, noun, adjective and adverb) can help you to understand texts more easily and improve your accuracy when writing.

Verb	Noun	Adjective	Adverb
–	1	mythical	–
2	belief	3	believably
–	4	heroic	heroically
5	representation	representative	representatively
–	6	traditional	7
transform	8	transformational	–

B Complete the sentences with the correct form of the words in parentheses.

1 The minotaur is a ________________ (*myth*) creature with the head of a bull and the body of a man.

2 The main character usually ________________ (*hero*) saves a princess or someone else in distress.

3 Snakes are frequently used to ________________ (*represent*) danger.

4 ________________ (*tradition*), stories were told and not written down so there are frequently variations of a legend.

5 Many stories frequently include the ________________ (*transform*) of a person into some kind of monster.

PRONUNCIATION

Thought groups

8.2 **A** Listen to the first part of a story from the interview. Mark any pauses with (/). Why do you think the speaker pauses at these points?

As in many of the stories, Sinbad's ship is caught in a terrible storm and driven off course. They sail toward a small island but are attacked by a tribe of monkeys carrying spears. Fearing for their lives, Sinbad and his crew swim to the island and rush to a castle they see at the top of a hill.

8.3 **B** Read the next part of the story. Mark where you think the speaker will pause with (/). Then listen and check.

Tired and hungry from their escape, the crew falls asleep on the floor of the castle but is awoken to find the ground shaking. In the doorway to their room stands a giant over 20 meters tall. His eyes burn like fire, his teeth are long and sharp, and his huge mouth has the lips of a camel. Sinbad and his crew try to run away but one of them is caught and eaten by the giant.

C SPEAK Work in pairs. Practice telling the story from Exercise B. Remember to use pauses to make the story easier to follow.

SPEAKING HUB

A PREPARE Work in pairs. Look at the pictures and use the words in the box to discuss what you think each myth might be about.

Greeks hidden horse war

fake lake monster Scotland

accident coat forest hitchhiker

B PLAN Work in groups of three. Student A – Go to the Communication Hub on page 147. Student B – Go to the Communication Hub on page 149. Student C – Go to the Communication Hub on page 152.

C PRESENT Summarize the myth you have just read about to your group. Use your notes to help you.

D DISCUSS Work in pairs. Think about myths and legends in your own country. Tell your partner:

- who the myth was about
- what the origins of the myth were
- what happened in the myth

Speculate about past events

Summarize a cultural story

8.2 Who did it?

- Write and perform a short scene
- Speculate about the causes and consequences of a crime

V – easily confused verbs; crime
S – following an argument
G – order of adjectives
P – adding information

READING

A PREDICT Work in pairs. You are going to read part of a story called *The curse of the black falcon*. Look at the picture and discuss the questions.

1 What do you think the Black Falcon is?
2 What do you think happens in the story?

B SKIM Read the story quickly and check your predictions from Exercise A.

C READ FOR MAIN IDEA Read the story again. Are these sentences true (T) or false (F)? Correct the false sentences.

1 Professor Bainbridge was excited about having a party. *T / F*
2 Professor Bainbridge was most excited by the value of the necklace. *T / F*
3 He only got to keep the necklace for a short time. *T / F*
4 Only members of the family knew the code for the safe. *T / F*
5 The safe was hidden in the desk. *T / F*
6 The burglar broke the window immediately. *T / F*
7 The burglar searched the room calmly at first. *T / F*
8 A sudden noise alerted the professor to the burglar's presence. *T / F*

The Curse of the BLACK FALCON

'So, how do I look?'

Professor Bainbridge smiled as he turned to face his daughter. She was wearing a beautiful blue dress that had once belonged to his mother. Although Alice had recently turned 20, to him she'd always be the little girl who was too scared to sleep with the lights off. 'Like a million dollars,' he said, returning her smile.

Tonight was supposed to be a celebration, but he'd never liked parties, especially when he was the focus. He sighed, put his glasses down and rubbed his eyes. Seeing his reaction, Alice touched her father's arm and asked, 'Daddy, what's wrong? Aren't you excited to show everyone what you found?'

All of this fuss over an old necklace. True, it was worth a lot of money to the right collector, but to him its historical value was far more important. He'd heard stories about the mysterious Black Falcon all his life and after years of research and hard work, he'd finally found it in a muddy French field. It was such a significant find that his family had insisted that they hold a party to celebrate. On Monday, the professor would deliver the necklace to the British Museum, but for the weekend it would stay locked away in the safe above his desk. Nobody outside of the family knew the combination to the safe, but it still made him nervous to have such a valuable object in his house. He looked up at the large rectangular painting above the desk, tried to straighten it and turned back to his daughter.

'I'll be happier when this weekend is over,' he said angrily. Recognizing that her father was nervous, Alice began to straighten his bow tie. 'You never know, you might have fun.' The professor was just about to reply when the doorbell rang. 'That'll be the Joneses!' Alice said excitedly. 'They're always early. Come on!' The professor sighed again and followed her out into the hallway.

For an hour, the study lay empty. The fire had died out and the only sound came from the antique gold clock on the desk and the thunderstorm outside. Suddenly, a figure dressed in black appeared at the window. Cautiously, they looked into the study. Satisfied that the room was empty, they raised a fist to the window. Yet, instead of breaking the glass immediately, they stopped. For two long minutes they waited, patiently watching the sky until suddenly, the moment came. A loud crash of thunder echoed through the sky and the figure calmly smashed the window, felt for the handle and climbed inside.

Slowly, they began opening drawers and pulling books off the shelves, but as the minutes ticked by, they became more and more desperate. Frustrated, the figure leaned against the desk and stared at the painting above it. Noticing it was hanging at a strange angle, the figure moved the painting to the side, revealing the strong metal safe behind. After a few minutes, the safe was open and inside lay the ultimate prize – the Black Falcon.

Just as the figure reached inside to grab the necklace, they heard the professor's voice ringing through the hallway outside. 'I'll just go and fetch my pipe … See you outside.' In their hurry to find somewhere to hide, the figure sent a small Chinese vase crashing to the ground. Terrified, the figure hid behind the open door, holding the necklace as the professor appeared on the other side. 'Tommy? Is that you?' he called, looking into the darkness. He listened for a reply but there was nothing but silence.

D INFER MEANING **Work in pairs. Scan the story again and discuss the questions.**

1 What does the professor mean when he says that Alice looks 'like a million dollars'?
2 Why does the figure in black wait before breaking the window?
3 How does the burglar work out where the Black Falcon is?

VOCABULARY
Easily confused verbs

A Choose the correct options to complete the sentences. Then scan the story again to check your answers.

1 *Seeing / Watching* his reaction, Alice *felt / touched* her father's arm and asked …
2 For two long minutes they waited, patiently *watching / seeing* the sky until suddenly, …
3 … the figure calmly smashed the window, *touched / felt* for the handle and climbed inside.
4 … they *heard / listened* the professor's voice ringing through the hallway outside.
5 'Tommy? Is that you?' he called, *seeing / looking* into the darkness.
6 He *listened / heard* for a reply but there was nothing but silence.

B Complete the sentences with the correct form of the words in Exercise A.

1 Standing inside the room, he ________________ carefully to what they were saying outside.
2 He ________________ along the wall until he found the light switch.
3 He sat ________________ them to see what they would do.
4 ________________ the news, she rushed quickly to tell the others.
5 He ________________ in the direction of the safe and saw that the picture had been moved.
6 As he entered the room, he ________________ that the window had been smashed.
7 He carefully ________________ the necklace before picking it up.
8 ________________ a noise upstairs, she put down her broom and went to investigate.

C Work in pairs. Discuss the questions.

1 What's the most interesting piece of news you've heard this week?
2 Do you prefer to watch movies at the movie theater or stream them online? Why?
3 Do you think you could find your way around your home by touch alone?
4 Do you think listening to other people's conversations is a good way to learn English? Why/Why not?
5 What's the worst movie you've ever seen? Why was it so bad?

GRAMMAR
Order of adjectives

A Scan the story again. Underline sentences in which two or more adjectives are used to describe a noun.

B WORK IT OUT **Choose the correct options to complete the rules. Use the sentences in Exercise A to help you.**

Order of adjectives

When we use two or more adjectives to describe a noun, we usually put the adjectives in [1]***alphabetical order / a specific order***.

Opinion adjectives (e.g. *amazing, incredible*) are always used [2]***before / after*** descriptive adjectives (e.g. *ancient, leather*).

C Go to the Grammar Hub on page 136.

D PRACTICE **Rewrite the sentences using the adjectives in parentheses.**

1 He drives a car. (*expensive / old*)
____.
2 They walked slowly through the woods. (*dark / quiet*)
____.
3 She opened the door. (*wooden / noisy*)
____.
4 She had a bag. (*leather / red*)
____.
5 She was wearing shoes. (*Italian / beautiful*)
____.
6 In the living room there was a table. (*wooden / antique / stunning*)
____.
7 The house was surrounded by trees. (*old / tall*)
____.
8 In the garden there was a statue. (*stone / ancient*)
____.

E SPEAK **Student A – Go to the Communication Hub on page 150. Student B – Go to the Communication Hub on page 153.**

SPEAKING

A PREPARE **You are going to write and perform the next scene from *The curse of the black falcon*. With a partner, discuss what might happen next. Does the burglar escape or are they caught by the professor? Write notes about the key events in your scene.**

B PLAN **Write a conversation with one of you as the burglar and the other as the professor. Practice acting it out.**

C SPEAK **Perform your scene for the class. Vote on which pair has the best ending.**

VOCABULARY
Crime

A Work in groups. Look at the pictures and discuss the questions.

1 What do the pictures show? What's the connection between them?

2 Which do you think is more reliable? Why?

B Complete the definitions with the correct form of the words in bold.

1 There was a **burglary** here last night. The thieves took money, jewelry and electronic goods.

2 He tried to **bribe** the police with $5,000 to let him go.

3 I was a victim of **identity theft** when someone hacked into my computer and stole my bank details.

4 During the **robbery,** they threatened the sales clerk with a knife.

5 I was the victim of **fraud** when someone tricked me into giving them my bank details. They took $2,000.

6 I was **blackmailed** into helping the criminal gang to break into our offices.

a ____________ (v) to make someone give you money or do what you want by threatening to reveal compromising information about them

b ____________ (n) when someone illegally enters a building and steals things

c ____________ (n) the crime of obtaining money from someone by tricking them

d ____________ (v) to give money or presents to someone so that they will help you

e ____________ (n) the crime of taking money or property illegally by using threats or violence

f ____________ (n) the illegal use of somebody else's name and personal information to obtain goods, credit cards, etc.

C Go to the Vocabulary Hub on page 146.

D SPEAK Work in pairs. What do you think is the most effective way to catch the criminal in each example? Think about:

- CCTV
- digital footprints
- DNA
- eyewitnesses
- phone histories
- fingerprints

LISTENING

A SPEAK Work in pairs. Tell your partner about something interesting, unusual or frightening that has happened to you. Then discuss the questions.

1 How accurate do you think this memory is?

2 Think about other people there at the time. Would their memory of the event be the same?

8.4 **B** LISTEN FOR ORGANIZATION Listen to a talk about memory and eyewitness testimony. Put the topics in the order they are discussed.

___ using language to influence memory
___ creating false memories
___ how the human memory works
___ the impact on the real world
___ blocking out painful memories

8.5 **C** LISTEN FOR CONCLUSIONS Work in pairs. Listen to the last part of the talk again. What conclusion does the speaker make about eyewitness testimonies?

1

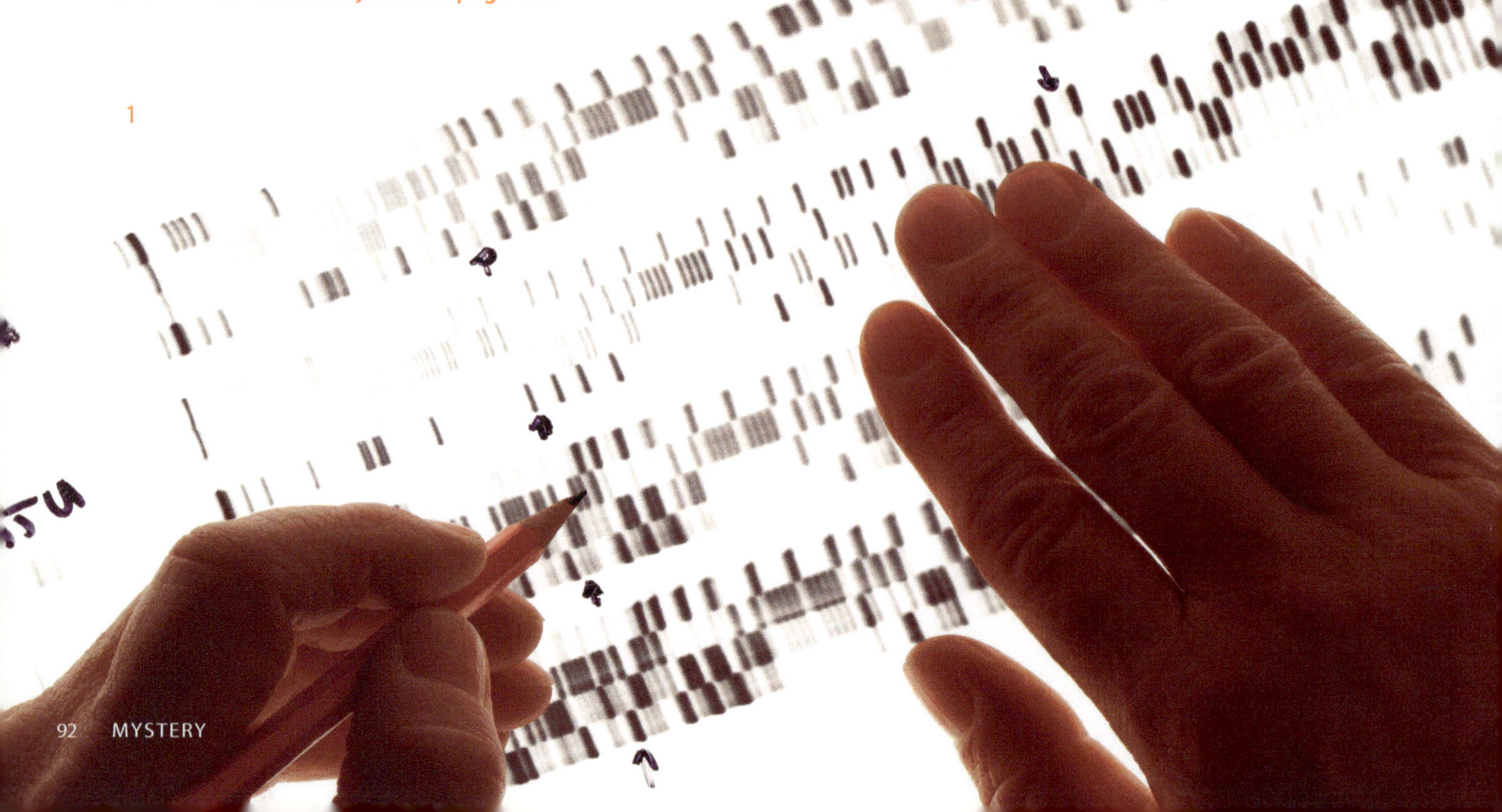

8.4 **D FOLLOW AN ARGUMENT** **Listen to the full talk again. Complete the summary of each section with no more than three words from the talk. Use the information in the box to help you.**

Following an argument

In talks, speakers usually build to one clear conclusion. To reach this point, they use each section of the talk to develop their argument. To help you follow an argument, listen for when the speaker:

- asks a question, then answers it – this helps them highlight the main ideas
- uses pronoun referencing – this helps them refer back to the main ideas
- gives a definition – this allows them to use key vocabulary

1 Our memories are unreliable because we rewrite or add to them each time we ________________.
2 Although the idea of repressed memories was popular in the 1980s, studies since strongly indicate that patients were encouraged to create false memories ________________.
3 The 1974 Loftus study showed that the way you ________________ or talk about an event can influence someone's memory of it.
4 To many, studies like this explained how patients in the 1980s might have been encouraged to ________________ their own childhood memories.
5 The 1995 Loftus study demonstrated that people can actually be convinced to create ________________ childhood memories.

E SPEAK **Work in pairs and follow these instructions:**

Student A – Turn to page 97. Look at the picture for 30 seconds. Close your book. Tell Student B as much that you can remember about the picture as possible.

Student B – Turn to page 97. Look at the picture and listen to your partner's description. How accurate is their memory?

F **Now change roles using the image on** page 109.

PRONUNCIATION
Adding information

8.6 **A** **Listen to an extract from the lecture. Is the phrase in bold said with a falling tone (↘), rising tone (↗) or fall-rising tone (↘↗)?**

The information presented by a witness may have been influenced by the way in which they were questioned after the event. **On top of that**, lawyers could encourage witnesses to add or change details.

B **Work in pairs. What is the function of the phrase in Exercise A?**

a to change the topic
b to give an explanation
c to add information

8.7 **C** **Listen and repeat the sentences.**

1 Sounds ridiculous, doesn't it? **But actually**, the way we question someone can have a dramatic effect on how they describe what happened.
2 Juries are asked to pay close attention to eyewitness testimonies, but they are arguably not a reliable source. **Furthermore**, they can be affected by the stress and anxiety of, for instance, a violent robbery.

SPEAKING HUB

A PLAN **Read the situation and write notes about the victim, crime and any other important details.**

On Saturday, December 23, the billionaire oil tycoon Magnus Baldursson held a dinner party at his house to celebrate his retirement. At around 10:00 pm, his daughter's body was found at the bottom of the main staircase with a broken neck. She's thought to have been murdered.

B PREPARE **Work in groups. Turn to** page 148.

C DISCUSS **In your groups, discuss who you think killed Sophia and why.**

A: It must have been Albert. He said he is happy that Sofia's dead!
B: Yes, but he has an alibi. He was eating dinner in the kitchen.

- Write and perform a short scene
- Speculate about the causes and consequences of a crime

8.3 Fact or fiction?

A– understatement S– maintaining a conversation

An urban legend

COMPREHENSION

A Work in groups. Which of the following do you think are true and which are urban legends?

1. If you drop a penny from the top of a skyscraper it will kill anyone it lands on.
2. Sharks can detect a single drop of blood from the other end of a swimming pool.
3. Using your cell phone at a gas station could trigger an explosion.

Glossary

crane (n) a tall machine with a long arm used for lifting and moving heavy objects

dummy (n) a model of a person, typically used for displaying clothes in a store window

Portaloo™ (n) a temporary toilet inside a small building that can be easily moved from place to place

B Watch a segment from a TV show about urban legends and answer the questions.

1. Which urban legend is discussed in the video?
2. How does the presenter and his team test the legend?
3. What is the conclusion of the experiment?

C Watch again. Complete the sentences with no more than three words from the segment.

1. The team dropped the Portaloo™ from a height of ____________ onto a concrete surface.
2. The first test showed that doing ____________ would result in serious injury.
3. The slow-motion video shows that the ____________ impact travels upward through the body.
4. For the second test, the team makes the ____________ body-double 'jump' before impact.
5. The second test showed it isn't possible to jump upward quick enough to make a real difference to the speed that ____________.

AUTHENTIC ENGLISH

A 00:47–01:12 Watch part of the video again. Do the reactions of the presenter and his colleague make the situation sound more or less serious than it is?

B Match the situations (1–5) with their understated descriptions (a–e). Use the information in the box to help you.

Understatement

An understatement is a sentence that makes a situation seem less important, serious, big, etc than it really is.

Two ways to make an understatement are by:

1 **modifying the noun**

*OK, so we have **a little** problem with the car – it's been stolen.*

*I'm afraid there's **a slight** issue with your card, sir. The payment has been declined.*

2 **rephrasing the sentence**

You've put me in a terrible position. → *This is not the best position to be in.*

I can't remember the last time I felt this bad! → *Well, I've definitely felt worse.*

1. You accidentally deleted an important document.
2. You almost died in a car crash.
3. Your house was robbed and everything was stolen.
4. It's minus thirty degrees outside.
5. You're so sick that you can't get out of bed.

a 'It's a little bit cold outside.'
b 'Yeah, it was pretty scary I guess.'
c 'So, I'm not really feeling 100% to be honest.'
d 'OK, don't worry, but there's been a little incident at home.'
e 'Uh, there's a slight issue with the report.'

C Work in pairs. Take turns describing an extreme situation, then giving an understated description of it.

A: You broke your leg in a climbing accident!
B: Yes, it was kind of painful …

Don't believe everything you hear

SAM MALCOLM AMANDA HARRY EMILY

A Work in pairs. Imagine that you are trapped in a room. What different methods might you use to try to escape?

B Watch the video and answer the questions.

1 Which of your ideas from Exercise A do Harry and Sam try?
2 Where are they getting their ideas from?
3 How do they eventually escape?

SPEAKING SKILL

A Work in pairs. Read the extract from the conversation and discuss the questions.

1 What is the function of the highlighted phrase?
2 Why is it appropriate in this situation?
3 What other phrases could you use?

Sam: What now?
Harry: OK. We'll just have to call someone and get them to open the door from the other side using the spare key. Does that sound like a plan?

B Watch the video again. Complete the box with examples from the conversation.

Maintaining a conversation

When we are working together to solve a problem, we frequently keep the discussion going by asking others what they think of our suggestions. To do this, we use phrases such as:

Does that sound like a plan?, ________________,
________________, ________________,
________________.

C Read the situation below and brainstorm possible solutions.

You are driving through the countryside at night when suddenly your car breaks down. There's no cell phone signal and you didn't pass any houses or other buildings for miles before you broke down. There are no streetlights and very little moonlight.

D Work in groups. Discuss your ideas from Exercise C and try to agree on one solution. Use phrases from the box to maintain the conversation.

SPEAKING HUB

A **PLAN** Look back at the urban legends at the beginning of the lesson. Brainstorm different ways to effectively test each legend.

B **PREPARE** Choose your best suggestion for each test in Exercise A. Write notes about:

- what equipment you would need
- why this is an effective test
- how many times you would run the test and why
- any potential issues

C **SPEAK** Work in groups. Discuss your ideas from Exercise B and try to agree on one test for each urban legend.

Well, we can't really drop a coin from a skyscraper onto someone's head! I mean, I think that would hurt a little!

D **PRESENT** Present your ideas to the class and answer any questions.

Discuss how to test an idea

➤ Turn to page 161 to learn how to write a complex essay.

Unit 8 Review

VOCABULARY

A Complete the text with the correct form of the words in bold.

The Kitsune is a [1]________ Japanese creature.	**MYTH**
It has the ability to [2]________ from a fox into a human, but it does not look like a normal fox.	**TRANSFORM**
In [3]________ stories, the Kitsune could fly, become invisible and produce fire and lightning. People had the [4]________ that as the creature got older, it became stronger and more intelligent. Once it reached one hundred, the creature could take a form that	**TRADITION** **BELIEVE**
[5]________ a human. It could also enter people's dreams and drive them mad. In many ways, the creature is similar to the	**REPRESENT**
[6]________ characters in Pokémon, but the Kitsune was much more evil and considered a great trickster.	**HERO**

B Complete the sentences with the correct form of the words from the box.

feel hear listen look see touch watch

1 The fog was so thick we couldn't ________ where we were going.
2 He hid behind the door, ________ as they argued about what to do.
3 They suddenly woke up. 'Did you ________ that noise?' she asked.
4 She reached out and gently ________ his hand.
5 They ________ in horror as the cars crashed into each other.
6 ________ closely, he noticed that some of the things on his desk had been moved.
7 They could ________ the cold draft coming through the door.

C Choose the correct options (a, b or c) to complete the sentences.

1 At the courthouse last night, Mr. Taylor was ___ to 15 years in prison.
a committed **b** charged **c** sentenced
2 He admitted to using sensitive information to ___ the former star.
a blackmail **b** bribe **c** charge
3 Police have released footage of the armed ___ at the gas station.
a robbery **b** burglary **c** identity theft
4 Mr. Baxter says he ___ for five hours without a break.
a was charged **b** was arrested **c** was questioned
5 The men are accused of ___ multiple crimes in the area.
a witnessing **b** committing **c** investigating

D Work in pairs. Discuss the questions.

1 What do you think is the most common crime in your country?
2 What could be done to address crime in your city?
3 How can you protect yourself against identity theft?

GRAMMAR

A Rewrite the underlined sentences with *must / might / can't* + *have* + past participle.

1 They should be here by now. Maybe they got lost on the way.
They ________
________.
2 I'm sure it wasn't Erin you saw last night. She's in Madrid.
You ________
________.
3 I'm sure Max got the promotion. He was looking very happy earlier!
Max ________
________.
4 I was cleaning up earlier. It's possible I threw the letter away by accident.
I ________
________.
5 I'm sure I didn't leave my phone at work. I had it on the train.
I ________
________.
6 Oh, no! I'm sure you booked the wrong tickets by mistake!
You ________
________.

B Work in pairs. Take turns reading the sentences below, then responding with a modal of deduction.

1 Where's Emily? She should be here by now.
2 Did you hear that weird noise this morning?
3 So I saw your best friend outside earlier.

C Choose the correct options to complete the sentences.

1 He collects *Japanese antique / antique Japanese* vases.
2 They found some *ancient gold / gold ancient* coins in the field.
3 We're staying in a *wonderful little / little wonderful* town on the coast.
4 The town is full of *amazing French / French amazing* architecture.
5 They've rented a *luxury huge / huge luxury* villa for their vacation.
6 It's a *beautiful 19th century / 19th century beautiful* mirror.
7 The *valuable Russian gold / valuable gold Russian* egg sold for millions.
8 He wore a *new blue / blue new* shirt for their date.

9 BUSINESS

> The highest use of capital is not to make more money, but make money do more for the betterment of life.
>
> Henry Ford

A Vietnamese entrepreneur transports her products in Haiphong, Vietnam.

OBJECTIVES

- talk about the risks and benefits of apps
- make an effective complaint about a product or service
- conduct a survey about what influences our purchases
- design and present an ad campaign
- discuss investment opportunities
- write a proposal

Work with a partner. Discuss the questions.

1 Read the quote. What roles in society do you think businesses have other than making money?

2 Do you think the future belongs to big businesses or to start-up companies and entrepreneurs? Explain your reasoning.

3 When looking for a new job are you more attracted to a high salary or challenging work? Why?

9.1 Customers

- Talk about the risks and benefits of apps
- Make an effective complaint about a product or service

G adjective clauses **P** pitch on non-essential adjective clauses
S fronting **V** dependent prepositions: verbs

READING

A SPEAK Work in groups. Would you trust a stranger to do the following? Why/Why not?

- drive you somewhere
- stay at your house
- recommend something
- give you advice
- rate your skills
- judge your interactions

B READ FOR MAIN IDEA Read *Who would you trust?* Complete the article with the headings below.

- affecting your career
- new technology, new economy
- the influence of the consumer
- the benefits of and need for reviews
- the future of ratings

Who would you trust?

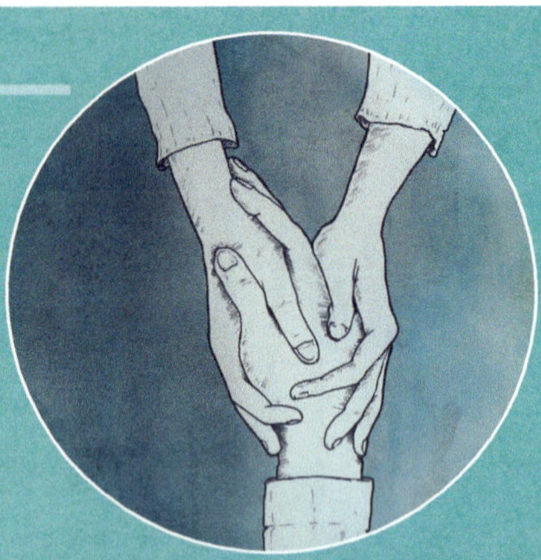

[1]Who are the people in your life that you place your trust in? What does someone have to do to earn your trust? In today's technology-driven world, it seems we are more willing than ever to trust the word of complete strangers.

By Leonard Jackson | July 16, 2018

a ______________________

Trust has always played an essential role in the economy. [2]In the past, we placed our trust in our neighbors – people in our local community that had developed a good reputation for the products and services they offered. As major cities grew, we came to trust the reputation of companies and institutions. Individuals could start businesses, but it took time for them to establish a good reputation. Technology, and the way that it has enabled individuals to set up businesses and allowed others to rate them, has changed all of this. Just a few years ago, neither of the online services Uber or Airbnb existed, but both are now hugely popular. [3]Thanks to Uber, which lets people use an app to order a ride at a generally much lower rate than a normal taxi firm, we are all potential taxi drivers. And the website Airbnb, which lets you stay in other people's houses or apartments, means that a spare bedroom in your house is a money-making opportunity.

b ______________________

Star-rating systems have been around for decades on Amazon and eBay, but mobile technology has made them much more accessible. Online shopping, which is clearly quicker and more efficient than regular shopping, doesn't allow us to physically try out the products. Ratings have helped to fill this gap. Consumers also tend to be good judges of how authentic a review is. For example, a product that doesn't have any negative reviews is likely to be viewed with some suspicion. Allowing customers to see both the good and bad in a product usually means they trust the reviews more – much more than something that constantly gets five stars.

c ______________________

Mobile technology has given people much more power to influence the reputation of a company. When Kylie Jenner sent a negative tweet about Snapchat, the company's value fell by over $1 billion in one day. [4]Of course, we don't all have the influence of famous celebrities, but companies now hire people whose job is to monitor mentions of their brands so they can provide instant customer support. Those companies that fail to react quickly run the risk of negative opinions and experiences going viral. In the past, complaining may have involved going into a store or writing a series of letters, but now good companies respond in minutes.

d ______________________

Our own online reputation can also have a significant effect on our real-world prospects. [5]Recruiters now regularly check out people's online profiles before interviewing or hiring them and the first thing they see are social media profiles. LinkedIn – the professional networking site – can have a huge influence on people's careers. In the past, employers posted job ads online hoping to attract the best talent; now they actively seek out prospective employees via endorsements on LinkedIn. Companies trust the accuracy of these online reviews of our experience and abilities even though they may have never met the people that wrote them.

e ______________________

So, how might our reputation be measured in the future? [6]Well, it's not difficult to imagine a world where our every interaction affects a social credit score. What we share or buy online, the content we 'like', even the people we connect with could all contribute to an overall rating that affects what we're able to do in the real world. Although this may sound like science fiction, a future in which we are rated on everything may not be that unrealistic.

C READ FOR DETAIL **Read again. Complete the sentences with no more than two words from the article.**

1 New technology has allowed customers to ________ new businesses.

2 A rating system can reduce the ________ between customers and sellers.

3 People are unlikely to trust a product with no ________.

4 Customers can now ________ what a company does.

5 Businesses employ people to monitor ________ of their company online so that they can deal with issues quickly.

6 Our own personal online ________ could affect our future job prospects.

7 Companies look for ________ using networking sites like LinkedIn.

8 The writer believes that in the future we may use a ________ based on how we interact online.

D SPEAK **Work in groups. Discuss the questions.**

1 Do you usually check online reviews before buying or doing something? Why/Why not?

2 Have you ever complained about a product or service via social media?

3 What can you do to protect or improve your online reputation?

GRAMMAR

Adjective clauses

A **Look at the highlighted sentences in the article. Underline the adjective clauses in each.**

B SPEAK **Work in pairs. Are the clauses you underlined in Exercise A essential or non-essential? How do you know?**

C WORK IT OUT **Match the sentences (1–6) from Exercise A to the rules (a–f).**

Adjective clauses

In essential adjective clauses:

- we can use *that* instead of *who* or *which* [a] ___
- we can omit the relative pronoun when it's the object of the adjective clause [b] ___

In non-essential adjective clauses:

- we use commas to separate the clause from the rest of the sentence [c] ___

In both types of adjective clause:

- we use *where* to talk about places [d] ___ and *whose* to talk about possession [e] ___ – neither of which can be omitted
- we use prepositions at the beginning of a clause in formal English and at the end in informal English [f] ___

D Go to the **Grammar Hub** on **page 138**.

E SPEAK **Work in groups. Try to improve the following review using adjective clauses like the one in the example.**

Apps Games Reviews

★★★★☆

Meal Maker is a great app!

ClaireP | 2 days ago

This is the best app *that I've ever downloaded!* It has a lot of useful features including a meal tracker. I also like the recipes. Another good feature is the fitness section. There's also a community space. I was actually sent a recipe by an old friend! Anyway, I'd definitely recommend this app.

PRONUNCIATION

Pitch on non-essential adjective clauses

9.1 **A** **Listen to this extract from a radio show about apps. Does the speaker's pitch step up or down on the non-essential adjective clause?**

Trello, which I use to stay organized at work, is the most useful app on my phone.

9.2 **B** **Listen and repeat the sentences.**

1 MyFitnessPal, which records daily food and exercise, is a good app for helping you lose weight.

2 Spotify, which allows you to stream music offline, is something I use every day.

3 Mint, which links all your bank cards, is a great app for keeping track of your finances.

SPEAKING

A PLAN **Make a list of apps that you use regularly on your phone or tablet.**

B PRESENT **Work in pairs. Compare your lists from Exercise A. Explain any apps that your partner doesn't know or use.**

A: I've heard of most of these, but what's Strava?
B: Uh, It's a fitness app that tracks how far you run.

C DISCUSS **Work in pairs. Rank the apps in Exercise B from most to least useful. Then discuss any risks involved with each and how they might be improved.**

LISTENING

A SPEAK Complete *Are you a good complainer?* Compare your answers with a partner. Give reasons for your approach.

B Go to the Communication Hub on page 153 to find out what type of complainer you are.

9.3 **C LISTEN FOR GIST** Listen to a customer make a complaint about something they ordered online. Answer the questions.

1. What does the customer want to complain about?
2. What two solutions does the customer service representative offer?
3. Is the customer happy with these solutions? Why/Why not?
4. Why can't the customer service representative resolve the issue now?

9.3 **D LISTEN FOR FRONTING** Listen again. Choose the correct options (a, b or c) to complete the sentences. Use the information in the box to help you.

Fronting

In informal spoken English, speakers sometimes move part of a clause from its normal position to the beginning of a sentence.

How you thought you'd get away with it, I'll never know.

Never have I been so disappointed.

This non-standard word order is called fronting and is used for emphasis or dramatic effect.

1. The customer had to wait for ___ to speak to a customer service representative.
   - a two minutes
   - b five minutes
   - c 40 minutes
2. The customer doesn't think the delivery should have been left ___
   - a in the backyard.
   - b under the patio table.
   - c in the children's playhouse.
3. The customer expects the company to ___
   - a issue a full refund for the damaged books.
   - b offer a discount on his next purchase.
   - c replace the most damaged books.
4. The customer paid ___ for the books.
   - a $10
   - b $150
   - c $100
5. The customer thinks ___ is ridiculous.
   - a the customer service representative
   - b the company's terms of service
   - c the company's refunds and exchange policy

E SPEAK In some cultures, people prefer not to complain directly. How common is it to complain in your culture? How do you think people react to bad service or faulty products?

Are you a good complainer?

In some countries, complaining could almost be a national sport. In others, people rarely complain about anything. To find out what type of complainer you are, decide what you would do in the following situations.

1 You order some books from a well-known online retailer, but when they arrive most of them are damaged.

- a Say nothing and keep the books. It's still possible to read them; they just don't look very nice.
- b Share the story on social media, swearing to never use the company again.
- c Contact the company directly and ask for a refund or a replacement.

2 You order a cup of coffee at a well-known chain, but when it arrives it's the wrong drink.

- a Drink it anyway. It might not be what you ordered, but it's still delicious.
- b Post a comment publicly shaming the company on their social media page.
- c Politely point out the mistake to staff and ask for a new drink.

3 You accidentally sit in the first class section of train and are caught by the ticket inspector.

- a Pay the fine. You made a mistake, so you should face the consequences.
- b Refuse to pay and post a video of the argument that follows on social media.
- c Accept responsibility, but send an email to the train company suggesting they use clearer signs in first class.

4 You order a tuna sandwich from Andy's Café, but ask them to remove the cucumber because you don't like it. When you take your first bite, you realize they haven't done what you asked.

- a Remove the cucumber yourself and eat the sandwich anyway.
- b Share a picture of the sandwich online with the hashtag '#avoidandyscafe'
- c Politely explain the issue to staff and ask for a new sandwich.

5 You oversleep on a business trip and miss an early morning flight. The airline company won't let you on the next flight without a new ticket.

- a Buy a new ticket. It's your fault that you missed the flight.
- b Post a video of your argument with the airline company on social media.
- c Accept responsibility, but email the airline company suggesting they offer more support to customers in your situation.

VOCABULARY
Dependent prepositions: verbs

Dependent prepositions: verbs

Some verbs and prepositions are commonly used together. These are called dependent prepositions and they are followed by either a noun or *-ing*.
For example:
How do you intend to deal with this issue? NOT ~~*How do you intend to deal about this issue?*~~

9.4 **A** **Complete the extracts from the phone call with the prepositions in the box. Then listen and check.**

about (x2) for (x2) on to (x2) with

1 Thank you ________ holding; we appreciate your call.
2 I'm calling to complain ________ the condition of the books I received.
3 I understand that, but at no point did I consent ________ the books being left somewhere they could get damaged!
4 I understand that, but I really must insist ________ a full refund.
5 I'm afraid that since we have adhered ________ your delivery instructions, the most I'd be able to offer is $10 off your next purchase.
6 Look, I don't want to argue ________ this anymore!
7 24 hours? Why can't this be dealt ________ right now?
8 I can only apologize ________ any inconvenience caused.

B **Are these sentences correct or incorrect? Rewrite the incorrect sentences.**

1 Cheap Flights would like to apologize for any inconvenience caused by this delay.
2 You should have complained at having to wait so long to be served.
3 I'm sick of being passed between different people – I just want someone to deal with this issue!
4 I realize you've adhered in company policy, but I'm still not satisfied.
5 Gary, can you help me? There's a customer downstairs who keeps insisting at speaking to the manager.
6 Look, we've been arguing on this for the past 45 minutes. Either issue a refund or let me speak to your manager.
7 When you completed the purchase online, you consented with our terms and conditions.
8 Let me take this opportunity to thank all of you for giving us your feedback today.

SPEAKING HUB

A **PLAN** **Work in pairs. Think of phrases you could use to complain about a product and how you could respond to these complaints.**

B **SPEAK** **Student A – Imagine you are a customer service representative. Use the stages below to help you resolve your partner's complaint. Student B – Imagine you are a customer. Go to the Communication Hub on page 149.**

1 Find out how you can help the customer.
2 Find out if the product is broken.
3 Ask if something else could be causing the fault, e.g. the internet provider.
4 Check if the product is still under warranty.
5 Suggest sending someone out to repair the product.
6 Tell the customer that exchanges are not part of the company policy.
7 Tell the customer you will refer the complaint to your supervisor.

C **REPEAT** **Change roles. Student A – Go to the Communication Hub on page 150.**
Student B – Use the stages in Exercise B to help you resolve your partner's complaint.

D **DISCUSS** **Who had the most successful complaint? Tell the class and give reasons.**

– Talk about the risks and benefits of apps
– Make an effective complaint about a product or service

9.2 Products

- Conduct a survey about what influences our purchases
- Design and present an ad campaign

V science; advertising
P connected speech: determiners and quantifiers
G determiners and quantifiers
S topic sentences

VOCABULARY
Science

A Read *The book club*. Complete the definitions with the words in bold.

1 ________________ (n) a process of studying or examining something in order to understand or explain it
2 ________________ (n) people who study something carefully to discover new information about it
3 ________________ (n) one or more ideas that explain how or why something happens
4 ________________ (n) facts or signs that make you believe something is true
5 ________________ (n) facts or information used for making calculations or decisions

B Complete the sentences with words from Exercise A.

1 The company has collected ________________ from over 20,000 people worldwide.
2 ________________ claim the results indicate a clear link between stress and high blood pressure.
3 I'm sorry, but there simply isn't enough ________________ to support that claim.
4 ________________ of the data showed a link between the consumption of fish and improved memory.
5 One ________________ is that consumers don't actually question the claims made in advertising.

The Book Club

Episode 402: Science fact or fiction?

According to **researchers** from the McCallun Institute, over 80% of Americans still believe that Vitamin C cures the common cold, despite the fact that there is little to no **evidence** to support this **theory**. In her new book, *Science fact or fiction?*, Professor Dawn Jackson uses her **analysis** of hundreds of consumer studies to argue that believing in health myths may actually affect the products we buy. She goes on to claim that companies take advantage of this fact in their marketing campaigns. But are Jackson's observations really supported by the research **data**? Michael Evans spoke to her earlier this week to find out.

LISTENING

A SPEAK Work in pairs. Do you think the following sentences are facts (F) or myths (M)? Explain your reasoning.

1 We should drink eight glasses of water a day. ___
2 Eggs are bad for your heart. ___
3 Yogurt is good for digestion. ___
4 Eat less food when you have a fever. ___
5 Eating cheese can give you nightmares. ___
6 Natural sugar is better for us than processed sugar. ___

9.5 **B LISTEN FOR MAIN IDEA** Listen to a radio interview about health myths. According to the scientist, which three of the claims in Exercise A are myths?

Glossary

dehydration (n) a dangerous lack of water in the body

9.5 **C LISTEN FOR DETAIL** Listen again. Complete the sentences with no more than three words or a number from the podcast.

1 According to the professor, the ________________ benefits from the commonly held belief that we need to drink eight glasses of water a day.
2 There's no evidence that increasing your intake of ________________ will help the body fight infections such as the common cold.
3 The professor argues that we can only be confident of a health claim if there is a large body of ________________ to support it.
4 Probiotics, also known as '________________ bacteria', are generally thought to be beneficial to the digestive system.
5 Companies need to be careful about ________________ ________________ used in advertising as they cannot legally make claims that aren't supported by evidence.
6 While ________________ are associated with a number of negative health effects, the professor says we don't need to worry about how much fruit we consume.

D SPEAK Work in pairs. Why do you think so many companies focus on health? How do companies try to promote unhealthy products?

GRAMMAR

Determiners and quantifiers

A Work in pairs. Read the sentences. Which of the determiners or quantifiers in bold describe 100%, a large amount, a medium to small amount or 0%?

1. There's **little** evidence to support many of the health claims made about yogurt.
2. You need **plenty of** fruits and vegetables in your diet.
3. It's not true that we need to drink **several** glasses of water a day.
4. There is **no** evidence to support that claim.
5. **All** companies have to be careful with the wording of their ads.
6. **Neither** ad was particularly accurate.
7. **Every** claim must be supported by evidence.
8. There isn't really **any** evidence to support that claim.
9. **None** of those claims are based on real data.

B **WORK IT OUT** Choose the correct options to complete the rules.

Determiners and quantifiers

few, much, many, a little, etc

- We use *many, few, a few, several, a large number of* with [1]*countable / uncountable / countable and uncountable* nouns.
- We use *much, a little, little, a great deal of, a large amount of* with [2]*countable / uncountable / countable and uncountable* nouns.
- We use *a lot of, lots of, plenty of, some* and *any* with [3]*countable / uncountable / countable and uncountable* nouns.

all, each and *every*

- We use *all* with [4]*singular / plural* nouns.
- We use *each* and *every* with [5]*singular / plural* nouns.

both, either and *neither*

- We use *both* with [6]*singular / plural* nouns.
- We use *either* and *neither* with [7]*singular / plural* nouns.

no, none and *any*

- We use *no* + noun in [8]*positive / negative* sentences and *any* + noun in [9]*positive / negative* sentences.
- We use *none* in short answers, in [10]*positive / negative* sentences, or with *of* + pronoun / countable or uncountable nouns.

C Go to the Grammar Hub on page 138.

PRONUNCIATION

Connected speech: determiners and quantifiers

9.6 **A** Listen to the extracts from the radio show. Is there a pause between the words in bold? Is the pronunciation of *of* strong or weak?

1. We get **plenty of water** through food.
2. You'd have to eat **a lot of** fruit to get the same amount of sugar as you'd get from, say, a soda.

9.7 **B** Draw (‿) to show the connected speech in the determiners and quantifiers below. Then listen and check.

1. A large number of people pay attention to claims in advertising.
2. A lot of people are influenced by product reviews.
3. Plenty of respondents don't pay attention to the wording of an ad.
4. A few of the people interviewed said that price wasn't a factor when choosing clothes.
5. Hundreds of people buy products because of celebrity endorsements.

SPEAKING

A **PLAN** Work in pairs. You are going to conduct a survey on factors that influence people's shopping habits. Adapt the sample questions to fit one of the topics in the box.

clothes   food   vacations   technology

1 **Do you regularly eat out in restaurants? Yes/No**

2 **Which factors are the most important when choosing a restaurant?**

	not significant						significant
price	1	2	3	4	5	6	7
location	1	2	3	4	5	6	7
décor	1	2	3	4	5	6	7
type of food	1	2	3	4	5	6	7

3 **Restaurant reviews have an influence on my choice of restaurant.**

strongly agree — agree — neutral — disagree — strongly disagree

4 **Which ONE of these has the most influence when you write your own review of a restaurant?**

value for money   service   quality of the food

B **SPEAK** Ask your questions from Exercise A to as many people as possible in ten minutes. Write down their answers.

C **DISCUSS** Work in pairs. Analyze your answers from Exercise B.

Our results show that the most important thing when eating out is the quality of the food ...

D **PRESENT** Present your findings to the class.

- founder of The Oprah Winfrey Network (OWN)
- grew up in extreme poverty
- net worth = $2.9 billion

- co-founder of Amazon
- quit a well-paid job on Wall Street to develop Amazon
- net worth = $157.4 billion

- founder of Lens Technology
- left school at 16 to work in a factory
- net worth = $5.4 billion

READING

A SPEAK Work in groups. Look at the infographic and discuss the questions.

1. Can you think of any other famous entrepreneurs? What products or services did they create?
2. What qualities do you think make a good entrepreneur?
3. Would you like to start your own business? Why/Why not?

B READ FOR GIST Read *The path to success* and choose the best sub-heading (1–3).

1. Setting up a new fashion label can be difficult, especially with minimal advertising.
2. How the courage to follow a childhood dream led to an international success story.
3. How celebrities can help promote your values.

C TOPIC SENTENCES Read the article again. Match the topic sentences (1–5) to the blanks (a–e). Use the information in the box to help you.

Topic sentences

Topic sentences express the main idea of a paragraph. They are usually found at the beginning of a paragraph and are frequently supported by further related information or examples. Identifying topic sentences can help you get a quick overall understanding of a text without having to read in detail.

1. The brand has since become known for its colorful floral prints, which are inspired by Nicola's happy childhood memories of the summer in the English countryside.
2. The story of many successful entrepreneurs is the stuff of Hollywood – rags-to-riches tales of people who overcame great challenges in order to succeed.
3. In an age where so many of us seem content to remain in well-paid, but ultimately dissatisfying jobs, it's refreshing to see someone have the courage to make a dramatic lifestyle change.
4. Yet like many of us, Nicola felt that something was missing and decided to do something about it.
5. In the past decade, Beautiful Soul has used a variety of techniques to raise brand awareness.

THE PATH TO SUCCESS

a___ Oprah Winfrey was born into extreme poverty, yet recently became the world's first black female billionaire. Bill Gates and Mark Zuckerburg both dropped out of college, but went on to create two of the most influential companies in modern history. Starting out on the wrong foot seems to be the inspiration many entrepreneurs need to create an empire, and Nicola Woods is no exception.

For 11 years, Nicola built a successful career in the fast-paced world of corporate insurance. She wore designer clothing, drove sports cars and went on dream vacations.

b___ Looking for inspiration, she took a six-month sabbatical to travel around the world. Sitting among the cherry blossom in a park in central Tokyo, Nicola's thoughts turned to her childhood dream of working in the fashion industry. Realizing that she needed a radical change of lifestyle, Nicola enrolled in college and earned a BA in Fashion, Design and Technology. She then went on to launch the luxury womenswear **brand**, Beautiful Soul, in 2008.

D READ FOR DETAIL Read the article again and answer the questions. Underline the parts of the text that give you the answers.

1 Why did Nicola take six months off work to go traveling?
2 What lifestyle change did Nicola make when she returned from Japan?
3 Which two values is the brand built upon?
4 How do these values influence their use of materials?
5 Who has helped to raise the brand's international profile?
6 What has brought the company to the attention of the media?
7 What do the private fittings allow Nicola to do?
8 What does the writer think Nicola should be congratulated for?

E SPEAK Work in groups. Nicola had a successful career in corporate insurance that made her wealthy, yet she was still dissatisfied. What do you think are the most important factors in career satisfaction?

c___ Her clothes are proudly feminine and offer a modern interpretation of classic British designs. However, maybe as interesting as the designs themselves are the values that lie behind them. There is an industry-wide **trend** toward clothing that does not damage the environment and Nicola is excited to lead the charge. The brand is committed to sustainability and the regeneration of the British manufacturing and textiles industries. Materials are organic, locally sourced and fair trade, proving to the **consumer** that luxury clothing can still be produced ethically. The company also operates a zero-waste policy, using leftover fabric from one season in the creation of the next.

d___ Rather than expensive **ad campaigns**, the fashion label has largely relied on word of mouth, driven to a large extent by the support of **high-profile** celebrities. Pippa Middleton, Taylor Swift and Katy Perry are among those to publicly **endorse** the brand, helping to raise its international profile. Beautiful Soul has also attracted vast media attention through its involvement in the London, Milan and Paris fashion weeks and is now stocked at high-end boutiques around the world. However, Nicola is also eager to connect with her customers face-to-face, so the brand has recently begun offering private fittings at their studio in Portobello, West London. The hope is that **marketing strategies** like these, as well as studio open days, will allow Nicola to better understand her **target market** and adapt accordingly.

e___ Nicola Woods may not have been born into poverty, nor did she drop out of college before becoming successful. Yet like all entrepreneurs, she too had to show great strength of character to get where she is today.

Glossary

fair trade (n) a system that ensures the original producer receives a fair price for their goods

sabbatical (n) a period of time when someone (usually a college professor) is allowed to stop working in order to travel or study

sustainability (n) the use of methods that cause little to no damage to the environment and can therefore continue for a long period of time

VOCABULARY

Advertising

A Scan the article again. Complete the definitions with the words in bold.

1 ________ (n) a series of advertisements that share a single idea or theme
2 ________ (n) a plan of how to encourage people to buy a product or service
3 ________ (n) someone who buys or uses goods and services
4 ________ (v) to express support for someone or something, especially in public
5 ________ (n) a product or group of products that has its own name and is made by one company
6 ________ (n) the group of people that a product or service is directed toward
7 ________ (adj) frequently seen in public, mentioned in newspapers or appearing on television
8 ________ (n) a gradual development or change in a situation

B Complete the sentences with the correct form of the words in Exercise A.

1 Which recent TV ________ do you think have been most effective? Why?
2 Do you think ________ celebrities should be involved in advertising? Why/Why not?
3 Are you more likely to buy a product if it's ________ by a celebrity? Why/Why not?
4 Who do you think is the ________ for the following products – energy drinks, electric cars, video game consoles, high-end sports equipment? Why?
5 Which ________ do you associate with luxury and quality? Why?
6 How can ________ influence the way products or services are advertised?
7 Which ________ would discourage you from buying a product or service? Why?
8 Do you follow the latest fashion ________? Why/Why not?

C SPEAK Work in pairs. Ask and answer the questions in Exercise B.

SPEAKING HUB

A PLAN Work in groups. Go to the Communication Hub on page 153.

B PRESENT Present your campaign to the class and answer their follow-up questions.

- Conduct a survey about what influences our purchases
- Design and present an ad campaign

Café Hub

9.3 Raising capital

A – illustrating your argument S – reformulating and paraphrasing

Crowdfunding

Glossary

film (n) (British) = movie **(n) (American)**

COMPREHENSION

A Work in pairs. What do you think is the best way to raise money for a new business or project? Why?

Glossary

commission (n) a payment made to someone that is directly related to the amount they sell of something

donor (n) someone who gives money or goods to an organization that needs help

B Watch a news report about getting investment for new projects. Answer the questions.

1 How did the director raise money for his film?

2 How does this system work?

3 Why do people donate money like this?

C 00:00–01:42 Watch the first part of the report again. Are these sentences true (T) or false (F)? Correct the false sentences.

1 The director produced a video about the project as part of his Kickstarter campaign. *T / F*

2 To date, the campaign has raised over two thousand dollars more than its original goal. *T / F*

3 Some donors are given the opportunity to appear in the films they support. *T / F*

4 Kickstarter only makes money if a project is successful. *T / F*

D 01:43–02:37 Watch the second part of the report again. Choose the best options to complete the sentences.

1 Kickstarter CEO, Yancey Strickler, says most ideas *wouldn't be profitable / aren't interesting* enough to gain traditional investment.

2 Michael Moore has *successfully funded projects on / publicly endorsed* Kickstarter.

3 Moore states that he *would be happy to invest / has previously invested* in film projects via Kickstarter.

4 A major issue of crowdfunding is that many projects *are never finished / cost more than estimated*.

AUTHENTIC ENGLISH

A Work in pairs. Read the extract from the report. What is the speaker's main argument? How does he illustrate it?

99% of ideas will never be a good fit for investment because they're not going to make a lot of money. But if instead the notion is, 'What do we want to see exist? What do we think would be cool and interesting? What would we want to see?', there's a lot more things that become possible.

B Match the arguments (1–3) with the questions that could be used to illustrate them (a–c). Use the information in the box to help you.

Illustrating your argument

In natural spoken English, we frequently ask rhetorical questions to emphasize or support our arguments:

We have to ask ourselves, 'What do we want to highlight about our project? How can people benefit from supporting us?'

1 Almost two thirds of the people surveyed still believe Vitamin C cures the common cold.

2 The results of the survey indicate that unemployment is still on the rise.

3 Over the past year, we've seen a 60% increase in profits.

a The obvious question is, 'What influenced such a positive performance?'

b Which begs the question, 'What steps can be taken to get people back into work?'

c This raises the question, 'How can we better inform the public?'

C Work in pairs. Take turns making sentences about the topics below, then illustrating your ideas with a question.

- sports
- health
- employment

A: Arsenal has admitted that they need a better striker to compete at the highest level.

B: The only question is, 'How much are they willing to pay for one?'

Starting positions

A Work in pairs. Think of the steps that are involved in starting a new business. What order do they have to be done in?

B Watch the video. Choose the best summary (1 or 2).

1. Inspired by Sam's advice, Emily decides to take a traditional route to funding her new business venture.
2. Despite Sam's advice, Emily decides to take a more modern approach to funding her new business venture.

SPEAKING SKILL

A Watch the video again. Answer the questions.

1. What is the function of the phrases *I just meant …*, *What I meant to say was …* and *What I meant is …*?
2. What is the function of *essentially* and *basically*?

B Read the information in the box and check your answers to Exercise A.

Reformulating and paraphrasing

Sometimes in conversation we need to explain something in a different way to help the listener understand. This is called reformulating.

To do this, we use phrases such as: *I just mean (that) …, What I'm trying to say is …, What I meant to say was …, In other words …, What I mean is (that) …, That's to say …*

Sometimes the listener doesn't understand because we've used a word or phrase that they're unfamiliar with. Rather than give a long explanation, we usually focus on the essential details. This is called paraphrasing.

To do this, we use phrases such as: *(So) essentially/basically …*

C Choose a topic that you know a lot about (e.g. a particular subject, sport, etc) and brainstorm a list of interesting, technical terms associated with it.

D Work in pairs. Tell each other about the topic you chose in Exercise A, using technical language. Reformulate or paraphrase when necessary.

SPEAKING HUB

A PREPARE Look at the following ideas that people are hoping to crowdfund. Brainstorm the strengths and weaknesses of each.

- Idea A: a chip that is inserted in your brain to allow you to access the internet with your mind. Will allow users to access the internet instantly without using a device. Will be very expensive.
- Idea B: wireless electricity. No more power cables in the home or across the country. There are concerns about electromagnetic radiation damaging people's health.
- Idea C: a tablet that turns a container of ocean water into drinking water. Will help stop water shortages. Production process of tablets creates toxic pollution.

B SPEAK Work in groups. You have $50,000 to invest in crowdfunding projects. Discuss each of the projects in Exercise A and decide how much, if anything, to invest in them.

We should be asking, 'Which idea is tackling the most important issue of the day?' And it seems to me that renewable energy is the most important.

C REFLECT As a class, discuss which ideas got the most/least funding and why.

Discuss investment opportunities

➤ Turn to page 162 to learn how to write a proposal.

Unit 9 Review

VOCABULARY

A Match the numbers (1–8) to the letters (a–h) to form full sentences.

1 I am responsible …
2 Our brand is associated …
3 All of our products are made …
4 I'm sick …
5 It is important for businesses to show that they care …
6 When the dress arrived, I was really dissatisfied …
7 The success of a company is dependent …
8 I'm interested …

a with luxury and success.
b with it. It looked nothing like the pictures.
c from locally sourced materials.
d on many factors.
e for a team of 20 people at work.
f about the people who work for them.
g in the idea of moving to a new house but my husband wants to stay where we are.
h of people on social media showing off about their lives.

B Complete the text with the words in the box.

analysis data evidence researchers theory

The pursuit of happiness

For decades, the simplest way to address unhappiness has been to go shopping. But does retail therapy actually work? Can we buy our way to happiness?

To test the [1]__________, a group of [2]__________ from the Institute for Social Sciences interviewed thousands of shoppers before and after a spending spree. [3]__________ of the [4]__________ seemed to indicate that retail therapy does make us happier immediately after the purchase. However, as yet, there is no [5]__________ to suggest that shopping can buy you long-term happiness. The key to this, it seems, remains a mystery!

C Work in groups. Discuss the questions.

1 Why do you think people frequently continue to believe something, despite a large amount of scientific evidence against it?
2 What kind of research do you think governments should fund? Why?

D Choose the correct options (a, b or c) to complete the sentences.

1 To work in fashion, it's important to keep up with ___ and influencers.
a brands b trends c campaigns
2 We are trying to ___ young males from a professional background.
a target b advertise c campaign
3 ___ social media stars are paid a lot of money to advertise particular brands.
a Consumers b High-profile c Trend
4 We hired six athletes to ___ our new health-food range.
a campaign b target c endorse
5 Our company is going to try to raise our ___ awareness by sponsoring national sporting events.
a campaign b advertise c brand
6 ___ frequently buy products that represent a certain lifestyle.
a Consumers b Brands c High profile

E Work in pairs. Discuss the questions.

1 Which brands are you most loyal to? Why?
2 How can consumers influence the products and services they use?
3 Which products do you think are marketed at your age range? Why?

GRAMMAR

A Rewrite the sentences as one sentence using an adjective clause. Leave out the relative pronoun where possible.

1 Have you read the book? The one I lent you.
Have ____________________?
2 There was some leftover pizza in the fridge. Where is it?
Where's ____________________?
3 That's the boy. His brother has joined our soccer team.
That's ____________________.
4 I bought a new cell phone. It's really good.
The ____________________.
5 Here's the beach. My family had our first vacation here.
This is ____________________.

B Are these sentences correct or incorrect? Rewrite the incorrect sentences.

1 I think every city should have bike lanes.
2 It was a great game of tennis. Either players played amazingly.
3 Any of you can leave until the exam is finished.
4 Every person is influenced by advertising to at least some degree.
5 Not many people came. Just few friends from college.
6 We haven't received any positive reviews for over a week.
7 I'm happy with neither restaurant since both look nice.
8 Did you do many sightseeing on vacation?

10 MEDIA

> Ignorance, the root and stem of all evil.
>
> Plato

A Japanese commuter on the Yamanote Rail Line in Tokyo, Japan.

OBJECTIVES

- give opinions on recent news stories
- intervene appropriately in a discussion
- report a conversation
- plan and create a viral marketing ad
- give your opinion on streaming services
- write a persuasive essay

Work with a partner. Discuss the questions.

1. Read the quote. Do you think the internet makes us more or less ignorant? Why?
2. Should the media respect the privacy of famous people? Why/Why not?
3. What media sources do you read on a regular basis? Why do you read those ones?

10.1 Reporting the news

- Give opinions on recent news stories
- Intervene appropriately in a discussion

G– reported speech S– listening for repair and elaboration V– traditional media P– avoiding interruption

READING

A SPEAK Work in pairs. Discuss the questions below.

1 When was the last time you bought a magazine or newspaper?

2 Why do you think people now get more of their news online than in the traditional media?

10.1 **B Listen to a press conference with the editor of a lifestyle magazine called *Healthy Me*. Answer the questions.**

1 What is the announcement about?
   a a new print and digital magazine coming out
   b a print magazine becoming digital-only
   c an online magazine releasing a print version

2 What trend inspired the new business model?
   a the increased popularity of digital content in general
   b the increased popularity of the magazine
   c the increased popularity of health-based apps

3 According to the speaker, what type of print media will be affected by digital?
   a lifestyle magazines
   b fiction
   c reference books

C READ FOR MAIN IDEA Read *The death of print?* and choose the best summary of the writer's opinion (1–3).

1 The shift toward digital content is the beginning of the end for print products.

2 Sales of print products may actually be improved by the shift toward digital content.

3 Despite the shift toward digital content, there is still a market for print products.

D READ FOR DETAIL Read the article again and answer the questions. Underline the parts of the text that give you the answers.

1 What two things prompted LMI Media to make their magazine digital-only?

2 What method do online publications use to try to generate income?

3 How do the public feel about this?

4 What type of magazine is thriving?

5 What type of magazine does the author think will struggle?

6 What types of print media are still successful?

E SPEAK Work in groups. Discuss the questions.

1 Do you prefer print or digital media? Why?

2 What type of magazines, if any, do you think will survive in the future?

3 Do you think all online content should be free? Why/Why not?

GRAMMAR

Reported speech

A Scan the article again. Underline the reported speech that matches the following extracts from the press conference.

1 'We've gone from a distribution of just over 500,000 copies a month to under 100,000.'

2 'In fact, yesterday saw the total number of registered users reach over one million.'

3 'Will other publications from LMI Media make the same transition?'

4 'I'm sure all magazine publishers will start to re-evaluate their options over the next five to ten years.'

5 'What does this trend mean for print media in general?'

6 'However, for lifestyle magazines like ours, which are predominantly directed toward a younger audience, it simply doesn't make any financial sense to produce print media any longer.'

The DEATH of PRINT?

Lucy Morgan | 04/29/2019

As *Healthy Me* becomes the latest high-profile magazine to abandon print, Lucy Morgan makes the case against the digital revolution.

LMI Media has recently announced that January's issue of the lifestyle magazine *Healthy Me* will be the final print edition, making it the latest in a long line of publications to go digital-only. Yet is this really the right approach or do print magazines simply need to adapt to the changing marketplace?

B WORK IT OUT Complete the rules in the box. Use the examples in Exercise A to help you.

Reported speech

- When we report what someone said, we usually change the verb by moving it back one tense into the past.
  - present progressive → past progressive
  - simple past / present perfect → [1] ______________
  - *will* → [2] ______________
  - *can* → *could*
- We usually need to change time and place references.
  - *yesterday* → [3] ______________
  - *here* → *there*
- It isn't necessary to change the tense when:
  - the information is still true or relevant now.
  - the reporting verb is in the [4] ______________ tense.
- When we report questions, we don't use the auxiliary verb [5] ______________.
- With *yes/no* questions we use *if* or [6] ______________.

C Go to the **Grammar Hub** on **page 140**.

D SPEAK Work in pairs. Use the prompts below to interview your partner about their print and digital reading habits. Write notes about their answers.

- How often / read magazines?
- Which magazines?
- Print or digital? Why?
- Which / online magazines?

E DISCUSS Work in groups. Report your findings from Exercise D. What similarities or trends can you identify?

SPEAKING

A PLAN Think about an interesting news story you read recently. Write notes about:

- the main ideas / key events
- things that people said

B SPEAK Work in pairs. Explain your news stories and give your opinions on them.

In a press conference yesterday morning, an emotional Sally Ronson, editor-in-chief of *Healthy Me*, stated that a combination of declining sales over the past five years and the increased popularity of digital content had motivated the change. She told reporters that the publication had gone from a distribution of just over 500,000 copies a month to under 100,000 – a huge number of readers to lose in such a short period of time. However, the magazine is still popular. Since 2014, downloads of the *Healthy Me* app have increased by 300%. In fact, Ronson said that the previous day had seen the total number of registered users reach over one million. The issue for publications like this is how to turn this interest into sales. One method is to introduce paywalls – a feature in an app or website that stops people who have not paid a subscription from accessing some or all of the content. However, the general perception of the public seems to be that online content should be free and, as a result, few are willing to pay to access their favorite publications.

When asked whether other publications from LMI Media would make the same transition, Ronson said no. Yet it's clear that she believes the future of magazine publishing is digital. In fact, she said she was sure that all magazine publishers would start to re-evaluate their options over the next five to ten years. However, I'm not sure this is true. Magazines with highly specialized content, such as the *Spectator*, *The Economist* and *Prospect* have all seen significant growth. However, I do agree with Ronson when she says that for lifestyle magazines like hers, which are predominantly directed toward a younger audience, it simply doesn't make any financial sense to produce print media any longer. Not surprisingly, people aren't willing to pay for 'empty' news about barely famous people or to read articles about serious content produced by barely credible journalists.

The press also asked Ronson what this digital trend meant for print media in general and she very rightly pointed out that this depends entirely on the type of publication. Print media is thriving in many areas. E-book sales are now falling while the sales of printed fiction are actually increasing. E-books also never really had any serious impact on the sales of reference books. Furthermore, local papers with content focused on a small region still tend to be popular.

Magazines and newspapers will no doubt have to evolve and those that do so innovatively will prosper. Those that focus on celebrity gossip and news found more easily on the internet will almost certainly disappear, but specialist magazines and local news are likely to continue to thrive.

LISTENING

A SPEAK Work in pairs. Look at the news headlines and discuss which you think are from real news stories and which are fake.

B PREDICT Work in groups. How big is the problem of fake news? What can be done to help people deal with fake news?

10.2 **C LISTEN FOR GIST** Listen to an interview with a journalist about fake news. Do they mention any of your ideas from Exercise B?

10.2 **D LISTEN FOR DETAIL** Listen again. Complete the sentences with no more than three words from the interview.

1 Some fake news is for fun but many articles want you to believe the content is ________________ news.
2 The internet, specifically ________________, has changed the way we consume media.
3 Internet advertising comes from ________________ understanding the things you read and look at.
4 People have less ________________ in sources like CNN or the BBC than they used to.
5 People rarely ________________ behind the stories they read.
6 Teaching students ________________ would help them better identify fake news.

10.2 **E LISTEN FOR REPAIR AND ELABORATION** Listen again. Are these sentences true (T) or false (F)? Correct the false sentences. Use the information in the box to help you.

Listening for repair and elaboration

In presentations and interviews, speakers sometimes make mistakes and need to correct themselves. When making a repair like this, we frequently use phrases such as:

Let me rephrase that …, Sorry, what I meant to say was …

At other points, the speaker may feel that their point has been misunderstood and try to give more detail or explain something in a different way. When elaborating like this, we frequently use phrases such as:

What I mean is …, In other words …, To be more precise …

According to the speaker …

1 it's easier to publish fake news online. *T / F*
2 opinion has no place in real journalism. *T / F*
3 there is no agreement on the extent of the damage climate change will cause. *T / F*
4 the government is ultimately responsible for content published online. *T / F*
5 75% of students can't spot fake news. *T / F*

F SPEAK Work in groups. Discuss the questions.

1 Have you ever been tricked by fake news?
2 Whose responsibility is it to deal with fake news?
3 Do you think it should be illegal to publish fake news stories? Why/Why not?

VOCABULARY
Traditional media

A **Complete the definitions with the words in bold.**

1 The **editor** lost his job after the paper was accused of publishing fake news.
2 The **headline** was misleading because it said they had found a long-term cure.
3 **Tabloid** newspapers are mainly full of photos and celebrity gossip.
4 The press **coverage** of the royal wedding lasted all day.
5 The newspaper was accused of being **biased** in favor of the president.
6 The journalist refused to reveal the **source** of their story.
7 Her views are highly **subjective** and rarely based on hard evidence.
8 The **broadsheet** newspapers all included an in-depth analysis of the situation.

a ________________ (n) a small newspaper with a lot of pictures and short articles, frequently about famous people
b ________________ (n) the way news is reported on television or radio or in the newspapers
c ________________ (n) a person who is in charge of a newspaper or magazine
d ________________ (n) where information comes from
e ________________ (adj) based on your own feelings and beliefs, not facts
f ________________ (n) a large newspaper generally considered to be more serious than smaller newspapers
g ________________ (adj) preferring one person, thing, or idea to another in a way that is unfair
h ________________ (n) the title of a newspaper story that is printed in large letters

B **Complete the questions with the correct form of the words in Exercise A.**

1 Is it OK for journalists to write articles that are ________________ or should they be objective?
2 Do you prefer to read serious ________________ newspapers or less serious ________________ papers?
3 Should an ________________ take responsibility for all stories in their paper?
4 Sensationalist ________________ are written to encourage people to buy papers and click on articles online. Should they be banned?
5 Should press ________________ of people's lives be controlled to allow more privacy?
6 Why should we pay attention to the ________________ of a newspaper article?
7 Newspapers are frequently ________________ toward certain political parties. Should this be banned?

C **SPEAK** **Work in pairs. Discuss the questions in Exercise B. Explain your reasoning.**

PRONUNCIATION
Avoiding interruption

10.3 **A** **Listen to this extract from the interview. What intonation is used on the highlighted words – falling (↘) or rise-fall-rise (↗↘↗)? Why?**

I think we used to have more faith in sources like CNN, but now people don't know who to trust.

10.4 **B** **Underline the word(s) you think will have a rise-fall-rise tone. Then listen and check.**

1 Governments need to take much stronger action against companies that circulate fake news stories; it's just not OK to misinform the public.
2 In other words, unlike bloggers and people writing on social media, large newspapers can't just lie or make things up.

SPEAKING HUB

A **PLAN** **Read the questions. Write notes about your opinions on the following questions:**

1 Do large media organizations have too much influence?
2 Do you think the government should be involved in making sure the media isn't biased?
3 What are the advantages and disadvantages of people getting news from the internet?
4 Whose responsibility is it to fact-check content that is produced online?
5 Do you think less fake news would exist if the individual writers were held responsible for the content they produced?
6 Do you think journalists and the media should be allowed to say they can't reveal their sources?

B **PREPARE** **Think about other possible viewpoints and how you would respond to them.**

C **SPEAK** **Work in groups. Take turns answering the questions while politely waiting for an opportunity to ask a follow-up question to explore different points of view.**

Give opinions on recent news stories
Intervene appropriately in a discussion

10.2 Digital media

- Report a conversation
- Plan and create a viral marketing ad

S – substitution
V – social media; adjective + noun collocations
G – reporting verbs
P – using intonation to attract and keep interest

READING

A SPEAK Work in groups. Discuss the questions.

1 How do you know that an article you are reading comes from a credible source?
2 How can your own bias affect what you read and how you interpret it?

B PREDICT Work in pairs. Read the headlines from three different news stories and look at the pictures. What do you think each story is about?

C SKIM Skim the news stories and check your predictions from Exercise B.

D SUBSTITUTION Read again. What do the words in bold refer to? Use the information in the box to help you.

Substitution

To avoid repetition, writers frequently replace phrases, clauses or ideas with other words. This is called substitution. Common substitutes are:

- *one, ones, some*
  There are many reasons to doubt the statement, but ***one*** *of the most important is that the timings just don't add up.*
  (*one* = a reason to doubt the statement)
- *do*
  While Mr. Evans didn't have access to the property, the investigation has revealed that his partner ***did***.
  (*did* = have access to the property)
- *either/neither*
  I've never seen him before in my life. ***Neither*** *has my husband.*
  (*neither* = not seen him before)

1 '… but apparently Mr. Rodriguez **did**.'
2 '**Some** even work all night…'
3 '… yet **neither** have been named as part of the investigation.'
4 '… **one** being how the chocolate could have possibly survived for over 3,000 years.'
5 'Believe me, **so do I**.'

E SPEAK Work in groups. Do you think any of the stories are true? Why/Why not?

GRAMMAR

Reporting verbs

A Read the news stories again. Match the highlighted sentences (1–5) to the direct speech (a–e).

a 'No, I'm sorry. I cannot discuss an on-going investigation.' ___
b 'We simply need to run a lot of tests. Until then, this is nothing more than a fun news item.' ___
c 'I'm sorry the police were called out unnecessarily.' ___
d 'That's correct. The animal was delivered home safely.' ___
e 'Earlier today my team discovered two additional bars nearby – both in a similar state.' ___

Terrified New Yorker sees 'bear'

CALLS 911

Brooklyn Heights, New York –

Brooklyn Heights resident Anthony Rodriguez was terrified to see a bear rummaging through the trash cans outside his apartment early yesterday morning. Rodriguez called the NYPD and officers were soon at the scene. Fortunately for attending officers Liam Henderson and Alyssa Romano, the 'bear' turned out to be a hungry but harmless domestic dog. 'We arrived at approximately 6:30 am to find a large brown dog checking trash cans on the street for leftover food,' Officer Romano told reporters. She added, 'I have no idea how anyone could confuse the animal for a bear, but apparently Mr. Rodriguez did. [1]Rodriguez later apologized for wasting police time. The story has prompted a number of animal rights groups to raise concerns over the dog's welfare. [2]In response, a spokesperson for the police department confirmed that the animal had been safely returned to its owners.

TECH CRIMINAL CAUGHT HANGING AROUND

An employee of IT giant FTP Systems was arrested last night following a failed burglary attempt at the company's head office.

Neil Aitken broke into the London office shortly after midnight in order to steal sensitive computer data. Having downloaded over five terabytes of confidential information to his personal laptop, Mr. Aitken got stuck in the elevator on the 54th floor and was forced to use the alarm to call for help. 'I wasn't surprised to hear the alarm,' said Geoff Payton, the maintenance worker on duty that night. 'A lot of programmers work late and some even work all night. But Mr. Aitken kept asking me not to call the police, which seemed suspicious, so I called the authorities.' When Mr. Aitken was finally rescued from the elevator over two hours later, he was promptly arrested and will stand trial for burglary next month. [3]Although investigators have refused to comment on their current progress, it is widely believed that Mr. Aitken had intended to sell the stolen data to FTP Systems' biggest competitor, BIOS Technologies. Our sources have also suggested that the police are eager to talk to two current employees of BIOS Technologies, about their dealings with Mr. Aitken, yet neither has been named as part of the investigation.

EGYPTIAN DISCOVERY MAY CHANGE THE HISTORY OF CHOCOLATE

Human civilization has a long history with chocolate. As far back as 1900 BCE, the Mayans of Central America prepared a bitter, frothy drink with crushed cocoa beans, cornmeal and chili peppers. The Aztecs used cocoa beans as currency and drank chocolate at royal feasts.

However, it wasn't until 1847 that Fry & Sons produced the first bar of chocolate as we know it. At least, that's what historians thought until a ground-breaking discovery made 10 km north of Cairo last month.

A team of archeologists digging outside the tomb of a wealthy Egyptian official from the 13th century were amazed to find what appeared to be several ancient chocolate bars buried in the sand. 'We discovered four bars in total, each wrapped in white fabric,' explained lead researcher Arnaud Laurent. 'Each bar appears to be divided into five sections, maybe to make them easier to eat.' [4]Laurent later informed local journalists that his team had found two more bars in a similar condition.

Although images of all six chocolate bars have been widely shared online, not everyone is convinced of their authenticity. In an article published in the Journal of Archaeological Studies, [5]Professor Richard Hamilton advised historians not to take the discovery seriously until further research has been conducted. 'It's certainly an interesting discovery,' writes Professor Hamilton, 'but there are still a lot of things we don't know – one being how the chocolate could have possibly survived for over 3,000 years.' In a response on Twitter posted late last night, Laurent wrote, 'Everyone has a lot of questions. Believe me, so do I.'

B WORK IT OUT Complete the rules with verbs from Exercise A.

Reporting verbs

We can use reporting verbs to explain the way in which something was said. Reporting verbs are followed by a range of different structures:

a *argue*, [1]__________, *state, suggest* + (*that*) + clause

b *assure*, [2]__________, *tell, warn* + object + (*that*)

c *agree, demand, offer*, [3]__________, *threaten* + infinitive

d [4]__________, *encourage, persuade, remind, warn, convince* + object + infinitive

e *admit*, [5]__________, *deny, insist, suggest* + (preposition) + verb + *-ing*

C Go to the **Grammar Hub** on **page 140**.

D PRACTICE Rewrite the quotes in reported speech using the verbs in the box.

apologize blame encourage refuse threaten

1 'We won't leave until our demands are met.'
The protestors ____________________.

2 'We will fire any employee who is one minute late.'
The company ____________________.

3 'We want to say we're sorry to the 100 people who got food poisoning last week.'
The restaurant ____________________.

4 'Can anyone who saw anything please contact us?'
The police ____________________.

5 'The service is slow because of the internet provider.'
The TV company ____________________.

SPEAKING

A PLAN You are going to discuss the following questions with a partner. You must tell the truth in response to three of the questions and lie in response to the other. Write notes about what you want to say.

1 Have you ever blamed someone else for something that you did?
2 Have you ever cheated on a test?
3 What's your biggest regret?
4 Have you ever been persuaded to do something stupid?

B SPEAK Work in pairs. Discuss the questions in Exercise A. Remember to tell one lie.

C DISCUSS Work with another pair. Report your partner's answers from Exercise B and explain which one you think was a lie and why.

Luis denied ever cheating on a test, but that can't be true!

VOCABULARY
Social media

A Work in pairs. Look at the pictures (1–3). What do they have in common? Have you done any of these things?

B Complete the definitions with the correct form of the words in bold in *#nomakeupselfie*.

1 When something goes ________________ it becomes very popular and spreads quickly, especially on the internet.

2 A ________________ is a series of organized activities designed to achieve a particular social, commercial or political result.

3 When something is ________________, it is frequently being mentioned or discussed on the internet, particularly on social media platforms.

4 To ________________ people with a message or program means they see or hear it.

5 A ________________ is someone who chooses to receive updates and messages from another person on a social media platform.

6 A ________________ is a symbol used on social media to describe the general subject of a post.

7 An ________________ is someone who changes the way people behave, especially through social media.

#nomakeupselfie

The no make-up selfie **campaign** was developed to raise awareness of cancer research in the UK. The **hashtag** nomakeupselfie started **trending** on various social media websites asking women to post a selfie with no make-up and to donate money to Cancer Research UK. The campaign quickly spread across the internet especially when celebrities such as Lady Gaga, Alicia Keys and Heidi Klum also shared selfies with their **followers** on Instagram. This, along with other social media **influencers** following suit, helped the campaign to **reach** a much wider audience. The trend went **viral** and donations reached $8 million in six days.

2

1

C Go to the Vocabulary Hub on page 146.

D **SPEAK** Work in groups. Discuss the questions.

1 Who do you follow on social media? Why?
2 Which hashtags have you seen trending lately?
3 What do you think makes a campaign go viral?

LISTENING

10.5 **A** **LISTEN FOR ORGANIZATION** Listen to a talk on viral marketing campaigns. Put the topics in the order they're discussed.

___ the research behind viral success
___ create content which affects people's emotions
___ successful charity campaigns that went viral
___ understand the people you are hoping to reach
___ social media influencers can help raise awareness
___ build relationships with donors to ensure long-term success

10.5 **B** **LISTEN FOR DETAIL** Listen again. Complete the sentences with no more than three words or a number from the talk.

1 The Ice Bucket Challenge had ________________ mentions online and 15 million videos were watched ________________ times online.

2 People will react similarly when they see an ________________.

3 The speaker suggests using Pinterest in a campaign directed toward younger ________________.

4 Videos go viral when they affect people's ________________.

5 Frequent ________________ are integral to a charity's continued success.

6 A ________________ is a great way to get people involved because it affects people's emotions and is fun.

C **SPEAK** Work in pairs. Do you think viral campaigns are an effective way to raise awareness of an issue? Why/Why not?

VOCABULARY

Adjective + noun collocations

Adjective + noun collocations

Some adjectives and nouns are commonly used together. For example, we say *negative attitude* NOT ~~*negative belief*~~.

Match the numbers (1–6) with the letters (a–f) to form adjective + noun collocations.

1 The number of **online** …
2 There has been a **positive** …
3 One **key** …
4 Hashtags are a great way to raise **public** …
5 Using Twitter allows us to reach a **wider** …
6 The company has made a **substantial** …

a **awareness** of a new campaign.
b **comments** posted is a good measure of success.
c **audience** than through other social media platforms.
d **factor** was the use of social media influencers.
e **reaction** both online and in print media.
f **donation** to the campaign.

PRONUNCIATION

Using intonation to attract and keep interest

10.6 **A Listen to the sentence below being said in two different ways. Check (✓) the one that sounds more engaging.**

By 2014, it had exploded and garnered 1.2 million mentions on social media, with participants in over twenty countries.

☐ Speaker 1 ☐ Speaker 2

B Underline the words you think will be stressed and draw arrows to show where you think the intonation will rise.

1 It's important to show that they aren't alone, that they do have someone to turn to.
2 Just one small donation from you could change the lives of these children forever.
3 It's time we put a stop to this unnecessary suffering. It's time we took a stand.

10.7 **C Listen and check your answers to Exercise B.**

SPEAKING HUB

A PLAN Work in groups of four. You are going to create a viral marketing campaign for a charity or to raise awareness of an issue (e.g. mental health, homelessness, etc). To help you plan, discuss the questions below.

1 Which charity are you going to raise awareness of and try to get regular donations for?
2 How are you going to get more online mentions for your chosen charity?
3 What key factors will hook your audience into the video?
4 Who is going to be your target audience?
5 How are you going to get higher engagement and create viral content?

B PREPARE Film your viral ad.

C PRESENT Play your viral ad to the class. Take a class vote for the ad most likely to go viral.

- Report a conversation
- Plan and create a viral marketing ad

Café Hub

10.3 Watch on demand

A– *from … to* S– circumlocution

The rise of streaming

COMPREHENSION

A Work in groups. Discuss the questions.

1 Do you prefer streaming movies on platforms like Netflix and Amazon Prime or going to the movie theater?

2 Overall, do you think streaming services have had a positive or negative effect on the movie industry?

3 How do you think movie theaters could adapt to survive the rise of 'on demand' content?

Glossary

influx (n) the arrival of a large amount of people or things at the same time

metric (n) a system or standard for measuring things

B Watch a news report about the rise of video streaming services. Choose the best summary (1 or 2).

1 Streaming services like Netflix have provided a platform for films that might not otherwise have been made.

2 Streaming services like Netflix are now forcing people in the film and TV industry to rethink their approach.

C Watch the report again and answer the questions.

1 According to the presenter, what is usually essential to the success of large film franchises?

2 According to the first interviewee, what won't audiences be able to stream online?

3 Which two examples does the presenter give of cinemas diversifying their business?

4 According to the independent producer, why are many people leaving the film industry to work in TV?

D Work in pairs. Read the extract from the report. What do you think might explain lower ticket sales but higher overall attendance?

Box office sales are no longer the sole metric of success. In fact, so far this year, box office receipts are down, whilst cinema admissions are up.

Glossary

cinema **(n) (British)** = movie theater **(n) (American)**

mum **(n) (British)** = mom **(n) (American)**

AUTHENTIC ENGLISH

A Work in pairs. Read the extract from the report. Why do you think the speaker uses *from … to*? What does this emphasize?

As a result of this revolution, cinemas are changing. They're diversifying to become hubs for community events, **from** live conversation **to** meeting places for new mums.

B Read the information in the box and check your answer to Exercise A.

from … to

In natural spoken English, *from … to* is generally used when talking about the highest and lowest points in a range:

Subscription packages cost anywhere ***from*** *$22* ***to*** *$65 a month.*

However, it can also be used to make arguments sound more persuasive by giving two very different examples that show how big the range of something is.

These days, we can stream everything ***from*** *the latest blockbuster movies* ***to*** *children's cartoons.*

Although this structure usually follows the main claim or argument, it can also be used to introduce it:

From *the atmosphere* ***to*** *the size of the screen, a movie theater offers a great deal that streaming services simply cannot match.*

C Work in pairs. Take turns completing the sentence prompts with *from … to* and your own ideas.

1 My hometown has a lot to offer, …

2 … , there are many clear benefits of social media.

3 There are a lot of people who could play me in a movie, …

4 There's a lot we can do to tackle climate change, …

5 … , there are a lot of advantages to being self-employed.

6 There are multiple reasons to go vegetarian, …

My hometown has a lot to offer, from world-class theater to excellent burgers and fries.

Some big news

A Work in pairs. To what extent would the following factors affect your decision to take a new job?

- length of the commute
- salary
- working hours
- vacation time, benefits and perks

B Watch the video and answer the questions.

1. What are the advantages of Amanda's new job?
2. Why do you think she is reluctant to take it?

SPEAKING SKILL

A Match the extracts (1–3) to their meanings (a–c).

1. Well, that's certainly not near here.
2. And I know that I certainly wouldn't be disappointed if you decided not to go.
3. I guess I just need to be given a good reason to stay by someone, really.

a. I don't want you to go.
b. Give me a reason to stay.
c. It's really far away.

B Work in pairs. Are Harry and Amanda being vague or direct? Why?

C Read the information in the box and check your answers to Exercise A.

> **Circumlocution**
>
> Using more words than is necessary when fewer would do is called circumlocution. This is something we do to be vague or evasive, usually because we are embarrassed, uncomfortable or simply want to avoid saying something. Circumlocution is typically signaled by phrases such as: *I guess what I'm trying to say is …, I just kind of want you to know that …, I suppose what I mean is …*

D Work in pairs. Take turns breaking the bad news below to each other using circumlocution.

- All the money has been stolen out of their bank account.
- You have spilled coffee on their brand-new white carpet.
- You had said that they could have the day off tomorrow, but now you need them to come in to work.
- You have forgotten to send the important letter that they asked you to mail.
- They are going on vacation tomorrow, but the airline they are flying with has gone out of business.

SPEAKING HUB

A PREPARE Work in pairs. Brainstorm the advantages and disadvantages of video streaming services.

B PLAN Work in two groups. You are going to debate the following:

Video streaming services have had a negative impact on the movie and television industry.

Group A – You agree with the idea above.

Group B – You disagree with the idea above.

Plan your arguments. Think about how to support your position, as well as what the other group might say.

C SPEAK Hold your debate.

Give your opinion on streaming services

➤ Turn to page 163 to learn how to write a persuasive essay.

Unit 10 Review

VOCABULARY

A Complete the text with the correct form of the words in the box.

bias   broadsheet   coverage   editor   headline   tabloid

What your newspaper says about you

The newspaper a person reads says a lot about who they are. In the US and many other countries, [1] ______________ newspapers are traditionally smaller in size and their stories are shorter. The [2] ______________ are usually more shocking and many of the stories focus on people and celebrities. [3] ______________, on the other hand, are usually larger in size and much of the [4] ______________ in these newspapers focuses on serious stories rather than celebrity gossip. In both cases, the paper's [5] ______________ decides what gets published and can have a huge influence on their readers. Many newspapers in the US tend to be [6] ______________ toward one of the two main political parties and people will usually not buy a paper that supports the other party.

B Complete the infographic with the correct form of the words in the box.

campaign   follower   hashtag   influencer   meme   reach   trend   viral

The power of Social Media

Katy Perry, Justin Bieber and Barack Obama all have over **100 million** [1] ______________ on Twitter.

[2] ______________ are used **125 million** times a day on Twitter.

PewDiePie is, without a doubt, one of the **biggest** [3] ______________ on social media, with over **60 million** subscribers to his YouTube channel.

When a music video goes [4] ______________ it can [5] ______________ **billions** of people. 'Despacito' has had over **5 billion** views.

A short [6] ______________ is much more likely to be **successful** than a long one.

A social media marketing [7] ______________ is a cheap and quick way to reach **millions** of people.

'Stranger Things' was the **highest** [8] ______________ search for a TV show on Google in 2017.

C Choose the correct options to complete the sentences.

1 Celebrity endorsement is a great way to raise public ***awareness / understanding*** of a campaign.
2 Going viral was a ***key / main*** factor in the charity's success.
3 The charity has received a lot of positive online ***posts / comments*** recently.
4 Overall, we've had a pretty ***positive / affirmative*** reaction from the public.
5 The actress made a ***consequential / substantial*** donation to charity.
6 In order to reach a ***wider / deeper*** audience, you need a good hashtag.
7 We need to carry out a ***thorough / deep*** investigation into why this campaign failed.
8 I don't understand why there was such a ***negative / poor*** reaction to our ad.

GRAMMAR

A Rewrite the sentences in reported speech.

1 'I've been working every night this week.'
Nicki said ______________________________.
2 'I'm going to be about ten minutes late.'
Jonas says ______________________________.
3 'Have you always wanted to go to college?'
He asked ______________________________.
4 'We were trying to find somewhere to park.'
She said ______________________________.
5 'I'll let you know when I'm finished.'
Marco said ______________________________.
6 'I'd wanted to tell her for months.'
Alex said ______________________________.
7 'I will need some help with my project.'
Pablo says ______________________________.
8 'Where can I find a good seafood restaurant?'
Sofia asked ______________________________.

B Are these sentences correct or incorrect? Rewrite the incorrect sentences.

1 Piotr agreed coming to the meeting.
2 She refused to apologize for being late.
3 Maria offered working this weekend.
4 They insisted on to pay for dinner.
5 He congratulated her on passing the exam.
6 She reminded me sending the email.
7 They invited us having dinner with them.
8 They advised me to get there fifteen minutes early.

Irregular Verbs

Base form	Simple past	Past participle
be	was/were	been
become	became	become
begin	began	begun
break	broke	broken
bring	brought	brought
build	built	built
buy	bought	bought
can	could	(been able to)
catch	caught	caught
choose	chose	chosen
come	came	come
cost	cost	cost
cut	cut	cut
do	did	done
drink	drank	drunk
eat	ate	eaten
fall	fell	fallen
feel	felt	felt
find	found	found
forget	forgot	forgotten
get	got	got
give	gave	given
go	went	gone/been
grow	grew	grown
have	had	had
hear	heard	heard
hit	hit	hit
hold	held	held
hurt	hurt	hurt
keep	kept	kept
know	knew	known
leave	left	left
lend	lent	lent

Base form	Simple past	Past participle
let	let	let
lose	lost	lost
make	made	made
mean	meant	meant
meet	met	met
must	had to	(had to)
pay	paid	paid
put	put	put
read	read	read
ride	rode	ridden
run	ran	run
say	said	said
see	saw	seen
sell	sold	sold
set	set	set
shut	shut	shut
sing	sang	sung
sit	sat	sat
sleep	slept	slept
speak	spoke	spoken
spell	spelled	spelled
spend	spent	spent
stand	stood	stood
steal	stole	stolen
take	took	taken
teach	taught	taught
tell	told	told
think	thought	thought
throw	threw	thrown
understand	understood	understood
wear	wore	worn
win	won	won
write	wrote	written

PHONETIC SYMBOLS											
Single vowels			Diphthongs			Consonants					
/ɪ/	fish	/fɪʃ/	/uw/	new	/nuw/	/p/	pen	/pen/	/s/	snake	/sneɪk/
/iː/	bean	/biːn/	/eɪ/	face	/feɪs/	/b/	bag	/bæg/	/z/	zoo	/zuː/
/ʊ/	foot	/fʊt/	/ɔɪ/	boy	/bɔɪ/	/t/	tea	/tiː/	/ʃ/	shop	/ʃɒp/
/uː/	shoe	/ʃuː/	/oʊ/	nose	/noʊz/	/d/	dog	/dɒg/	/ʒ/	television	/'telɪvɪʒən/
/e/	egg	/eg/	/ju/	use	/juz/	/ʧ/	chip	/ʧɪp/	/m/	map	/mæp/
/ə/	mother	/'mʌðər/	/aɪ/	eye	/aɪ/	/ʤ/	jazz	/ʤæz/	/n/	name	/neɪm/
/ɜː/	word	/wɜːrd/	/aʊ/	mouth	/maʊθ/	/k/	cake	/keɪk/	/ŋ/	ring	/rɪŋ/
/ɔː/	talk	/tɔːk/				/g/	girl	/gɜːrl/	/h/	house	/haʊs/
/æ/	back	/bæk/				/f/	film	/fɪlm/	/l/	leg	/leg/
/ʌ/	bus	/bʌs/				/v/	verb	/vɜːrb/	/r/	road	/roʊd/
/ɑː/	arm	/ɑːrm/				/θ/	thing	/θɪŋ/	/w/	want	/wɒnt/
/ɒ/	top	/tɒp/				/ð/	these	/ðiːz/	/j/	yes	/jes/

Grammar Hub

1.1 Question forms

Questions with *be, have* and *do*

- We usually use the auxiliary verbs *be*, *have* and *do* to form questions. These come before the main verb.

Question word	Auxiliary	Subject	Main verb	
	Is	he	coming	this weekend?
	Have	you	seen	her?
When	did	they	move	in?

Subject questions

- When the question word (*who*, *what*, etc) is the subject, we don't use an auxiliary.

Question word	Main verb	
What	happened	to you?
How	are	you?

Indirect questions

- Indirect questions begin with phrases such as *Can you tell me …?* After the phrase, we use the same word order as a sentence, not a question.

  Do you think it will rain? NOT ~~*Do you think will it rain?*~~

  Can you tell me where you live? NOT ~~*Can you tell me where do you live?*~~

Questions ending in a preposition

- When a question word is the object of a preposition, the preposition usually comes at the end of the sentence.

  Who did you brother live with?

  What did you use it for?

Questions with negative auxiliaries

- When we ask negative *wh-* questions, we use the auxiliary verb, even in subject questions. Negative *wh-* questions can be used to confirm something you believe to be true, to express an opinion in a more formal manner or to focus on a smaller number of answers.

  *OK, who **doesn't** want pizza? (= I think most people **will** want pizza)*

1.2 Tense review

Simple present	**He enjoys** parties.
Present progressive	**I'm watching** the news.
Simple past	**He got up** early this morning.
Past progressive	**I was walking** the dog.
Present perfect	**I've lived** here for 12 years.
Past perfect	**I'd seen** the movie several times.

- We use the simple present to talk about general truths or actions that always/usually/never happen as part of our daily routines.
- We use the present progressive for things that are happening now or around now.
- We use the simple past to talk about past states or completed actions in the past.
- We use the past progressive to describe the background to a story or something that was in progress at a particular time in the past. We also use it with the simple past to describe an action that was interrupted.

  We were driving home when we had an unexpected phone call.

- We use the present perfect to talk about a state or action that started in the past and is still happening now. We also use it to announce news.
- We use the past perfect to talk about a past action that occurred before another past action. This tense is frequently used with the simple past.
- With the negative and question forms of these tenses, we use an auxiliary verb (*be*, *do* or *have*, depending on the tense).

  She doesn't feel well.

  It didn't cost a lot.

  I haven't finished yet.

  Had they been there before?

Be careful!

- Certain time words and expressions, such as *now*, *just*, *already*, *recently*, *every day*, etc, help us to identify which tense we need to use.

  *I was traveling across the country **at the time**.*

  *I have **just** finished the last series on Netflix.*

  *Actually, I saw him at the gym **yesterday**.*

1.1 Question forms

A Correct the mistakes in each question.

1 Does he lives near here?
2 What she has done to her hair?
3 Where you work?
4 Which is team winning?
5 Haven't you already be on vacation?
6 Who with do you live?
7 When he told you that?
8 What was happened next?

B Rewrite the direct questions as indirect questions.

1 Where did you get your information?
Can you tell me ________________________?
2 Is it going to snow later, do you think?
Do you think ________________________?
3 What do you think of the new recycling laws?
Can I ask you ________________________?
4 Where does Alejandro come from?
Do you know ________________________?
5 Has the mail arrived yet?
Could you see if ________________________?

C Complete the questions in the interview.

Interviewer: Where [1] ________________________?
Mia: I'm from Seattle, Washington.
Interviewer: How long [2] ________________________?
Mia: I've been here for about five years now.
Interviewer: Who [3] ________________________?
Mia: With friends, but I'm looking to find an apartment of my own.
Interviewer: So when [4] ________________________?
Mia: I guess I decided to become an actor when I was about five!
Interviewer: What [5] ________________________?
Mia: I don't have much free time, but when I am free, I like spending time with friends and family.
Interviewer: Do you think [6] ________________________?
Mia: Oh yes. I think I'll always be an actor. I can't imagine doing anything else!

➤ Go back to page 5.

1.2 Tense review

A Choose the correct options to complete the sentences.

1 I ***am / was*** watching television when I started to feel sick.
2 Joanna was ashamed because she ***has / had*** done something wrong.
3 I ***am never feeling / have never felt*** relaxed around him – I don't know why.
4 We ***were taking / had taken*** the wrong turn and were now completely lost.
5 I'm pretty sure I ***met / have met*** you at Jenna's party last year.
6 While I ***was walking / had walked*** home, I slipped on some ice and broke my ankle.
7 I ***live / have lived*** here for about a year and a half now.
8 James ***studies / is studying*** French at Harvard next year.

B Complete the sentences with the correct form of the verb in parentheses.

1 Jochen is an anxious person who ________________________ (*not like*) doing new things.
2 It wasn't awkward at the party because I ________________________ (*already meet*) everyone there.
3 The question is: why was Tom there – who ________________________ (*wait*) for?
4 I have some really exciting news – I ________________________ (*start*) a new job!
5 We ________________________ (*work*) on a secret project these days.
6 Tell me about yourself. How long ________________________ (*work*) for this company?

C Complete the sentences with the correct form of the verbs in the box. Use contractions where possible.

forget	have	know	meet
snow	think	walk	work

1 It ________________________ heavily and I wasn't wearing a winter coat.
2 She ________________________ for the company for almost five years now.
3 It's difficult because he ________________________ many people in the area.
4 We ________________________ much money back then, but we were happy.
5 I knew I ________________________ her before, but I couldn't figure out where.
6 I ________________________ about starting my own company.
7 I ________________________ down the road in the sunshine when out of nowhere, it suddenly started pouring rain.
8 She only realized she ________________________ her passport when she got to the airport.

➤ Go back to page 7.

Grammar Hub

2.1 Present perfect and present perfect progressive

	Positive	Negative	Question
Present perfect	**He's improved** his fitness level.	**They haven't finished** their meeting yet.	**Have you lost** weight?
Present perfect progressive	**I've been trying** to give up sugar.	**She hasn't been sleeping** very well.	**Have you been avoiding** me?

- We use the present perfect for finished actions with a present effect, and the present perfect progressive for unfinished actions.

  I've read that book before, actually.
  (= I finished the book.)
  I've been reading a great book recently.
  (= I started it and I'm still reading it.)
- We use the present perfect to emphasize the result of an action, and the present perfect progressive to emphasize the action itself.

  I've cleaned the bathroom.
  (emphasizing the result: the bathroom's now clean)
  I've been cleaning the bathroom all morning.
  (emphasizing the action: the cleaning)
- We use the present perfect to suggest that something is permanent and the present perfect progressive to suggest that something is temporary.

  I've lived here my whole life. (= long-term/permanent)
  I've been living here while I look for a new apartment.
  (= short-term/temporary)
- We use the present perfect to say how often something has happened and the present perfect progressive to say how long something has been happening.

  I've been to the gym every day this week. (= number of times)
  I've been going to the gym for the past two months.
  (= length of time)

Be careful!

- We don't usually use state verbs such as *be*, *have*, *know* and *seem* in the present perfect progressive.

  She's had short hair for several months now.
  NOT ~~She's been having short hair for several months now.~~

2.2 *used to / would / be used to / get used to*

	Positive	Negative	Question
used to	**I used to work** in a hotel.	**He didn't use to get** so stressed.	**Did she use to have** long hair?
would	**They would take** the bus to work.	**She wouldn't have** anything for breakfast.	**Would he usually come** home late?
be used to	**He's used to getting** up early.	**I'm not used to eating** such spicy food.	**Are you used to driving** on the right now?
get used to	**He** soon **got used to wearing** glasses.	**I haven't gotten used to** the cold weather.	**Are you getting used to living** in the country?

- We use *used to* + base form to talk about past habits, repeated actions and states or situations that have changed.

  I used to get up really early on the weekend.
  He didn't use to have a beard.
- We also use *would* + base form to talk about past habits and repeated actions.

  The children would spend hours playing in the yard.
- We use *be used to* + verb + *-ing*/noun to talk about a situation which is now normal or familiar. We use the negative form to talk about a situation which is new or strange.

  I'm used to living on my own.
  I'm not used to the cold weather.
- We use *get used to* + verb + *-ing*/noun to talk about a situation which is becoming more familiar.

  I'm getting used to working in an office.
  I haven't gotten used to the food yet.

Be careful!

- We cannot use *would* to talk about past states.

  They used to live in Panama. NOT ~~They would live in Panama.~~

2.1 Present perfect and present perfect progressive

A Choose the correct options to complete the conversations.

1 **A:** How long have you ***known*** / ***been knowing*** Emily?
B: Uh, about five years now, I think.

2 **A:** Did you tell everyone about the change of venue?
B: I think so. Oh no! I've just ***realized*** / ***been realizing*** that I forgot to tell Piotr!

3 **A:** How's your essay going?
B: I've ***planned*** / ***been planning*** it for the past three hours so I'm almost ready to start writing.

4 **A:** Who'll be there this evening?
B: Just me and my sister. She's ***stayed*** / ***been staying*** with me while her apartment is being redecorated.

5 **A:** I saw Toby in town today.
B: Yes, his boss has ***given*** / ***been giving*** him a week off from work.

6 **A:** So, what have you been up to?
B: I've been ***working*** / ***worked*** on a new book. I should finish it by the end of the year.

B Complete the sentences with the present perfect or present perfect progressive form of the verbs in the box. Add pronouns if necessary.

avoid	be	decide	do	find	know	leave	notice	only go out	think	use	wait

1 They ______________ about moving now that their son ______________ home.
2 Ren ______________ the new shampoo for six months and she ______________ a big improvement in her hair.
3 Lucia ______________ to quit her job because she ______________ it more and more stressful over the last few months.
4 Why ______________ me? ______________ something to upset you?
5 I ______________ Farid for years, but we ______________ for a few weeks!
6 I ______________ for you for hours! Where ______________ all this time?

C Use the prompts to write sentences in the present perfect or present perfect progressive.

1 Kim / not work / here for long, so she / not met / all of her colleagues yet
______________.
2 I think Jamila and Kalid / already / send out / the invitations
______________.
3 I'm afraid I / not clean / the living room yet because I just / not have / time
______________.
4 Jimmy / drive / for hours, so he must / be / exhausted
______________.
5 I / know / about this for a long time
______________.
6 How long / it / be / since you / quit / your job
______________?
7 You / visit / this museum before
______________?
8 We / eat / vegan food for two months now
______________.

➤ Go back to page 17.

2.2 *used to / would / be used to / get used to*

A Choose the correct options to complete the sentences.

1 People ***didn't use to*** / ***wouldn't*** be able to look everything up on Google.
2 Sofia is slowly ***used*** / ***getting used*** to living back home with her parents.
3 ***Did you use to*** / ***Would you*** have a smartphone when you were younger?
4 ***I'm still not used*** / ***I didn't use*** to having short hair!
5 The children always ***got used*** / ***used*** to spend their allowance on candy.
6 Jakob ***got*** / ***was*** used to wearing glasses fairly quickly.
7 ***Were you*** / ***Have you gotten*** used to the new software yet?
8 As a child, Milo ***would*** / ***was used to*** become demotivated very easily.

B Complete the text messages with the correct form of *used to*, *be used to* and *get used to*.

How's the new job going? Have you [1] ______________ the commute yet?

Not really. It [2] ______________ take about 20 minutes to get to work. Now it takes over an hour!

I know the feeling! I [3] ______________ having a long drive to work – I've been doing it for a while now – but I still [4] ______________ getting up so early!

It's horrible, isn't it? I [5] ______________ get up at seven thirty. These days, that's when I have to leave the house. And I'm still [6] ______________ getting home so late, either.

➤ Go back to page 19.

Grammar Hub

3.1 Narrative tenses

	Positive	Negative	Question
Simple past	**The rescue team found** Jose and **carried** him to safety.	Unfortunately, **the rescue team didn't see** the survivors.	So what **did you do** next?
Past progressive	At the time, **most of us were trying** to get some sleep.	**I wasn't looking forward to** the trip.	What **were you doing** when the storm hit?
Past perfect	They returned to find that **the tornado had destroyed** their house.	They suddenly realized that **the helicopter hadn't seen** their signal.	**Had you been** in that kind of situation before?
Past perfect progressive	**She'd been swimming** for hours by the time she was rescued.	Although **they hadn't been driving** long, everyone was exhausted.	How long **had you been climbing** for?

- We use the simple past for completed actions that are the main events in a story.

  After some hours alone in the woods, Wei ate his last chocolate bar.
- We use the past progressive (*was/were* + verb + *-ing*) to describe:

  a actions in progress at a particular point in a story.

  He was charging his phone at the time.

  b longer actions or situations that are interrupted by a shorter action.

  They weren't wearing life jackets when the boat capsized. NOT ~~*They didn't wear life jackets when the boat capsized.*~~

  c the general background of a story.

  The skies were getting dark, the winds were picking up and the passengers were beginning to worry.
- We use the past perfect (*had* + past participle) to describe past actions or situations that happened before one of the main events in the story, or before the story began.

  A lot of insects had bitten Francesco before he decided to use the insect repellent.
- We use the past perfect progressive (*had* + *been* + verb + *-ing*) to describe longer actions or situations that started before one of the main events and have continued up to that point.

  We'd been waiting for hours before we were rescued.

Be careful!

- We usually use the past progressive after *while* and *as*.

  While she was standing by the side of the road, a car with dark windows pulled up.
- We can usually use either the simple past or past perfect after *as soon as* and *by the time*.

  By the time I'd realized what was happening, Jilly had left.

3.2 Alternatives to *if* in conditionals

- We use *unless* to mean *if … not*.

  Generally, bears won't attack you unless they think you're a threat. (= They won't attack you if they don't think you're a threat.)

  Unless this weather improves, we'll be stuck in the camp all day. (= If the weather doesn't improve, we'll be stuck in the camp all day.)
- We use *provided (that)* and *as long as* to mean *only if*.

  They should be back soon provided (that) they don't take a wrong turn. (= They should be back soon, but only if they don't take a wrong turn.)

  As long as you stay on the path, you won't get lost. (= You won't get lost, but only if you stay on the path.)
- We use *in case* to talk about doing something now to prepare for a possible future situation.

  I'll take a waterproof jacket in case it starts raining. (= because it's possible it will start raining)

  She's going to stay in a safe spot in case she encounters a bear. (= because it's possible that she will encounter a bear)
- We use *as soon as* to mean *in the shortest possible time / immediately*.

  I'll call you as soon as I hear anything. (= I'll call you immediately after I hear something.)

Be careful!

- Even though we're talking about the future, we use a present tense after future time clauses.

  We'll leave as soon as the storm clears. NOT ~~*We'll leave as soon as the storm will clear.*~~

  Elephants won't attack you unless you run toward them. NOT ~~*Elephants won't attack you unless you will run toward them.*~~

3.1 Narrative tenses

A Choose the correct options (a, b or c) to complete the sentences.

1 Nozomi ___ her bike when it started raining.
a was riding b rode c had ridden

2 We ___ down the side of the mountain when our rope snapped.
a had climbed b were climbing c climbed

3 The ship ___ into a rock, but no one was hurt.
a had crashed b was crashing c crashed

4 I ___ my tent when suddenly I heard a strange noise in the forest behind me.
a packed away b had packed away c was packing away

5 The next day, they saw that the hurricane ___ the house off the ground!
a was lifting b had lifted c lifted

6 When the wave hit the ship, everyone ___ to panic.
a had started b started c was starting

7 The sun ___ and the conditions were perfect for hiking.
a was shining b had shone c shone

8 We ___ for eight hours when the captain told us to prepare for an emergency landing.
a were flying b had been flying c flew

B Complete the story with the correct form of the verbs in the box.

approach carry faint fall fly happen serve take off

Something strange [1] ________ the last time I was on a plane. I [2] ________ to Moscow on a business trip. We [3] ________ from Frankfurt about an hour before, and the cabin crew [4] ________ drinks. Suddenly, one of the cabin crew near me just [5] ________ to the floor. We didn't know if he [6] ________ or had had a heart attack. Other members of the crew rushed to help him, and [7] ________ him to the back of the plane. Just as we [8] ________ Moscow, the captain made an announcement, telling us that the crew member was fine. I was very relieved.

➤ Go back to page 27.

3.2 Alternatives to *if* in conditionals

A Choose the correct options to complete the sentences.

1 They'll survive in the woods ***provided / unless*** they have enough food.
2 ***Unless / Provided*** we leave right now, we'll never make it back to the camp before dark.
3 I'll let you start the fire ***as soon as / as long as*** you know what you're doing!
4 Do Yoon is bringing extra water ***as long as / in case*** we run out.
5 Let's give Margie a call ***as soon as / as long as*** we reach the cabin.
6 ***As long as / Unless*** you have a better suggestion, let's have pizza tonight.
7 I wrote their number on a piece of paper ***in case / unless*** my phone battery dies.
8 We'll go fishing at the river tomorrow ***as long as / in case*** it doesn't rain.

B Are these sentences correct or incorrect? Rewrite the incorrect sentences.

1 We'll call the police as soon as we will get to safety.
2 I'll cancel the trip unless Tara will decide to go with me.
3 You can go to the party provided you're back home by 11 o'clock.
4 Unless the taxi doesn't come soon, we're going to be late.
5 Take some seasickness pills with you in case the ocean will be rough.
6 Will you call me as soon as you arrive at the airport?
7 He'll sleep on the ship as long as the weather won't be too bad.
8 I'll take the risk provided you think it's worth it.

C Match the numbers (1–10) with the letters (a–j) to make conditional sentences.

1 Provided you don't make any sudden movements, ___
2 She won't use her credit card ___
3 You won't get into trouble ___
4 Astrid should give David the money now ___
5 As long as you promise to pay him back, ___
6 I'll come with you as ___
7 Unless we stay late, ___
8 I'm going to take a map with me ___
9 Provided that we stay somewhere cheap, ___
10 I'll buy the tickets ___

a provided you tell the truth.
b I'd love to come with you to Paris.
c in case she doesn't see him later.
d in case we get lost.
e we'll never get all this work done on time.
f he said that he would get the food for the party.
g unless it's an emergency.
h as soon as they're available online.
i you should be perfectly safe.
j long as we make sure we're back home by five.

➤ Go back to page 31.

Grammar Hub

4.1 Future forms

- We use *will* + base form:

  a for decisions made at the moment of speaking (including promises, offers, plans and requests).

  That's a good idea – I'll call him now.

  That looks heavy – I'll carry it for you.

  b to make predictions based on personal opinions or feelings (usually with adverbs like *definitely, certainly, possibly*, etc to show how sure we are).

  Tom will definitely be late – he always is!

  Mom won't like that movie. It's not her sort of thing.

- We use *be going to* + base form:

  a to talk about general intentions and plans made before the moment of speaking.

  I'm going to look for a new job.

  b to make predictions based on present evidence.

  The traffic's not moving – we're going to be late!

- We use the simple present to talk about a timetabled or scheduled event.

  Our flight leaves at 8:30 am on Monday.

  My job interview is tomorrow morning.

- We use the present progressive to talk about future arrangements and fixed plans.

  We're staying in a hostel for the first three nights.
  (= We've already booked the hostel.)

  I'm meeting Sarah at 7:30 pm outside the restaurant.
  (= We've already arranged to meet at that time and place.)

4.2 Future perfect, future progressive and future perfect progressive

	Positive	Negative	Question
Future perfect	**The movie will have started** by the time we get there!	**I won't have finished** the report by tomorrow morning.	**Will you have left** by then?
Future progressive	**I'll be seeing** her on Monday, so I could ask her then.	**We won't be using** driverless cars for at least another 50 years.	So, what **will you be doing** this time tomorrow?
Future perfect progressive	In 2041, **we'll have been using** the internet for 50 years.	**I won't have been running** long enough to try a half-marathon in July.	How long **will you have been traveling** by then?

- We use the future perfect (*will* + *have* + past participle) to talk about something that will be finished before a specific time in the future.

  By 2050, we will have greatly improved the air quality in our cities.

- We use the future progressive (*will* + *be* + verb + *-ing*) to talk about an action that will be in progress at a specific time in the future.

  Hopefully, I'll be working in New York by then.

- We use the future perfect progressive (*will* + *have* + *been* + verb + *-ing*) to talk about an action or situation that will continue up to a specific time in the future.

  On July 9th, I'll have been working here for seven years.

- Certain time words and expressions are used with these tenses.

  In 50 years, we'll have stopped using gas-powered vehicles.

  This time next year, we'll be studying in France.

  By 2020, we will have been living together for 20 years.

Be careful!

- Do not confuse these three tenses. The future perfect is used for *completed* actions in the future, while the future progressive is used for actions *in progress* at a certain point in the future. The future perfect progressive refers to how long something will be in progress before a certain point in the future.

  I will have paid for my house by 2025. NOT ~~*I will be paying for my house by 2025.*~~

  I will be living in the US in five years. NOT ~~*I will have lived in the US in five years.*~~

  I will have been living here for 15 years in 2025. NOT ~~*I will be living here for 15 years in 2025.*~~

4.1 Future forms

A Choose the correct options to complete the sentences.

1 I *have* / *am having* French class every Monday night at seven o'clock.
2 *I'm meeting* / *I will meet* friends for lunch on Sunday.
3 *We'll probably* / *We're going to* move this year but I'm not certain.
4 It looks like they *will* / *are going to* win. They're 4–0 up with only a minute left to play.
5 I think the plane *arrives* / *will arrive* late.
6 I've had enough of this job! I'm *looking for* / *going to look for* a new one.

B Complete the post with the correct future form of the verbs in parentheses. Use contractions where possible.

Emily | 20 mins ago

So, big news! I have a place at NYU to study Performing Arts, so
1 ________________ (*I / move*) to New York in September! Apparently, I can stay in the residence halls near the main campus, but I've decided 2 ________________ (*I / look for*) my own apartment. Wouldn't that be amazing?
3 ________________ (*I / definitely / have to*) get a job to pay the rent, but it would be nice to have my own space. I've never lived in another country before, so 4 ________________ (*it / be*) difficult to be so far away from my family. But everyone's been so supportive! Anyway, my 5 ________________ (*flight / leave*) early on August 28th so if any of you want to meet up before then, just send me a message and
6 ________________ (*I / get back*) to you.

C Are these sentences correct or incorrect? Rewrite the incorrect sentences.

1 Having my young nephews to stay in the house next week is being exhausting!
2 The lecture starts at seven tomorrow evening, not eight.
3 I'm afraid that we aren't going on a cruise this year.
4 I'm feeling really tired, so I think I go to bed soon.
5 Are you starting looking for a job anytime soon?
6 We meet Andy and Karim for lunch on May 12th.
7 I probably won't get there until at least ten thirty.
8 I'm helping you do the dishes, if you like.

➤ Go back to page 39.

4.2 Future perfect, future progressive and future perfect progressive

A Choose the correct options (a, b or c) to complete the sentences.

1 It's a nine-hour flight. My plane leaves at 9 am, so at 11 am, I ___.
   a 'll be flying over the Atlantic   **b** 'll have landed in New York
2 Do you really think you'll ___ at the same company in ten years?
   a have worked   **b** be working
3 This time next year, he ___ for Real Madrid for ten years.
   a 'll have been playing   **b** 'll be playing
4 Do you think you ___ English in five years?
   a 'll have studied   **b** 'll still be studying
5 Is it possible that they ___ the use of fossil fuels by the time our children grow up?
   a 'll be banning   **b** 'll have banned
6 What will you ___ at three tomorrow? If you're free, let's meet up for coffee.
   a have done   **b** be doing
7 Next Sunday, I ___ here for two years.
   a 'll have been living   **b** 'll be living

B Complete the sentences with the future perfect, future progressive or future perfect progressive form of the verb in parentheses.

1 ________________ (*you / finish*) your studies by the end of the year?
2 I started learning English over four years ago, so in December, I will ________________ (*study*) it for exactly five years.
3 Within the next ten years, robots ________________ (*take*) over a lot of tasks.
4 What kind of world do you think we ________________ (*live*) in 50 years from now?
5 If the sea level rises, these cities ________________ (*completely / disappear*) in 100 years.
6 In June of next year, you ________________ (*work*) here for five years.

➤ Go back to page 43.

Grammar Hub

5.1 The passive voice; causative *have* and *get*

The passive voice

Simple present	**Most of the children are taken** to school by bus.
Present progressive	**We aren't being told** the truth about the extent of the damage.
Present perfect	**Has the amount of waste been reduced**?
Simple past	**The deer was killed** by a hunter.
Past progressive	**The forest was being cut down** by construction companies.
Past perfect	**The law hadn't been changed** for years.
will	How **will the park be affected** by the road?
Modals	**The plans can't be changed** now.
The infinitive	**This area** is too polluted **to be used**.

- We use the passive voice (*be* + past participle) when:
  - **a** we don't know who or what caused something to happen, or when this is not important.
    A fire was started in a small area of forest near the park entrance. (= We don't know who started the fire.)
  - **b** we want to focus on the action, not what caused it.
    Huge amounts of CO_2 are being added to the atmosphere every year. (= The focus here is the CO_2 – we aren't really interested in who or what is adding it.)
  - **c** it's obvious from the context who or what caused the action.
    The law has already been changed in many countries. (= It's obvious that it was the government of these countries that changed the law.)

Be careful!

- When we say who performed an action, we use *by*.
  The research is being carried out ***by*** *the US National Park Service.*

Causative *have* and *get*

Positive	Negative	Question
I'm having solar panels **installed**.	**We haven't had** the windows **replaced** yet.	**Are you getting** a smart meter **fitted**?

- We use causative *have* and *get (have/get* + object + past participle) to say that someone does something for us – typically for tasks we can't or don't know how to do ourselves.
  My parents are having a new garage built.
- We can also use causative *have* to describe something unwelcome or negative happening to us.
  I've had my bike stolen twice this month!

5.2 *-ing* and the infinitive

- We use verb + *-ing*:
  - **a** after prepositions.
    I'm thinking ***about moving*** *to another company.*
  - **b** as the subject or object of a sentence.
    Traveling *around South Korea was amazing.*
  - **c** after certain verbs (e.g. *admit, avoid, finish, mind*, etc).
    I ***don't mind living*** *in the suburbs.*
- We use the infinitive:
  - **a** after adjectives.
    It can be ***difficult to find*** *your dream job.*
  - **b** to talk about purpose (i.e. what someone wants to achieve).
    I came to New York to improve my level of English. (= This explains why I came here.)
  - **c** after certain verbs (e.g. *agree, attempt, decide, hope, manage, promise*, etc).
    Has the City Council ***agreed to build*** *more housing?*
- The base form is always used after modal verbs (e.g. *may, might, would*, etc) and after the verbs *let* and *make*.
  I think I ***would make*** *an excellent candidate for the Mars One program.*

Be careful!

- Some verbs can be followed by either verb + *-ing* or the infinitive, but with a change of meaning (e.g. *forget, go on, regret, remember, stop, try*, etc)
  I'll never forget ***waking up*** *in Tokyo for the first time. (= I have a memory of this.)*
  My daughter never forgets ***to call*** *me on my birthday. (= She doesn't forget to do this.)*

5.1 The passive voice

A Rewrite the sentences in the passive voice, omitting the agent where appropriate.

1 Millions of people watch the World Cup final.
The World Cup final ______________________.

2 High CO_2 levels are causing global warming.
Global warming ______________________.

3 We've recently fitted our attic with insulation.
Our attic ______________________.

4 When did they announce the winners of the competition?
When ______________________?

5 The council is going to cut down the tree.
The tree ______________________.

6 A plumber needs to install this kind of shower.
This kind of shower needs ______________________.

B Complete the paragraph with the correct passive form of the verbs in the box.

pick up confirm deliver inform pack print send take

ONLINE SHOPPING
behind the scenes

Someone has just ordered some new clothes online. But what happens behind the scenes before the items can [1] ____________ to their door? Once the credit card payment [2] ____________, an order confirmation email [3] ____________ automatically to the customer, and the people on the packing team [4] ____________ of the order. One of them then picks up the items from the warehouse in order for them to [5] ____________. Next the shipping label [6] ____________, and either the package [7] ____________ by a courier or it [8] ____________ to the post office for its trip to the customer.

➤ Go back to page 51.

Causative *have* and *get*

Put the words in the correct order to make sentences with causative *have* and *get*.

1 getting / I'm / the / locally. / posters / printed

____

2 to / bike / going / get / repaired? / your / When / you / are

____

3 the heating system / at / an electrician. / by / need / get / looked / I / to

____

4 has / her / hair / wife / six weeks. / My / every / cut

____

5 teeth / tomorrow. / having / checked / are / their / The dogs

____

6 new / expensive? / Will / very / having / installed / a / kitchen / be

____

7 having / After / better. / painted, / house / it / much / so / looked / our

____

8 had / their / neighbors / house / night. / into / Our / last / broken

____

➤ Go back to page 53.

5.2 *-ing* and infinitive forms

A Choose the correct options to complete the sentences.

1 We agreed ***to do / doing*** our project on the topic of megacities.
2 He really appreciates ***to be / being*** able to travel so much.
3 The council has passed a law ***protect / to protect*** old buildings.
4 They let us ***walk / to walk*** around the museum at night.
5 Did you manage ***to book / booking*** the tickets for the tour?
6 They made her ***completing / complete*** an online application form.
7 I'm really looking forward to ***having / have*** a few days off from work.
8 ***Invite / Inviting*** so many people to dinner really wasn't a good idea.

B Are these sentences correct or incorrect? Rewrite the incorrect sentences.

1 After a poor start, he went on winning the game in the end.
2 I fondly remember to visit Abu Dhabi when I was about your age.
3 I forgot to tell you that I entered that photography competition.
4 We regret informing passengers that the flight to Seoul has been delayed.
5 Stop to talk about your vacations all the time – it's making me jealous!
6 We tried to book tickets for the Coffee Museum in Dubai but it was closed.

➤ Go back to page 57.

Grammar Hub

6.1 Obligation, prohibition and permission

Strong obligation

- We use *have to, must, need to, be obliged to* and *be required to* to talk about things that we are obligated to do / are necessary.

  The meeting starts at 9:00 am, so you must be here before then.
  (= It's necessary for you to be here before 9:00 am.)
  You need to buy a ticket before boarding.
  (= It's necessary to buy a ticket.)

Lack of obligation

- We use *don't have to, don't need to, be not obliged to* and *be not required to* to talk about things that we aren't obligated to do / aren't necessary.

  The dress code is semi-formal, but staff members aren't required to wear ties. (= They can wear ties if they want to, but it's not necessary.)

Be careful!

- We cannot use *must not* in this way.

  They don't have to study music if they don't want to. NOT ~~They must not study music if they don't want to.~~

Weak obligation

- We use *should* to talk about things that are advised, recommended or suggested, but aren't necessary.

  You should read the report before our meeting with Alex tomorrow. (= It isn't necessary to read the report, but it's a good idea.)

- We use *be supposed to* to talk about things we're expected to do according to a rule or arrangement.

  I'm supposed to go to that meeting at 2:00 pm, but I really don't want to!

Prohibition

- We use *must not, can't* and *be not allowed to* to talk about things that are prohibited / not permitted.

  You can't smoke anywhere inside the building. (= You're not permitted to smoke.)

6.2 Articles

- We use the indefinite article (*a/an*):

  a when we talk about something for the first time.
  My sister-in-law just bought a new car.

  b when it's not clear or important which exact thing is being talked about (e.g. when something is one of many).
  *I'm going to **a study group** later with **a friend**.*
  *I actually read **a really interesting book** about entrepreneurs.*

- We use the definite article (*the*):

  a when there's only one of something.
  *Sorry, could you close **the door**? (= There's only one door in the room.)*

  b when it's clear to both speaker and listener which specific thing is being talked about.
  *What do you think of **the new science teacher**?*

  c with superlatives.
  *Jupiter is **the biggest** planet in the solar system.*

  d with rivers, some mountains, oceans, seas, plural country names, groups of islands and deserts.
  *Amazingly, he managed to land on **the Hudson River**.*

- We use no article:

  a to talk about things in general.
  More money needs to be spent on education in this country.

  b with most towns, cities, countries, continents, states, lakes and mountains.
  *Yale is an American university in **New Haven**, **Connecticut**.*

6.1 Obligation, prohibition and permission

A Complete the conversations with the correct form of the words and phrases in the box.

be required to | be supposed to | have to | must not | not need to

1 **A:** You ______ tell anyone that I'm here. I want it to be a surprise!
B: OK, I promise!

2 **A:** ______ visitors legally ______ wear helmets?
B: Absolutely! It's far too dangerous not to.

3 **A:** What do you ______ get in town today?
B: A new suit for my job interview next week.

4 **A:** Do you want to play tennis tomorrow?
B: No, I can't. I ______ not ______ put pressure on my wrist until it heals properly.

5 **A:** Should we plan to get to the airport at two?
B: We ______ get there so early. Three should be fine.

B Complete the second sentence so it has a similar meaning to the first using the words in bold.

1 Booking our flights soon is probably a good idea. **should**
I think ______ our flights soon.

2 A high level of English is essential for all applicants. **obliged**
All applicants ______ a high level of English.

3 My parents said I could stay up to watch the final. **let**
My parents ______ stay up to watch the final.

4 I don't know why they didn't let us take our bikes on the train. **allowed**
I don't know why we ______ take our bikes on the train.

5 Taking food and drink into the library isn't permitted. **can't**
You ______ food and drink into the library.

6 It's your choice whether you come with us. **have**
If you don't want to, you ______ come with us.

➤ Go back to page 63.

6.2 Articles

A Choose the correct articles to complete the sentences.

1 How long have you lived in *a* / *the* / – US, Misha?
2 I saw *an* / *the* / – amazing documentary on Netflix last night.
3 For their wedding anniversary this year, my parents are going to *a* / *the* / – Paris.
4 What do you think of *a* / *the* / – new sound equipment in the lecture hall?
5 My roommate Idris is a nurse at *an* / *the* / – hospital on Jones Street.
6 It's not a bad idea to do away with *a* / *the* / – meat in your diet.
7 This is by far *a* / *the* / – worst food I've ever eaten!
8 My dad's school wasn't in New York City; it was in *a* / *the* / – small town out in the country.

B Complete the sentences with *a*, *an*, *the* or – (no article).

1 Seeing kids in school uniforms is ___ unusual sight around here.
2 Lizzie, just do your best on ___ exam tomorrow – that's all you can do.
3 Imagine riding a camel in the burning heat of ___ Sahara Desert.
4 I've never been to ___ job interview before.
5 One thing I could never do without is ___ books.
6 How cold does it get in ___ Antarctica in the winter?
7 I was really excited to see that ___ book Sean gave me for my birthday is signed by the author.
8 How old were you when you first went to ___ college?

C Are these sentences correct or incorrect? Rewrite the incorrect sentences.

1 Lina will be waiting for us once we get off a bus.
2 Aisha got accepted by the university in the US – in California, I believe.
3 It was a successful meeting despite all the interruptions.
4 The Houses of Parliament in London are right next to the River Thames.
5 An exercise is always hard, but it's worth it if you value your health.
6 Most people these days have the smartphone, don't they?
7 Fran is very good at finding the bargains.
8 I'm simply too scared to try a bungee jumping.

➤ Go back to page 67.

Grammar Hub

7.1 First conditional with different future forms; Unreal conditionals

First conditional

- We use the first conditional (*if* + present + future) to talk about something that will probably happen in the future.
- We can use any present tense in the *if* clause (e.g. simple present, present progressive, present perfect, etc) and any future form in the main clause (e.g. *will*, *be going to*, future progressive, etc).

  If the weather improves, we're going to hold the event outside.

  If you're staying in tonight, I'll order us a pizza.

  They're going to let us know if their train is delayed.

  I'll be amazed if we've finished the meeting by three o'clock.
- We can also use an imperative in the main clause.

  Come and meet us later if you finish early.

Be careful!

- We can put the *if* clause or the result clause first. The only difference is we do not use a comma if we begin with the result clause.

  If the weather's nice tomorrow, we'll go to the beach.

  We'll go to the beach tomorrow if the weather's nice.

Unreal conditionals

Second conditional

- We use the second conditional (*if* + simple past + *would/might/could* + base form) to talk about imaginary or hypothetical situations in the present or future and their consequences.

  If I had enough money, I'd open a restaurant.
  (= I don't have enough money; I'm just imagining.)

  We couldn't order things online if credit and debit cards didn't exist. (= This is hypothetical, because credit and debit cards do exist.)

Third conditional

- We use the third conditional (*if* + past perfect + *would/could/might have* + past participle) to talk about a hypothetical situation in the past and its consequences.

  If I had known about the event, I'd definitely have gone to it. (= I didn't know about the event so I didn't go to it.)

Mixed conditionals

- We can also use a mixture of second and third conditionals (*if* + past perfect + *would/might/could* + base form) to talk about a hypothetical past situation with a present result.

  If you'd spent more time studying, you wouldn't be so nervous now.

7.2 *wish* and *if only*

- We use *wish* + simple past to talk about things we would like to be different in the present or future, but are impossible or unlikely to change.

  I wish my brother lived closer to Chicago. (= This is unlikely to change – I'm just imagining.)

  I wish I could speak Japanese. (= This is unlikely to change soon – I'm just imagining.)
- We use *wish* + past perfect to talk about things we regret in the past.

  I wish I'd told Yuko how I felt before she moved back to Japan. (= but I didn't tell her)

  I feel sick! I wish I hadn't eaten so much at lunchtime! (= but I did eat too much)
- We use *wish* + object + *would* + base form to talk about things we want to happen or stop happening in the present, usually because they annoy us.

  I wish you'd stop talking with your mouth full – it's disgusting!

  I wish people wouldn't just throw their garbage in the street.
- We can use *if only* instead of *wish* in all of the structures above to sound more dramatic/ emphatic.

  If only I'd paid more attention in school!
- We can use *were* instead of *was* after *I/he/she/it* in the *if* clause.

  I wish I was/were a little bit taller.
  (= This is impossible – I'm just imagining.)

Be careful!

- When you want to make a wish about yourself, or you and other people, use *could* instead of *would*.

  I wish I could sit at home all day. NOT ~~*I wish I would sit at home all day.*~~

7.1 First conditional with different future forms

Correct the mistakes in the sentences.

1 Let me know if you'll need any help with anything.
2 We're going to miss the beginning if we won't leave soon.
3 If everything goes well, we'll have been finishing by Friday.
4 Could I borrow that book if you won't be using it?
5 Don't go to work if you won't be feeling well.
6 If I'll get a bonus this year, I'm going to go to Hawaii.
7 I'll have let you know if I think I'm going to be late.
8 If you'll have been there before, you'll know how busy it gets.

➤ Go back to page 75.

Unreal conditionals

A Choose the correct options to complete the conditional sentences.

1 If you found a better job, you ***can*** / ***could*** start saving some money.
2 Ellie would prefer it if she ***didn't have*** / ***hadn't had*** to share a room.
3 ***We'll*** / ***We'd*** have been waiting for hours if you hadn't stopped to give us a ride.
4 If the car had gone over the cliff, we wouldn't ***get*** / ***have gotten*** out alive.
5 I'd join a gym if I ***wasn't*** / ***hadn't been*** so lazy!
6 If she ***saw*** / ***'d seen*** me, she'd have waved.
7 You ***won't*** / ***wouldn't*** be standing here talking to me now if you'd actually won the lottery.
8 If I'd entered the competition, I'm sure ***I'd*** / ***I'll*** have done better than Mo did.

B Complete the profile with the correct form of the verbs in the box. Add modal verbs where appropriate.

attract be can do still have succeed turn out

Business profile: Sean Taylor / the restaurant *Pie*

Sean no longer has *Pie*, the restaurant in Orlando, Florida he opened two years ago, but says that if he [1] ________ things differently in the past, maybe he [2] ________ it today. The first mistake Sean made was to prepare the food himself. If he'd employed a chef, maybe it [3] ________ better for the business. Sean says that if he [4] ________, he would go back in time and spend more time running the restaurant. He strongly believes the business [5] ________ if he'd spent more time with his customers. Second, he didn't promote and market it effectively. If he had done that, he [6] ________ more diners. Third, if he had tried to sell the restaurant rather than just closing it, he [7] ________ in the poor financial situation he's in now.

➤ Go back to page 77.

7.2 *wish* and *if only*

A Complete the sentences with the correct form of the verb in parentheses. Use contractions where possible.

1 I've been dreaming about getting a new car. If only I ________ (*have*) enough money!
2 I sent an email to the wrong person today. I wish I ________ (*not make*) such a silly mistake.
3 You really should ________ (*buy*) that cheap laptop when you had the opportunity.
4 I wish you ________ (*stop*) doing that – it's so annoying!
5 I love my job. If only I ________ (*not have to*) work weekends!
6 I wish I ________ (*can*) go with you tomorrow!
7 If only my grades ________ (*be*) better. Then I would have gone to college, but it's too late now.
8 I wonder where Patrícia is now. I wish I ________ (*ask*) her out all those years ago.

B Correct the mistakes in the sentences.

1 If only I've spent more time studying when I was a student.
2 I wish I didn't miss out on that opportunity to teach at a summer camp last year.
3 I find it hard to meet people. If only I'm not so painfully shy.
4 You're really hard to talk to today. I wish you hadn't been in such a bad mood.
5 I wish I would move back to where I grew up but I can't afford a house there.
6 I wish he had stop thinking about himself.
7 I really wish we had moved here – it was a big mistake.
8 You shouldn't tell Mei Xing that you were leaving. Now she's upset.

➤ Go back to page 79.

Grammar Hub

8.1 Past modals of deduction

- We use *must have* + past participle to say that we are almost sure that something happened or was true.

  She's pale and her hands are shaking – she must have had a substantial shock. (= I'm sure she had a shock.)
  Being alone on a mountain all night must have been terrifying! (= I'm sure it was terrifying.)
- We use *can't have* + past participle to say that we are almost sure something didn't happen or wasn't true.

  It can't have been easy living in such an isolated village. (= I'm sure it wasn't easy.)
- We use *may/might/could have* + past participle to say that we think it's possible that something happened or was true.

  Héctor isn't here yet – he may/might/could have gotten stuck in traffic.
  (= It's possible he got stuck in traffic.)
- We use *may/might* + *not* + *have* + past participle to say that we think it's possible that something hasn't happened but we are not certain.

  I'll call Agnes because she may/might not have heard the news yet.
  (= It's possible she hasn't heard the news yet.)

Be careful!

- *Could have* means that something possibly happened in the past, but *couldn't have* means we are certain that something did not happen.

  You could have left your phone at the office. (= It is possible.)
  You couldn't have left your phone at the office, because you just called me. (= It's impossible.)

8.2 Order of adjectives

- When we use two or more adjectives before a noun, we usually put the adjectives in the following order:

Opinion	Size	Age	Shape	Color	Origin	Material
beautiful	huge	20th century	rectangular	blue	English	leather
great	long	ancient	round	green	Italian	silk
old-fashioned	tiny	up-to-date	square	white	Turkish	wooden

Monika bought a stunning old crystal vase. (= opinion → age → material)
We got some big heart-shaped gold balloons for the party. (= size → shape → color)
Rapini is a delicious green Italian vegetable. (= opinion → color → origin)

- Opinion adjectives (e.g. *unusual*, *disgusting*, etc) are always used before descriptive adjectives (e.g. *enormous*, *circular*, etc).

  He was wearing a disgusting pink silk shirt. NOT ~~He was wearing a pink silk disgusting shirt.~~
  They found a beautiful ancient golden crown. NOT ~~They found an ancient golden beautiful crown.~~
- We usually use *and* between two or more adjectives of the same type, especially with colors.

  He showed me an old black and white photograph of his family.
  I love Portugal's beautiful blue and white tiles.

Be careful!

- Although not grammatically incorrect, it's very unusual for a description to use more than three adjectives, so it's better to avoid this.

  She was sitting at a beautiful, long, modern, square table.

- Compound adjectives (e.g. *long-term*, *state-of-the-art*, etc) should also be used in this order.

  She bought a great state-of-the art computer.

8.1 Past modals of deduction

A Choose the correct options to complete the sentences.

1 They're more than an hour late. They *must have* / *can't have* gotten lost.
2 Patrick *can't have* / *could have* gone to the opera. He hates classical music!
3 You passed! You *might have* / *must have* been so happy when you heard the results!
4 It *must have* / *can't have* been food poisoning. Nobody else who ate the fish got sick.
5 You *can't have* / *might not have* seen Marco in town. He's on vacation in Spain right now.
6 Sasha *couldn't have* / *might not have* heard the news yet, so let's call her just in case.
7 I *must have* / *can't have* left my bank card at the café – I used it just now to pay for the coffee.
8 He hasn't answered his phone for two days. I suppose he *may have* / *can't have* lost it.
9 I *can't have* / *must have* left my hat at the restaurant. That's the last place I had it.
10 It's not very likely because she's 103, but I suppose it *can't have* / *might have* been Grandma you saw at the grocery store.

B Complete the conversations with a modal verb and the correct form of the verbs in the box.

be do finish land make see

1 **A:** Here's that report you asked for.
B: You ________________ already! You only started it yesterday.
2 **A:** $20 for two cups of coffee!
B: That can't be right. The waiter ________________ ________________ a mistake.
3 **A:** Did the children break the baby's toy?
B: They ________________ it. They were at school all day.
4 **A:** Do you think Kobi's still on the plane?
B: Uh, he ________________ by now. It depends if there was a delay or not.
5 **A:** I can't imagine what Julie went through when she lost her father.
B: Yes, it ________________ awful for her.
6 **A:** It's strange that Doug hasn't replied to my email.
B: He ________________ it yet. He doesn't always check his email on the weekend.

➤ Go back to page 87.

8.2 Order of adjectives

A Add the adjectives in bold in the correct place in each sentence.

1 So, apparently, Saga used to have long hair. **blond**
2 What a silver bracelet that is! **beautiful**
3 The rupee is a small Indian coin. **round**
4 We now have four delightful puppies to take care of. **tiny**
5 There are some huge ancient statues in the museum. **bronze**
6 She gently held the strange rectangular box in her hand. **wooden**
7 If it's a stunning pink flower, it's probably a lotus. **bright**
8 'What is this peculiar yellow fruit?' he wondered. **oval**
9 I have no idea what this odd-looking metal instrument was used for. **circular**
10 When I was younger, I had a green and red jacket that I wore almost every day. **ridiculous**
11 My brother got a new job at the hospital. **part-time**
12 They presented a comprehensive plan. **long-term**

B Correct five mistakes with the order of adjectives in the extract.

There was silence, except for the regular ticking of the Victorian tall grandfather clock in the hallway. Noah and Emily stood at the bottom of the wooden steep staircase, looking up into the darkness. Noah turned on his flashlight. Its strong bright beam lit up the wall. Hanging just above their heads was a painting – the medieval priceless portrait of Anne of Avalon which they had been searching for for so long.

As they stared at the picture, Emily felt something brush against her leg. 'What was that?' she said. Noah swung the flashlight around. By the large ancient stone fireplace was an old black and white cat, staring at them. Hanging from the cat's collar was a rusty strange-looking small key. 'I wonder if that key opens the old metal box we found in the kitchen,' said Emily.

'I was just thinking the same thing,' Noah replied.

➤ Go back to page 91.

Grammar Hub

9.1 Adjective clauses

Types of adjective clause

- We use essential adjective clauses to identify exactly which person or thing we are talking about.

  The woman who sits next to me at work is studying for an MA in her free time.
- We use non-essential adjective clauses to give extra, non-essential information about a person or thing. We use commas to separate this clause from the rest of the sentence.

  The band, whose debut album was released in 1991, has sold over 32 million records in the US alone.
  (= We don't need to know when their debut album was released – this is just extra information.)

Relative pronouns

- All adjective clauses begin with a relative pronoun. We use *who* for people, *which* for things, *where* for places, *when* for times and *whose* for possession.

  Apparently, the store where I bought my computer closed down recently.

  Sam, whose mom owns a business, wants to open his own store.

- In essential adjective clauses:

  a we can use *that* instead of *who* or *which*.

  We're really looking for someone who/that has experience teaching children.

  b we can omit *who, that* and *which* when they are the object of the adjective clause.

  The employee (that) we spoke to wasn't very helpful.

  c we can never omit *where* or *whose*.

  My parents have just sold the house where I grew up.
  NOT ~~My parents have just sold the house I grew up.~~
- In non-essential adjective clauses:

  a we cannot use *that* instead of *who* or *which*.

  My sister, who recently graduated from Harvard, just got a new job. NOT ~~My sister, that recently graduated from Harvard, just got a new job.~~

  b we cannot omit the relative pronoun.

  Michael Jackson, who died in 2009, was known as the 'King of Pop'. NOT ~~Michael Jackson, died in 2009, was known as the 'King of Pop'.~~

9.2 Determiners and quantifiers

few, much, many, a little, etc

- We use *(too) many, few, a few, several, a large number of* and *hundreds/thousands of* with countable nouns.

  Not many people can afford to buy designer clothes.
  There are hundreds of bargains to choose from.
- We use *(too) much, a little, little, a great deal of* and *a large amount of* with uncountable nouns.

  We spend a great deal of money on things we don't need!
- We can use *a lot of, lots of, plenty of, enough, some* and *any* with both countable and uncountable nouns.

  Plenty of successful people never went to college.
  Did I put enough milk in your coffee?

all, each, every

- We use *all, all the, all of the* with plural nouns to talk about every person or thing in a group.

  All participants were asked to complete an online survey about their phobias.
- We use *each* and *every* with singular nouns to talk about all of the people or things in a group when considered separately.

  Each competitor was given a medal for taking part.

both, either, neither

- We use *both* with plural nouns to talk about two people or things. *Both* or *both of* can be used before a determiner (e.g. *the, my, those*, etc), but we always use *both of* before pronouns (e.g. *her, their, its*, etc).

  Both restaurants offer a range of vegetarian options.
- We use *either* (… *or*) with singular nouns to talk about one of two people or things when it's not important which, or to mean *both*.

  Which color do you prefer? I'm happy with either.
- We use *neither* (… *nor*) with singular nouns to mean *not either* of two people or things.

  Neither side played very well in the last game.
- We use *either of / neither of* with plural pronouns or plural nouns with determiners.

  Neither of them could decide which car to buy.

no, none, any

- We use *no* or *none* in positive sentences and *any* in negative sentences to refer to zero quantity.

  It seems there are no tickets left for tonight's show.

Be careful!

- *Few* is negative, and means *not many. A few* is positive and means *some, but not many*.
- Similarly, *little* is negative, and means *not much. A little* is positive and means *some, but not much*.

9.1 Adjective clauses

A Choose the correct options to complete the sentences.

1 Last summer, I visited my cousin, ***who / whose*** lives in a nice apartment in New York.
2 There's the new store ***– / where*** I was telling you about.
3 The recruiter ***who / which*** helped is my cousin, Léo.
4 The woman ***whose / who*** house we stayed in had listed it on Airbnb.
5 It's usually late at night ***where / when*** I feel hungriest.
6 My car, ***that / which*** I've had since May, uses a lot of gas.
7 Thanks, Fiona. The recommendation ***– / who*** you gave me was a great idea.
8 The house ***which / in which*** I grew up is now a hotel.

B Combine the sentences using an adjective clause. Omit the relative pronoun where possible.

1 San Francisco is where the company was founded. It is also home to TechCorp.
San Francisco ______________________________.
2 I used to work in a call center. It's just gone out of business.
The call center ______________________________.
3 Mark Allen created the app in his bedroom. He is now worth $20 billion.
Mark Allen ______________________________.
4 Sadly it was no longer under warranty. This means I can't get my money back.
Sadly ______________________________.
5 The app allows users to order food 24 hours a day. It has received mixed reviews.
The app ______________________________.
6 I sit next to a woman at work who has a degree in customer service management.
The woman ______________________________.

C Are these sentences correct or incorrect? Rewrite the incorrect sentences.

1 My company that is based in New York has offices all over the world.
2 The slight problem, that you told me about, can't easily be fixed.
3 The movies that are playing at that movie theater are never very good.
4 My coffee maker, I paid a lot for, makes terrible coffee!
5 Where's the complaint form the customer filled out?
6 The customer called about the problem is still on the phone.
7 The woman, whose tablet I was borrowing, just told me to keep it!
8 The store I got bad service from which isn't getting my business anymore!

➤ Go back to page 99.

9.2 Determiners and quantifiers

A Choose the correct options to complete the sentences.

1 I know ***a little / a few*** brands in this store.
2 There isn't ***much / many*** information on this label.
3 ***A large amount / A large number*** of products were recalled.
4 ***Neither / Both*** the seller and the buyer are concerned about prices.
5 ***Either / Neither*** you exchange it or issue a refund!
6 ***A few / A little*** of the customers complained.
7 Sadly, there are ***none / no*** left.
8 ***All / Each*** products must be returned with a receipt.

B Choose the correct option (a, b or c) to complete the sentences.

1 Contrary to popular belief, ___ people make purchases based on online reviews.
a much b neither c few
2 It's important that you include at least ___ vegetables in your diet if you want to stay healthy.
a few b both c a few
3 ___ food bloggers have become very important because they can influence food trends.
a Plenty of b Much c Every
4 ___ food companies make health claims about their products to encourage consumers to buy them.
a Both b Neither c Either
5 Drinking a large ___ of coffee does not actually dehydrate you.
a amount b plenty c number
6 Drinking ___ coffee may help to improve your concentration, but don't drink too much.
a a little b little c plenty
7 ___ product was successful because they were considered to be too unhealthy.
a Both b Neither c Either
8 ___ of the products turned out to be healthy as they claimed to be.
a No b None c Any

➤ Go back to page 103.

Grammar Hub

10.1 Reported speech

- When we report what someone said, we usually change the main verb by moving it back one tense into the past.

Direct speech	Reported speech
simple present '**I'm** completely exhausted.'	simple past She said (that) **she was** completely exhausted.
present progressive '**We're trying** to find a solution.'	past progressive They said (that) **they were trying** to find a solution.
simple past '**Online hits went** up.'	past perfect He said (that) **online hits had gone** up.
past progressive '**We were finding** it hard.'	past perfect progressive She said (that) **they had been finding** it hard.
present perfect '**I've made** a decision.'	past perfect He said **he'd made** a decision.
present perfect progressive '**I've been working**.'	past perfect progressive She said (that) **she had been working**.
will/can/may '**I'll let** you know tomorrow.' '**I can double-check** for you.' '**You may need** to book early.'	*would/could/might* He said (that) **he'd let** me know the next day. She said (that) **she could double-check** for me. She said (that) **we might need** to book early.

- We don't need to change the tense in reported speech:
  - **a** when the direct speech is in the past perfect (simple or progressive).
    'We had wanted to move for some time.' → He said they had wanted to move for some time.
  - **b** with the modal verbs *could, should, would, might* and *need*.
    'You might be able to get some money back.' → He said that we might be able to get some money back.
    'You don't need to worry.' → She said that I don't need to worry.
  - **c** when the information is still true or relevant, or the reporting verb is in the present tense.
    'My sister lives in Japan.' → She told me that her sister lives in Japan. (= It's still true that her sister lives there.)
- We usually do need to change time references, pronouns, etc.
  'See you tomorrow.' → She told me that she would see me the next day.

Reported questions

- When we report questions, the tense of the main verb changes but we don't use the auxiliary verb *do*. We also use the same word order as a positive sentence.
  'Where did you grow up?' → She asked me where I had grown up.
  NOT ~~She asked me where did I grow up.~~
- When we report yes/no questions we use *if* or *whether*.
  'Did you enjoy it?' → She asked me if I had enjoyed it.
  'Does she usually finish at 4 pm?' → He asked me whether she usually finishes at 4 pm.

10.2 Reporting verbs

- As well as *say* or *tell*, we can also use other reporting verbs (e.g. *threaten, promise, warn*, etc) to help summarize the meaning of what was said, to describe the speaker's attitude, or to indicate our stance.
  'I'm sorry I'm late.' → She apologized for being late.
- Reporting verbs are followed by a range of different structures:
  - **a** *argue, claim, confirm, decide, recommend, state, suggest*, etc + (*that*) + clause.
    He claimed that he was innocent.
    The police stated that they have made an arrest.
  - **b** *assure, inform, promise, remind*, etc + object + (*that*) + clause.
    Sarah assured me that she would pay me back.
    She promised him that it would never happen again.
  - **c** *decide, promise, refuse, threaten*, etc + the infinitive.
    She refused to tell me why I had been unsuccessful.
    Neighbors threated to call the police.
  - **d** *advise, ask, convince, encourage, persuade, remind, warn*, etc + object + the infinitive.
    My wife encouraged me to apply for the position.
  - **e** *accuse (sb) of, admit, apologize (to sb) for, blame (sb) for, confess to, insist on, recommend, regret, report, suggest*, etc + verb + *-ing*.
    She insisted on paying for the meal.
- Some reporting verbs, such as *persuade, warn, tell* and *ask*, can be followed by a negative infinitive.
  They persuaded her not to say anything at the press conference.

10.1 Reported speech

A Complete the second sentence so it has a similar meaning to the first.

1 'I've been working here for almost six months.'
Francis said that she ______________________ at the company for almost six months.

2 'I'm going to be a little late for the meeting.'
Andy says he ______________________ a little late for the meeting.

3 'Can I have a quick word with you, please, Mr. Jenkins?'
Susie asked me if she ______________________ ______________________ a quick word with me.

4 'I'd been hoping you'd have found a solution by now.'
Their boss said he ______________________ we would have found a solution by then.

5 'What time did you get home from work yesterday, Sofia?'
He asked me what time I ______________________ ______________________ home from work the day before.

6 'I think I know someone who might be able to fix this.'
Thais said she ______________________ someone who might be able to fix the problem.

7 'I'll call you around seven o'clock.'
Lars told me that he ______________________ me around seven o'clock.

8 'We were driving around for a long time before we found a place to park.'
Mom said they ______________________ around for a long time before they found a place to park.

B Rewrite the sentences and questions in reported speech. Add any information necessary.

1 'I'm not interested in hearing your excuses.'
Olga told me ______________________.

2 'In the end, the event was a big success.'
Juan said that, in the end, ______________________.

3 'Do you want to meet for coffee after work?'
She asked me ______________________.

4 'I've decided I am going to move to a new house soon.'
Jonas said ______________________.

5 'What are you planning to do about your noisy neighbors?'
Daryl asked me ______________________.

6 'Can you play somewhere else? I'm trying to work!'
Mom asked the kids ______________________.

7 'Hi Mateo! I was looking for you yesterday.'
Renata told me that ______________________.

8 'I've been working on a secret project.'
He said ______________________.

➤ Go back to page 111.

10.2 Reporting verbs

A Complete the news story with the reporting verbs in the box.

apologized assured blamed confirmed decided insisted refused stated

XPS TO CLOSE ITS LONDON OFFICE AFTER 50 YEARS

In an announcement yesterday afternoon, Michael Winters, CEO of XPS, [1] ______________ rumors that the company would be closing its London offices after almost half a century in the capital. After talking about how important the site had been to the company, Winters [2] ______________ on reminding reporters that XPS was still one of the most profitable businesses in its sector. He said that the board had only [3] ______________ to do it because there was no alternative, and [4] ______________ the economy for falling sales. Winters [5] ______________ to the staff for causing them anxiety about the future but he [6] ______________ them that they would be offered jobs in different locations. He [7] ______________ to comment on whether more offices were going to be closed and [8] ______________ that he would give further information when it was available.

B Are these sentences correct or incorrect? Rewrite the incorrect sentences.

1 A confidential source revealed that the company had lost $10 billion.

2 The police refused comment on an open investigation.

3 She threatened calling the police if they didn't leave immediately.

4 His lawyers advised him not to publish the story until after the hearing.

5 They assured that his name wouldn't be mentioned in the article.

6 Under pressure, she admitted fabricating the entire story.

7 The company accused Ms. Hartmann with leaking information to the press.

8 In court, Mr. Petrov confessed to willingly mislead the public.

➤ Go back to page 115.

Vocabulary Hub

1.1 Feelings

A Label the pictures (1–8) with the adjectives in the box.

awkward devastated disgusted frustrated furious overwhelmed relieved stunned

1 ______

2 ______

3 ______

4 ______

5 ______

6 ______

7 ______

8 ______

B Choose the correct options (a, b or c) to complete the sentences.

1 I was so ___ I had to leave the room. I didn't want a serious argument.
  a furious b stunned c relieved

2 I was ___ when I lost my ring. My grandma had given it to me when I was little.
  a disgusted b relieved c devastated

3 I was ___ by the lack of help. How could people just watch and do nothing?
  a furious b overwhelmed c disgusted

4 To be honest I felt a little ___. We hadn't parted on good terms.
  a awkward b relieved c frustrated

5 I'm so ___ we didn't miss our flight! I don't know what we would have done if we had.
  a furious b stunned c relieved

6 I think my grandpa gets pretty ___ that he can't do everything for himself anymore.
  a furious b overwhelmed c frustrated

➤ Go back to page 3.

1.2 Personality adjectives

A **Match the personality adjectives (1–8) with the definitions (a–h).**

1 I loved his talk. He was so **passionate** about what he was saying. ___
2 You're always so **optimistic**. I wish I could be more positive like you. ___
3 Don't be so **pessimistic**. It might not be so bad. ___
4 She's really **ambitious**. She wants to own her own company in two years. ___
5 Try not to be so **sensitive**. I'm sure he didn't mean to upset you. ___
6 He's really **naïve**. He'll believe anything you tell him. ___
7 She was **determined** to finish the race, even though she was injured. ___
8 You need to be really **flexible** to work here. They are always changing our jobs. ___

a thinking that the worst thing will happen in every situation
b likely to become upset quickly
c lacking experience in life and too ready to trust or believe in others
d showing or expressing strong beliefs, interest or enthusiasm
e able to make changes or deal with a situation that is changing
f being hopeful about the future and expecting that good things will happen
g not willing to let anything prevent you from doing what you have decided to do
h wanting to be successful, rich, famous, etc

B **Complete the job ads with adjectives from Exercise A. Use each adjective only once.**

Salesperson

We are looking for a new salesperson to join our team. We need hard-working people who can reach our high targets. You should be 1 ________________, with big plans for your career. We work long hours, including weekends, so you will need to be 2 ________________ about when you work. Some of our products are challenging to sell so you will need to remain positive and not develop a 3 ________________ attitude.

CHARITY WORKER

Is someone being 4 ________________ and unrealistic when they think they can change the world? We don't think so! We welcome 5 ________________ people who believe that we really can make a difference and that even small things can have a huge impact. We are looking to hire someone who can be 6 ________________ toward people's needs and who is 7 ________________ to help make other people's lives better. If you are 8 ________________ about making the world a better place, then this could be the job for you!

➤ Go back to page 9.

2.1 Health and fitness

Complete the sentences with the words and phrases in the box.

level of fitness	life expectancy	mental health	physical	processed foods	reduce the risk	slow the aging process

1 To remain healthy, adults should do at least 150 minutes of moderate ________________ activity, like bike riding, every week.
2 The average ________________ for women is typically two or three years longer than for men.
3 Some ________________ contain high levels of salt, fat and sugar.
4 Eating a balanced diet and exercising regularly may help ________________.
5 A healthy diet and regular exercise can both significantly ________________ of high blood pressure.
6 Improving your ________________ can help to fight various heart-related diseases.
7 Surprisingly, exercise can also be good for your ________________ because it reduces levels of stress and anxiety.

➤ Go back to page 14.

3.1 Descriptive verbs

Complete the sentences (1–8) with the verbs in the box.

crackling creaked growling rumbled screeched slamming smashed whirring

1 It was pouring rain and thunder ________________ in the distance.

2 The tires ________________ as she tried to stop the car in time.

3 The floorboards ________________ under his weight as he tried to tiptoe down the stairs.

4 They sat around the ________________ fire, wondering what to do next.

5 He stormed out of the room, ________________ the door behind him.

6 Shining his flashlight through the chain link fence, Todd was greeted by an angry ________________ dog.

7 The figure ________________ the window and reached inside.

8 The fan was ________________ in the corner of the room.

➤ Go back to page 29.

4.2 Intensifiers

Choose the correct options (a, b or c) to complete the sentences.

1 The risks of this kind of technology are ___ greater than any potential benefit.
  a intensely b utterly c considerably
2 All of the medical professionals that we spoke to said that the idea robots could perform complex surgery was ___ ridiculous.
  a disastrously b extremely c utterly
3 To be honest, the results were ___ unexpected. I thought we'd need to run several more tests.
  a considerably b totally c painfully
4 Seeing a computer program that I designed beat a human competitor is ___ satisfying.
  a intensely b totally c disastrously
5 If we don't put the proper safety measures in place, the results could be ___ bad.
  a disastrously b utterly c intensely
6 I am ___ sorry to announce that Maria Sanchez will be retiring from the field of robotics.
  a utterly b totally c extremely

➤ Go back to page 45.

5.2 Prefixes

Choose the correct prefix to complete the sentences.

1 Levels of pollution were so high they needed to ***decontaminate*** / ***uncontaminate*** the river.
2 They were ***disqualified*** / ***unqualified*** from the race for cheating.
3 In order to improve travel times, they decided to ***upgrade*** / ***downgrade*** the subway system.
4 The solution was ***unpossible*** / ***impossible*** to put into place.
5 The company ***misled*** / ***disled*** the community about the development.
6 People don't use the train because they feel it is ***overpriced*** / ***underpriced***.
7 The cost of building new road networks was significantly ***underestimated*** / ***overestimated***.
8 The excellent infrastructure has allowed the city to ***overperform*** / ***outperform*** many similarly sized cities.

➤ Go back to page 55.

6.1 Education

Complete the sentences with words from the box.

campus	elementary schools	entrance exam	graduate	high schools	lectures	scholarship	seminar	vocational

1 The ________________ for All Souls College at Oxford University has been called the world's hardest test. It is impossible to study for because there are no right or wrong answers and the questions are very abstract. The prize is a seven-year ________________!
2 The Open University is designed for distance-learning students. Those who attend can watch ________________ online and write notes. They can also join in smaller online ________________ groups, where they can discuss ideas.
3 In American ________________, students take a traditional academic path. However, in college they can choose a ________________ path that leads to professions such as an electrician or beautician.
4 In China, there is a ________________ of the University of Nottingham. Some of the buildings are identical to the ones on the UK site. Students here ________________ with a University of Nottingham degree.
5 Some five to eleven-year-olds in Bangladesh study in ________________ on boats due to frequent flooding in the country.

➤ Go back to page 64.

Vocabulary Hub

7.2 Three-part phrasal verbs

A Match the words in bold to the definitions.

1 I can't **keep up with** all of the technological changes.
2 I think people need to **stand up for** the things they believe in.
3 We seem to **run out of** money every month. We can only just afford our rent!
4 We **teamed up with** a local company to design the gallery.
5 The event lets me **catch up with** old friends.
6 The shelter **takes care of** homeless people in the city.

a to not have any more of something
b to work together
c to continue to learn about something or find out about something
d to find out someone's news
e to look after someone or something
f to defend someone or something that is being criticized or attacked

B Complete the sentences with the correct form of the phrasal verbs in Exercise A.

1 We wanted to ________________ the rights of young people in the community.
2 The plans keep changing so frequently that it's hard to ________________ what is happening.
3 We have ________________ local cafés to provide free food for the homeless.
4 Giving people a more beautiful environment encourages them to ________________ it.
5 A street party is a great way to ________________ neighbors you haven't seen in a while.
6 Our project ________________ government funding, so we crowdsourced the rest of the money needed.

➤ Go back to page 80.

8.2 Crime

Complete the sentences with the correct form of the words in the box.

arrest catch charge commit innocent investigate punishment question sentence witness

1 The police ________________ him for two hours and then ________________ him with identity theft.
2 She claimed to be ________________ but three separate ________________ identified her as being responsible for the crime.
3 He was ________________ with people's credit card details on his computer and was ________________ for credit card fraud. After they ________________ further, he was taken to court, where the judge ________________ him to six years in prison.
4 Some people argue that imprisonment isn't the best ________________ for someone who ________________ a crime, because many go on to reoffend when released.

➤ Go back to page 92.

10.2 Social media

Match the words in bold (1–5) to the definitions (a–f).

1 I was trying to do some online research, but I kept on getting distracted by all the **clickbait** stories.
2 You will need to go further back in that **thread** to find the message about the changes to the schedule.
3 I used to enjoy social media until a **troll** started writing horrible comments on my posts.
4 I think everyone has seen that **meme** of the president dancing – it's hilarious.
5 Why don't you **DM** me so we can discuss this some more?
6 I think that message goes against **netiquette** – it's really aggressive.

a the polite way of expressing yourself or communicating with other people when you are using the internet
b to send a direct message to someone on the microblogging service Twitter
c a link on a website that is designed to catch people's attention and encourage them to read on
d a series of email messages or messages on a forum about a particular subject
e someone who writes negative and hostile comments on a website in order to provoke people
f an image, video or piece of text that spreads very quickly on the internet, typically one which people create different funny versions of

➤ Go back to page 116.

8.1 Student A

Read the story and write notes to help you summarize it for your group.

Trojan Horse

The Trojan horse was a huge hollow wooden horse made by the Greeks during the Trojan War. The Greeks had pretended to give up in the war but had secretly sailed to the island of Tenedos. They had left one soldier, Sinon, to persuade the Trojans that the horse was an offering from the Greek gods. Laocoön and Cassandra, who were both important people in the city of Troy, warned against taking the horse into the city, but the Trojans accepted it anyway. In the middle of the night, Greek soldiers, who were hidden inside, emerged from the horse and let the rest of the Greek army into the city. The Greeks then captured and destroyed the city of Troy.

➤ Go back to page 89.

5.2

A PLAN You're going to select three candidates to join the Mars One mission. Read the profiles and write notes on who you would like to select and why.

ADRIAN JENKINS

Leadership Has led teams of dozens of men in dangerous situations.
Personality traits Very determined and strong-minded. Always believes he is right. Not willing to listen to others.
Certifications An MBA.
Unique skills Worked as paramedic. Is an expert in emergency situations.

LINA WANG

Leadership No leadership experience.
Personality traits Quickly forms strong relationships with others. A very creative problem-solver.
Certifications Currently completing a PhD in Physics.
Unique Skills Is recognized as one of the most talented scientists in the world for her age. Three products she has designed have won international awards.

ANA RAMOS

Leadership Has led small teams of marine biologists.
Personality traits Excellent attention to detail. Very organized and well prepared.
Certifications A PhD in Marine Biology.
Unique Skills Experience at spending time in small spaces. Has been on many long research trips to isolated places.

NICOS ALEXOPOULOS

Leadership Has led teams of surgeons for over ten years.
Personality traits Hard-working, with a never-give-up attitude. A perfectionist.
Certifications Certified doctor.
Unique Skills Has worked in many hospitals including many years with Doctors Without Borders in very difficult environments.

VIKTOR POPOV

Leadership No leadership experience.
Personality traits Prefers to spend time on his own. Finds relationships with others difficult.
Certifications Engineering degree.
Unique Skills An experienced explorer. Has done survival training in the jungle and the desert.

GRACE ADEBAYO

Leadership Leads team of volunteers to help build schools and medical facilities in rural areas.
Personality traits Kind, caring and open-minded.
Certifications A degree in Agriculture.
Unique Skills Experienced at growing food in difficult climates.

B DISCUSS Work in groups. Compare your choices in Exercise A. Agree on two candidates to join the Mars One mission.

➤ Go back to page 57.

Communication Hub

8.2 Speaking Hub, Exercise B

Read the profiles and answer the questions for each suspect. Underline the part of the text that gives you the answers.

1 Where were they at the time of the murder?
2 Why might they have committed the murder?
3 What is their alibi and does anyone else confirm it?

MAGNUS BALDURSSON

- Swedish billionaire oil tycoon
- Mild-mannered, yet a ruthless businessman
- Hates family secrets getting out and works hard to ensure nothing is made public

ALIBI

'What an awful night! I told Sofia that she would be taking over the business when I retire and my son, Linus, was furious. He started shouting about how much debt Sofia was in – apparently she owed over a million dollars to some pretty bad people. Anyway, that's when Sofia ran out in tears. Linus said he was going to his room, but when I went to speak to him at about 9:50 pm, he wasn't there. I went downstairs to the study and found my son-in-law in there. He was furious about something. I was just about to sit down when we heard Sofia's scream.'

LINUS BALDURSSON

- Magnus Baldursson's eldest child
- Quick-tempered and loud, but generally fun to be around
- Bankrupt after several bad business deals

ALIBI

'Yeah, I told my father about Sofia's debts – he deserved to know. Anyway, after the three of us argued, I went up to my room to think. I came down as soon as I heard the scream. That's when I found my sister's body.'

JAMES RUTHERFORD

- Has been married to Sofia for nine years
- Caring and dependable, but prone to fits of jealousy
- Frequently argues with his wife, but has never been violent

ALIBI

'I went to find my wife and saw her talking to Max on the stairs. It must have been just before 10:00 pm. He had his arm around her! I was so angry that I had to get away, so I went straight to the study to calm down! Magnus had just come in when we heard the scream.'

MAX FISHER

- Internationally recognized movie star who went to school with Sofia and Linus
- Sociable, always fun at a party
- Has loved Sofia his entire life and has always been jealous of her husband

ALIBI

'I found Sofia crying on the stairs at around 9:45 pm. I gave her my jacket and we talked for about ten minutes. Then she went upstairs to redo her make-up and said she'd be back down in a minute. I was feeling hungry, so I went to the kitchen to get a snack and found Bletchley eating his dinner. That's when I heard that awful scream.'

ALBERT BLETCHLEY

- Has served as the family butler for 36 years
- Hard-working, loyal and well-dressed
- Would do anything to protect the family

ALIBI

'Frankly, I'm glad Sofia's dead. She was always horrible to me and I never liked her. But it wasn't me who killed her. Ask Mr. Fisher. He was with me in the kitchen when it happened.'

➤ Go back to page 93.

1.2 Student A

Read the text and write notes about:

- who the person is and why they're famous
- any challenges they faced and how they overcame them
- any other interesting/relevant information

Emily Blunt

Emily Blunt was born in London in 1983. As a young girl, she felt confident and had a lot to say but unfortunately, she struggled because of a stutter. The stutter made it very difficult for Emily to say anything and between the ages of 12 and 13, she was badly bullied by other children. Strangely, whenever she spoke in a different accent or a funny voice, she lost the stutter and was able to communicate. Spotting her talent for different voices and for making people laugh, one of her teachers encouraged her to take part in the school play. But how could someone who struggled to speak stand up in front of the whole school and perform? Emily did the play in one of her funny voices and caught the acting bug. She has since gone on to win a BAFTA and a Golden Globe for her acting and has starred in many successful movies such as *Sicario*, *The Girl on the Train* and *A Quiet Place*.

Glossary

stutter (n) to have difficulty saying something because you can't stop yourself from repeating the first sound of some words several times

➤ Go back to page 7.

8.1 Student B

Read the story and write notes to help you summarize it for your group.

The Loch Ness Monster

There are carvings from almost 1,500 years ago showing a huge monster in a Scottish lake and written reports from the 7th century describing the same creature. However, there were very few other reported sightings until 1933, when a doctor, Colonel Robert Wilson, took the famous photo of the supposed Loch Ness monster and sent it to a local newspaper in Inverness. They in turn then reported a sighting of an enormous creature in one of Scotland's largest lakes. However, in 1994, a man named Ian Wetherell confessed he had helped his father create the 'monster' using plastic and a toy submarine. His father had then given the photo to Wilson to submit to the papers because he thought people were more likely to believe a doctor. Despite the fact that people now know that the photo was a fake, there are still regular reports of sightings of the Loch Ness monster every year.

➤ Go back to page 89.

9.1 Student B

Read the situation below and role-play a conversation with your partner.

You have bought a new cell phone. It keeps turning off whenever you try to connect to wi-fi. The phone also crashes whenever you try to install a new operating system. The product is still under warranty. You don't want it repaired because you have read online that these faults are common. You would like it replaced with a different type of phone.

➤ Go back to page 101.

Communication Hub

3.1

A PREPARE Work in pairs. Use the pictures (a–g) to tell a story.

B PLAN Join another pair. Together work out the details of your story. Use narrative tenses to help describe the sequence of events.

➤ Go back to page 27.

8.2 Student A

Use adjectives to describe the objects in the picture to your partner. Are there any similarities between your pictures?

There's a large old-fashioned camera in the top left-hand corner.

➤ Go back to page 91.

9.1 Student A

Read the situation below and role-play a conversation with your partner.

You have bought a new TV and it hasn't been working properly. Many of the functions don't work and other functions work really slowly. It's not the internet provider because your laptop and phone work fine. The product is still under warranty. You don't want it repaired because you have read online that these faults are common. You would like it replaced with a different model TV.

➤ Go back to page 101.

6.2 Student A

A Complete the text with *a, an, the* or – (no article).

1___ Maasai of Kenya and Tanzania have several age traditions that lead into 2___ manhood. Boys between 3___ ages of 12 and 25 are taught to become 4___ new warriors of 5___ tribe. 6___ night before 7___ ceremony, they sleep outside in 8___ forest, and at 9___ sunrise they come back for singing and dancing. They drink 10___ special drink, while also eating large amounts of 11___ meat. For 12___ next ten years they stay at 13___ camp to learn to be warriors. After 14___ final ceremony takes place, they become 15___ senior warriors and can get married.

B You are going to explain the ceremony in Exercise A to your partner. Write notes to help you.

➤ Go back to page 67.

8.1

Answer
It can't have been aliens since there were no signs of anything landing nearby. The family provided a sketch of one of the aliens which showed it must have been a large bird, probably a great horned owl. The sounds of bullets hitting metal must have been the surrounding farm buildings being hit.

➤ Go back to page 87.

5.1

A Work in pairs. Read the scenario and predict the cause and effect relationships between the pictures (1–10).

A chemical was sprayed to kill the mosquitoes.

In the early 1950s, an outbreak of malaria threatened the survival of the Dayak people of Borneo. Not knowing how to control the spread of the disease, the islanders turned to the outside world for help.

B Work with another pair. Compare you ideas from Exercise A.

➤ Go back to page 51.

6.2 Student B

A Complete the text with *a, an, the* or – (no article).

The *fiesta de quince años* celebrates [1]___ girl's 15th birthday and is popular throughout [2]___ Latin America. In Argentina, Peru and some other countries, the girl traditionally arrives at the party with her father, wearing [3]___ elaborate dress. [4]___ pair then dance alone, before inviting [5]___ friends and family to join them. After this, the evening typically alternates between [6]___ three-course meal and more formal dances, before the father gives a speech and presents his daughter with [7]___ large cake. This stage of the evening usually involves [8]___ ritual in which female friends and family pull [9]___ ribbons from a bunch. Each of [10]___ ribbons has a lucky object attached to it, except for one which is attached to a ring. Whoever gets [11]___ ring is said to be the next person to get married.
In Cuba, the final dance involves dancing with 14 different people and blowing out [12]___ candle and collecting a rose after each dance. With each candle the girl gets [13]___ wish and then [14]___ flowers are given as [15]___ gift to her mother.

B You are going to explain the ceremony in Exercise A to your partner. Write notes to help you.

➤ Go back to page 67.

8.1 Student C

Read the story and write notes to help you summarize it for your group.

The Vanishing Hitchhiker

One night, a group of friends were driving to a dance when they spotted a young woman hitchhiking. The group decided to give the woman a ride and asked her to come to the party with them. She was obviously cold, so one of the group gave her a coat. They eventually got to the party and after a night of dancing, they drove the woman home. The next day, one of the friends remembered they had forgotten to ask for his coat back, so he drove to the woman's house. However, when he knocked on the door he was told by the couple that lived there that the woman had been killed in a car accident years before. Scared, the man drove back to the corner where he and his friends had met the woman the night before. There, hanging on a road sign, was his coat.

➤ Go back to page 89.

1.2 Student B

Read the text and write notes about:

- who the person is and why they're famous
- any challenges they faced and how they overcame them
- any other interesting/relevant information

Jean-Dominique Bauby

Jean-Dominique Bauby was born in France in 1952. He was an actor and author. He also edited the famous fashion magazine *Elle*. In December 1995, at the age of just 43, he suffered a massive stroke. When he finally woke up, he discovered he had been asleep for 20 days. Most of his body had been paralyzed by the stroke and he had lost his speech. Despite his physical problems, he started writing the book *The Diving Bell and the Butterfly*. He did this by blinking his left eye while someone was reading the alphabet very slowly. He wrote and edited the book completely in his head while dictating one letter at a time. Unfortunately, two days after the book was published, he died. The book went on to be made into a movie, which was nominated for four Oscars and won two Golden Globe Awards.

Glossary

stroke (n) a sudden change in the blood supply to the brain

➤ Go back to page 7.

9.1

Are you a good complainer? *quiz results*

Mostly A's You don't like making a fuss, especially over things that just aren't very important. You'd rather put up with the mistake and get on with your day than get into an argument. You're also more than happy to face the consequences of your mistakes and wouldn't dream of blaming anyone else.

Mostly B's You're tired of big companies getting away with terrible customer service and see social media as the perfect place to fight for your rights. It's important to you that you get what you paid for and you're more than happy to publicly complain if you don't. After all, if you don't stand up to these companies, who will?

Mostly C's You don't see complaining as a way to get revenge. You understand that everyone makes mistakes, but expect a quick resolution when they affect you. You're more than willing to face the consequences of your own mistakes, but want to make sure steps are taken to help others avoid making the same mistakes in the future.

➤ Go back to page 100.

8.2 Student B

Use adjectives to describe the objects in the picture to your partner. Are there any similarities between your pictures?

There's a modern black camera in the bottom left-hand corner.

➤ Go back to page 91.

9.2

A Choose one of the products below to design an ad campaign around.

1. an electric sports car that is one of the most eco-friendly on the market
2. a sports brand directed toward wealthy young and successful people
3. a range of health-food products that are low in calories but nutritionally balanced
4. a fitness app that tracks all your activities and sets you new physical challenges

B Design an ad campaign around the product you chose in Exercise A. Use the following questions to help you:

1. How are you going to raise awareness of your product?
2. What high-profile celebrities would you get to endorse your product?
3. What trends are you going to link your product to?
4. What features will make customers fall in love with your product brand?
5. What is unique about your product compared to other products on the market?

➤ Go back to page 105.

1 Writing — Write a formal letter asking for information

W — structuring formal letters

A Read the letter and answer the questions.

1. What is the purpose of the letter?
2. Who will read it?
3. Why does the writer use a formal register?

B Match the parts of the letter (1–5) with their function (a–e).

- **a** expected response
- **b** reason for writing
- **c** sign-off
- **d** salutation or greeting
- **e** information required

To: French language club
From: John

[1]Dear Sir / Madam,

[2]I am writing to inquire about the French language club you organize to find out whether the club is suitable for me or not.

[3]First, I was wondering if you could tell me how many members there are. Also, could you tell me when you meet and how often? I want to make sure it's possible for me to attend regularly. Could you also tell me how much it costs? Is there a fee to join and then a weekly fee to pay? Lastly, would it be possible to tell me the approximate level of the group members and whether we have any formal lessons as well?

[4]I would be grateful if you could let me know by email before the next meeting. Hopefully, I will be able to join before then. Thanks in advance for your help.

[5]Kind regards,
John

C Complete the box with sentences from the letter.

Structuring formal letters

Saying why you're writing
I am writing to apply for …
1 ______

Organizing information
Could you let me know …?
2 ______

Asking for a response
If you could …
3 ______

Sign-off
Yours truly …
4 ______

WRITING

A PREPARE Read the task below and write notes about who you are writing to, what you need to know and what action you expect them to take.

> You are interested in joining the hiking club in your area. Write a letter of inquiry and find out:
> - how many members there are in the club
> - how often they organize walks and where they go
> - ask whether there are any fees involved in joining
> - what specialist equipment you need.

B PLAN Organize your notes into an appropriate structure for a letter of inquiry.

C WRITE Write your letter of inquiry. Use your plan to help you.

D EDIT Work in pairs. Edit your partner's essay. Check:

- spelling and punctuation
- all information in the task has been covered
- an appropriate structure/tone has been used

 Write an article giving advice

Ⓦ Using different structures to give advice

A Work in pairs. You are going to read an article titled *Clear the mess and clear your mind*. What advice do you think the author might give?

B Read the article quickly. Which of your ideas from Exercise A does the author mention?

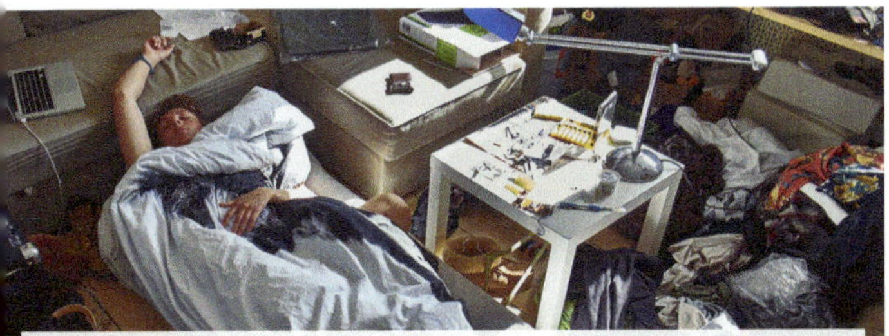

Clear the mess and clear your mind

What better way to start the new year than getting rid of some clutter? Doing so will not only make your house feel more organized, but could also lower your stress levels. Hopefully, the following tips should help you get started!

Throw things away

We keep far more things than we really need to and many of these can be thrown away or given to someone else to use.

- Do you really need or like all of your clothes? Why not go through your closet and see if there's anything you can donate to charity?
- If you don't watch it, listen to it or read it, sell it on eBay. You'll make a little bit of money and have more space!
- Don't forget to look in the garage. Most people use these areas to store things they just don't need or want.
- Don't keep broken things that you know you'll never fix.

Stay motivated

Decluttering can be hugely satisfying, but only if you can stay motivated. Use these basic rules to help you:

- Make sure you don't spend too long decluttering. If you are tired, take a break. It's much harder to make good decisions when you can't think properly!
- Don't leave a task incomplete. If you don't finish what you started, you're likely to become demotivated.

Good habits

Clutter can quickly build up again, so it's important to develop good habits for the future. Use these basic rules to help you:

- Avoid putting things into a pile. Putting them back where they belong will help keep things neat.
- Remember to never buy something on impulse. You can always buy it later if you really want it.

C Read the article again. Complete the table with examples from the text.

Using different structures to give advice
if + simple present + imperative
1 ______
2 ______
negative imperative
3 ______
4 ______
5 ______
positive imperative
6 ______
7 ______

D Rewrite the sentences using the words in bold.

1. Drinking coffee after 9 pm is not a good idea.
   Avoid ______.
2. Why not try putting $20 into a savings account every week?
   Try to ______.
3. If you don't use your gym membership, cancel it.
   It's a good idea to ______.
4. Maybe you could turn your phone off in the evenings.
   Try ______.
5. Try to exercise at least three times a week.
   Don't forget to ______.
6. Recording the food you eat every day is a good idea.
   Remember to ______.

WRITING

A PREPARE Work in pairs. Brainstorm advice you could give about one of these topics:

- reducing stress
- improving your diet
- getting in shape

B PLAN Organize your notes from Exercise A into a plan for an article. Think about the clearest way to present your ideas, using headings where appropriate.

C WRITE Write your advice article. Use your plan to help you.

D EDIT Work in pairs. Edit your partner's essay. Check:

- spelling and punctuation
- use of expressions to give advice
- appropriacy of the ideas (e.g. Is the advice clear? Is it good advice?)

W — using adverbs to add detail to a story

A Work in pairs. What is the worst vacation experience you have ever had?

B Read the story and answer the questions. Underline the parts of the text that gives you the answers.

1 What did they regret?

2 Did anyone fall into the sea?

3 Where did they have to sleep?

Vacation from HELL

Two years ago, my wife and I took a summer vacation in Sicily, Italy. The town we were staying in was beautiful, but there wasn't a lot to do. So, a few days into our stay, we decided to book a boat trip to the volcanic Aeolian islands. I'd just bought a new camera, so I was really looking forward to trying it out in such an amazing place. However, the night before we were due to leave, a terrible storm hit the south coast of Italy, so we assumed our trip would be canceled. The next morning, as we were strolling down to the harbor, the sea looked **incredibly** rough as the waves smashed against the rocks. **Surprisingly**, the trip went ahead anyway. We boarded the boat and waited **nervously** for it to leave. The waves were getting pretty violent and I thought about getting off several times but decided to wait and see if things would be better at sea. It was a decision that I was soon to regret as the boat rumbled out of the harbor.

At first, everything was **strangely** calm, and we wondered why we had been so nervous in the first place. But then the wind started to howl all around us. We rocked backward and forward as huge waves slammed **violently** against the boat, soaking us to the skin. Terrifyingly, benches were thrown from one side of the boat to the other and people all around us were sliding across the deck. **Fortunately**, no one fell over the side.

Finally, we reached the islands. We **rapidly** left the boat and sat shaking on the harbor wall. The staff assured us that the boat would return in three hours, but we were too terrified to go through that again. Strolling around the island, we tried **desperately** to find a hotel for the night so that we could return the next morning on the larger and safer car ferry. However, it was the peak of the summer and all of the hotels were booked up so we had no choice but to spend the night on the beach. An exciting day out had swiftly turned into the trip from hell!

C Read the story again and put the events in the order they happened.

___ arranged a boat trip
___ nervously boarded the boat
___ searched desperately for a hotel
___ a terrible storm erupted
___ waves smashed across the boat
___ slept on the sandy beach
___ walked to the harbor expecting the trip to be canceled
___ benches were thrown side to side and people slid across the deck

D SCAN Complete the box with the highlighted adverbs in the text.

Using adverbs to give detail to a story

We use adverbs of manner (e.g. *slowly*, ________, ________, ________, ________) to talk about how something happens.

We use adverbs of stance (e.g. *strangely*, ________, ________, ________, ________) to describe how we feel about something.

E Rewrite the sentences using the adverbs in bold.

1 It was incredible how dangerous the roads were on the island.
incredibly
The roads ________________.

2 We were nervous as we waited for the rescue team to come.
nervously
We waited ________________.

3 I was surprised the rescue team took such a long time to arrive.
surprisingly
The rescue team ________________.

4 It didn't take long for the fire to spread through the building.
rapidly
The fire ________________.

WRITING

A PREPARE You are going to write a short story about a nightmare trip or vacation. Write notes about:

- the location
- the people involved
- how you felt
- the key events
- contextual details (e.g. the weather, landscape, etc)

B PLAN Organize your notes from Exercise A into a plan for a short story.

C WRITE Write your short story. Use your plan to help you.

D EDIT Work in pairs. Edit your partner's story. Check:

- spelling and punctuation
- use of adverbs
- use of narrative tenses

4 Writing

Write a for and against blog post

W – structuring a for and against blog post

A Read the introduction to the blog post. What issue is the writer going to discuss?

B Work in pairs. Brainstorm ideas for and against the issue.

C Scan the blog post. Which of your ideas from Exercise B are mentioned?

About Blog Contact Search

In order to deal with congestion in cities, some people think that private vehicles should be banned from city centers. Others, however, feel that this is an unrealistic solution and that alternatives would work more effectively. This post will consider both perspectives.

[1]One of the arguments in favor of banning cars is that they are simply unnecessary if public transportation is effective. The needs of individuals can arguably be met by heavy investment in public transportation and the replacement of roads with bike paths. A good example of a city that has taken this idea to heart is Oslo, which plans to ban all cars from the city center by 2019 – approximately six years before a nationwide city ban comes into effect. Oslo is planning to replace almost 50 kilometers of road with bike lanes by the time the city goes car-free.

[2]On the one hand, banning cars seems like a simple way to address congestion in city centers. Yet, on the other hand, serious investment is required to make this feasible. One issue is that extensive public transportation networks would be required to replace cars in city centers. Many networks are seriously outdated or limited in their coverage. Furthermore, many countries simply do not have the financial means to build and extend their networks on such a scale.

[3]I believe that banning cars from city centers is only feasible in cities that already have an effective public transportation system. For everywhere else, cars are simply the most efficient way to get around.

[4]To conclude, while many cities are making steps toward banning cars from city centers, doing so requires heavy investment which many countries may not be able to afford. Realistically, we are a long way from car-free city centers.

D Match the paragraphs (1–4) to their functions (a–d).

a Arguments for ___ **c** Conclusion ___
b Personal opinion ___ **d** Arguments against ___

E Complete the box with phrases from the blog.

Structuring a for and against blog post

Introduction
Many people think that …
1 ______________________

To give arguments for and against
Some people argue that …
Others think …
2 ______________________
3 ______________________
4 ______________________

To give examples / more information
For example …
5 ______________________

To give your opinion
I am convinced that …
6 ______________________

Conclusion
In conclusion, …
7 ______________________

WRITING

A PREPARE Read the blog topic and write notes of arguments for and against.

Building more bicycle lanes is the best way to address pollution in city centers.

B PLAN Organize your notes from Exercise A into a plan for a for and against blog post.

C WRITE Write your blog post. Use your notes to help you.

D EDIT Work in pairs. Edit your partner's blog. Check:

- spelling and punctuation
- use of phrases to structure their argument
- strength of ideas

W describing problems and solutions

A Read the introduction to the problem/solution article. What is the main focus of the article?

> **Overcrowding in cities is among the principal dangers facing society today. This article will first look at some of the problems this causes and then suggest a number of possible solutions.**

B Work in pairs. Brainstorm possible problems and solutions for this topic.

C Scan the blog post. Which of your ideas from Exercise B are mentioned?

The main issue facing cities today is overcrowding, and the result is added pressure on public facilities. Schools, hospitals and roads are pushed to the breaking point as the city struggles to keep up with the rapid population increase. A good example of this is the pressure placed on hospitals and doctors, who are expected to deal with growing numbers of patients despite no increase in staff. One way to tackle the increased pressure on public facilities is to regulate building. When building new housing, rules should be put in place to ensure that enough new facilities are constructed at the same time. For instance, for every 1,000 new apartments, an elementary school and a doctor's office should be built by the construction firm.

One of the other foremost problems that occurs as a consequence of overcrowding is the increased levels of traffic. As a result, air pollution increases and traffic slows down. For example, in Mexico City, traffic has slowed to an average of around 10 kmph. One solution might be to build more bike lanes around city centers. This will allow commuters to navigate the city more quickly and will lower the CO_2 emissions. One example where this has been done successfully is Copenhagen in Denmark, where hundreds of meters of bike paths have been built.

In order to tackle the problems of overcrowding, cities should focus not only on building more housing but also on providing the infrastructure needed to support the growing population.

D Read the first paragraph again. Put the following in order to show the paragraph structure.

___ state the solution
_1_ state the problem
___ explain how this will solve the problem
___ show the results of the problem
___ give an example of the solution
___ give an example of the problem

E Complete the skills box with phrases from the article.

Describing problems and solutions

Introduction
X is one of the biggest issues we face ...
1 ____________________

Problems and results
The biggest threat to ...
The foremost problem ...
2 ____________________
3 ____________________

Examples and results
The result is ...
4 ____________________
A good example of this is ...

Solutions and explanations
One way to tackle the issue of X is to ...
5 ____________________
This will allow ...

WRITING

A PREPARE Work in pairs. Brainstorm problems and solutions in response to the following:

> **What are some of the difficulties of living and working in a megacity?**

B PLAN Organize your ideas from Exercise A into a plan for an article.

C WRITE Write your article. Use your plan to help you.

D EDIT Work in pairs. Edit your partner's article. Check:

- spelling and punctuation
- structure and organization
- strength of ideas

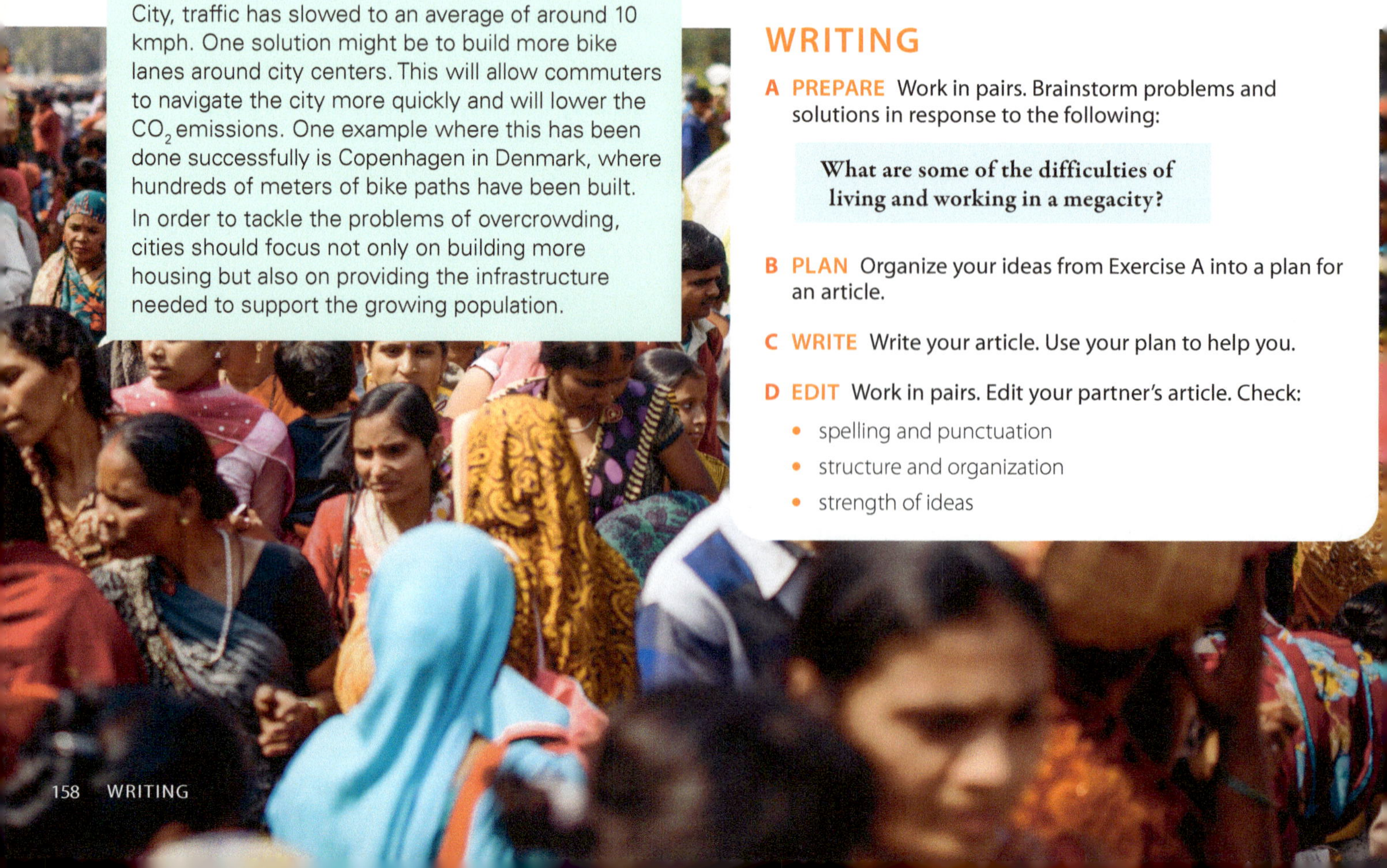

W – describing data

A Work in pairs. Which of these factors do you think are the most important things to consider when choosing a college or university? Why?

- quality of teaching
- college/university ranking
- friends at the college
- close to home
- good graduate employment rate
- cost of living

B Look at the bar chart. Which of the reasons in Exercise A is the most popular?

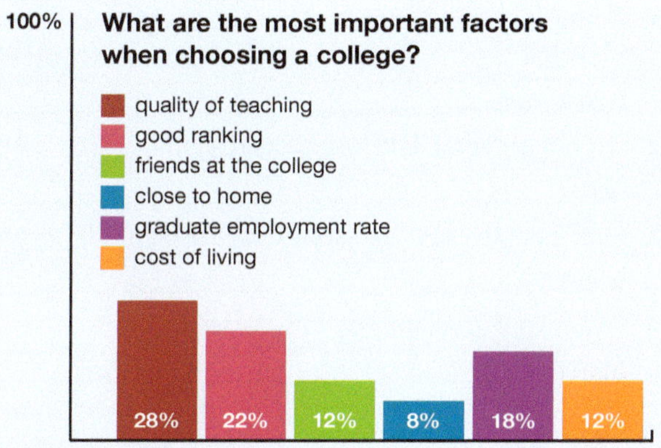

College choice

Introduction

The purpose of this report is to evaluate the results of a survey on reasons for choosing a college and to suggest areas for colleges to focus their efforts on to increase student recruitment.

Results

This graph illustrates the results of the student survey. The highest proportion of students chose the quality of teaching as the key factor. Almost one-third of students gave this as their primary reason for choosing which college or university to attend, with the institution's ranking being the second most import factor, according to almost a quarter of the students. The third most significant factor was employability of graduates, with friends and the cost of living more or less equal. The least important factor is closeness to home.

Interpretation

There are significant differences between two groups of factors in this data. Arguably, the first three factors are all interconnected. The ranking of a college can have an impact on employability and the standard of teaching has an impact on the ranking. Therefore, colleges need to focus not only on what is happening in the classroom, but also their connections with industry for internships and future employment. The other three factors are also potentially connected because they are clearly likely to have an impact on the students' lifestyle and happiness while attending college.

Recommendations

I would recommend that for colleges to increase their student recruitment and satisfaction they should invest in their staff and teaching facilities. They should also spend time developing their relationships with companies since employment opportunities are very important to students.

C Read the report and answer the questions.

1. How many sections are there to the report?
2. What is the difference between the results and interpretation sections?
3. What is the difference between the interpretation and recommendations sections?

D Complete the table with phrases from the report.

Describing data

Introduction

This report summarizes … and concludes with …

1 ______________________

Evaluating results

The majority of …

2 ______________________

The highest proportion of …

Several key trends indicated by the graph …

Comparing and contrasting

Similarly,

By contrast …

X and Y are 3 ______________________

There is no difference between X and Y.

4 ______________________ *X and Y.*

Making recommendations

It might also be useful to …

5 ______________________

WRITING

A PREPARE You are going to write a report describing the data in the chart below and make recommendations to colleges about how to promote their course. Write notes on the key results and your recommendations.

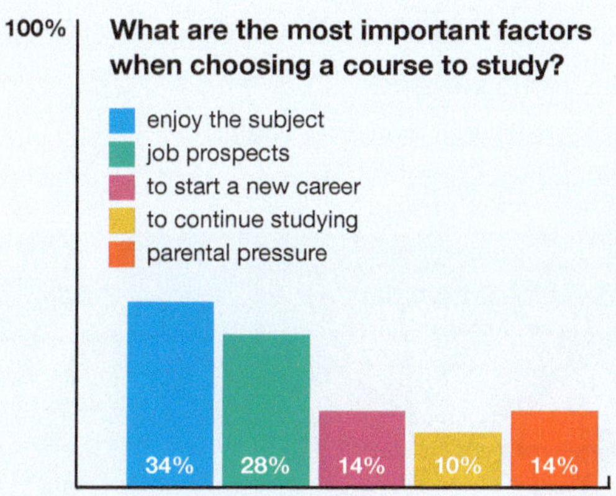

B PLAN Organize your notes into a report structure.

C WRITE Write your report. Use your plan to help you.

D EDIT Work in pairs. Edit your partner's report. Check:

- spelling and punctuation
- report structure
- strength of analysis and recommendations

Write a formal letter of complaint

W – hedging

A Work in pairs. Which of the following are issues in your neighborhood?

- graffiti
- trash
- crime
- noise pollution
- air pollution
- poor transportation systems
- lack of public spaces
- abandoned buildings

B Read the letter of complaint. What problem from Exercise A are mentioned?

> Dear Sir/Madam,
>
> [1]I am writing to you with regard to the proposal to knock down the old clothing factory and construct a new library in our area. While I agree that our neighborhood would benefit enormously from such a wonderful facility, I'm afraid I do not agree with the proposal for a number of reasons.
>
> [2]First, the clothing factory is a historical building and something we should be looking to preserve and restore, not demolish. Instead of demolishing the factory, I feel that proposals should look at converting it into the library instead. Simply destroying such a landmark and starting again is not something I expect many residents will find acceptable. Second, the current suggestion will create unacceptable levels of noise and take significantly longer than converting the factory. This is not something I feel residents will put up with and I have no option but to organize a campaign group against this.
>
> [3]I feel that local residents should be consulted on this project and I would appreciate an open discussion on these plans. I look forward to hearing from you on this matter.
>
> Kind regards,
>
> John Hadland

C Match the paragraphs (1–3) to their function (a–c).

a describing the issues ___

b explaining your reason for writing ___

c requesting action ___

D Rewrite the sentences using the words in parentheses. Use the information in the box and the letter to help you.

> **Hedging**
>
> Hedges are used to soften an opinion, rather than simply saying 'I don't agree.' Instead of directly disagreeing, which might be seen as being rude, people usually write something such as *I'm sorry but I don't agree*. Hedging like this makes your opinion or suggestion less direct and less likely to cause offense.

1 I know we need a new road but I don't agree with the proposal.
(*While / afraid*) ______________________.

2 It is not acceptable to lose a local park.
(*sorry*) ______________________.

3 Most people won't be happy with the plan.
(*expect*) ______________________.

4 I want your assistance on this matter.
(*appreciate*) ______________________.

WRITING

A PREPARE You are going to write a letter of complaint about a proposal to build a new road through your local park. Write notes about potential issues with this proposal and possible alternatives.

B PLAN Organize your notes into a formal letter structure.

C WRITE Write your letter of complaint. Use your plan to help you.

D EDIT Work in pairs. Edit your partner's letter. Check:

- spelling and punctuation
- strength of analysis and recommendations
- use of hedging language

W writing conclusions

A Read the essay prompt and answer the questions.

1 What claim is made in the prompt?

2 What does *this* refer to in the first question?

Many former criminals go on to reoffend following their release from prison. Is the prison system primarily to blame for this? Should more be done to support former criminals?

B Read the introduction and body of the essay. Choose the best summary (1 or 2) of the writer's position.

1 Support groups need to be established in local areas to help former criminals establish valuable roles in society.

2 The prison system needs to do more to provide criminals with the skills they need to succeed post release.

A large proportion of former criminals go on to reoffend when released from prison. This essay will explain that while the prison system certainly plays a role in this statistic, it is primarily the lack of employment opportunities on the outside that is to blame and, for this reason, support networks must be established to better integrate ex-convicts back into society.

One of the primary functions of the prison system is to reform criminals, not just punish them. To this end, most prisons offer training programs that provide inmates that are willing to learn with practical skills that should help them find employment post-release. However, many former criminals return to neighborhoods where opportunities are limited and they are forced to take low-paid jobs that don't reflect the skills they acquired while behind bars. Without a clear support network designed to help shape the careers of former criminals, many feel neglected by society. It is this lack of support that is the root of reoffending.

While most governments do offer guidance to former criminals, much more needs to be done to support sustainable reintegration into society. Support groups formed primarily of ex-convicts that have forged successful careers post-release should be founded in all major towns and cities. These groups should be given all of the funding and resources necessary to nurture the careers of former criminals, ensuring that they can play a valuable part in society.

C Work in pairs. Which is the best conclusion for the essay in Exercise B? Use the information in the box to help you.

Writing conclusions

Essays should finish with a simple conclusion summarizing the key arguments made in the body. Since no new ideas should be explored in the conclusion, it's easy to lose the interest of readers at this point. To avoid this, ensure your conclusions are short, simple and paraphrase your main ideas.

1

In conclusion, while most prisons offer training programs that provide inmates with valuable practical skills, many ex-convicts return to neighborhoods where opportunities are limited. All too frequently, they find themselves surrounded by others who have returned to a life of crime and cannot resist the urge to follow suit. By establishing support groups in major towns and cities, we would ensure that former criminals play a valuable part in society instead of turning back to a life of crime.

2

In conclusion, although the prison system should certainly shoulder some of the blame for the high volume of repeat offenders, it does provide inmates with the opportunity to acquire practical skills that are valuable to society. However, the existing networks available post-release do not offer former criminals the level of support they need in order to apply what they have learned. We need to establish well-resourced support networks throughout the country to help ex-convicts forge successful careers.

WRITING

A **PREPARE** Read the essay question below and brainstorm ideas.

Many ex-convicts struggle to adapt to life outside prison post-release. Is their attitude primarily to blame for this? Should more be done to help them adjust?

B **PLAN** Organize your ideas into paragraphs.

C **WRITE** Write your essay. Use your plan to help you.

D **EDIT** Work in pairs. Edit your partner's essay. Check:

- spelling and punctuation
- use of language
- strength of conclusion

W – using discourse markers in formal writing

A Read the proposal task below and answer the questions that follow.

> Your hotel has been getting low ratings from users on a popular travel website. Your boss has asked you to look at the reviews and to write a proposal for changes that can be made to the hotel. You should include information about the weaknesses reviewers have mentioned and suggest improvements.

1 What is the current problem?
2 What recommendations do you need to make?

Proposal for improvements to the hotel

Introduction

The purpose of this proposal is to examine weaknesses identified in the hotel's online reviews and to suggest ways to address them.

Hotel weaknesses

Analysis of the reviews has revealed that most customers feel the hotel décor is dated and in much need of modernization. In fact, many feel the old-fashioned look of the hotel makes it feel unclean. Furthermore, consumers usually leave poor reviews of the food in the hotel restaurant. The menu is considered to be too limited, and the service during breakfast too slow. Consequently, fewer and fewer guests are eating in the hotel itself.

Hotel improvements

Modernizing the look of the hotel would be hugely beneficial since there seems to be little doubt that we are attracting fewer customers as a result of the outdated décor. The hotel should be given a simple, fresh and clean look that is more in keeping with our competitors. The restaurant should be a way for the hotel to maximize profits, but due to the limited menu and poor service, people are choosing to eat elsewhere. Therefore, updating the menu and hiring more service staff is essential.

Recommendations

Implementation of the ideas outlined above would result in an increased level of customer satisfaction and more positive online reviews. Improving the restaurant would also encourage more guests to dine in, increasing overall profitability.

B Read the proposal. According to the writer, what are the main weaknesses of the hotel? What solutions do they recommend?

C Underline four formal discourse markers in the text. Use the information in the box to help you.

Using discourse markers in formal writing

In formal writing, we use a range of discourse markers to connect ideas. These include adding ideas (e.g. *additionally*), talking about effects and results (e.g. *subsequently*) and giving examples (e.g. *for instance*).

D Complete the sentences using discourse markers from Exercise C.

1 The hotel has had little investment in recent years. ________, the volume of reservations has fallen.
2 ________ the limited menu, customers are leaving negative reviews online.
3 A lot of our customers said they received poor service. ________, many complained our staff was rude.
4 The new menu simply isn't popular. ________, we should reinstate the old one.

WRITING

A PREPARE Work in pairs. Read the proposal task below. Brainstorm issues a coffee chain might experience and how to address them.

> You work for a large, successful coffee chain. However, lately your customer service department has been receiving increasingly negative reviews on social media. You have been asked to write a proposal highlighting the main issues and how to address them.

B PLAN Organize your ideas into appropriate sections.

C WRITE Write your proposal. Use your plan to help you.

D EDIT Work in pairs. Edit your partner's proposal. Check:

- spelling and punctuation
- strength of analysis and recommendations
- use of formal discourse markers

10 Writing

Write a persuasive essay

W concession

A Read the essay question below and answer the questions that follow.

> Some think social media has a negative impact on individuals and society as a whole. Others argue the effects have largely been positive. Discuss both views and give your opinion.

1 What two points of view do you need to discuss?

2 What else do you need to do?

B Work in pairs. What positive and negative effects do you think the writer might discuss?

C Read the essay. Were any of your ideas from Exercise B mentioned?

Social media has had a huge impact on people's lives, and in recent years, many have argued that this effect has been detrimental to both individuals and society as a whole. Although there are undeniably many negative effects of social media, I believe that its impact on society has been predominantly beneficial.

It must be acknowledged that social media brings with it a number of negative consequences. Arguably, as we spend more and more of our time online, we're engaging far less in the real world. As a result, as much as some people may feel they have a great deal of support from their online community, they are potentially losing touch with valuable support networks around them. Furthermore, because of the anonymous nature of online communities, interaction is frequently very confrontational, or worse – guided by people whose only agenda seems to be to cause conflict or to promote controversial views.

Nevertheless, despite these potential issues, the advantages of social media are apparent in many aspects of our lives. First, it has enabled people to stay in touch with a wider group of friends, which they might otherwise have lost contact with. Additionally, these platforms provide a simple way to connect and share content with people around the world that have common interests – something that, while possible before social media, was certainly far more difficult.

Overall, although social media can lead to conflict and the breakdown of face-to-face communication with those around us, it has also made many bonds stronger.

D Scan the essay again. Underline the words and phrases used to make concessions. Use the information in the box to help you.

Concession

In writing, concession means admitting that part or all of an opposing viewpoint is valid. Doing so not only shows you have a well-rounded view of the topic, but can also be used to further develop your own argument.

***While** it's true that social media can make some people feel isolated, the majority of us feel better connected in this day and age.*

E Rewrite the sentences using the words in bold.

1 Social media allows for more open discussion. It frequently leads to conflict.
While ... may
_______________________________________.

2 Social media divides some people. It brings many more together.
Although ... may
_______________________________________.

3 It's clear that many people enjoy using social media. It makes others feel isolated.
Many ... but
_______________________________________.

4 I don't like the idea of policing social media. It's an important next step.
Nevertheless
_______________________________________.

5 I don't like social media personally. I can understand its appeal.
As much as
_______________________________________.

WRITING

A **PREPARE** Read the essay question below and brainstorm your ideas.

> Today, many people prefer to socialize online rather than in person. Some people feel this is a positive development while others argue it has had a negative impact on our relationships. Discuss both views and give your opinion.

B **PLAN** Organize your notes from Exercise A into an appropriate essay structure.

C **WRITE** Write your essay. Use your plan to help you.

D **EDIT** Work in pairs. Edit your partner's essay. Check:

- spelling and punctuation
- strength of arguments
- use of concession phrases

Audio scripts

UNIT 1

Lesson 1.1 Listening, Exercise B

1.1 **Mk = Mark S = Sarah F = Fyodor A = Alana Mn = Martin Y = Yumi**

Conversation 1

Mk: Hello. I haven't seen you here before.

S: Uh, no, I've just joined actually. This is my first Get Together.

Mk: Oh, well, you chose a good group. Everyone here's pretty friendly and we all have a similar level of ability, which helps.

S: That's a relief. I've been learning for about a year or so now. How about you? Have you been playing long?

Mk: Uh, yeah a little bit longer ... for about two and a half years. I think I'm alright but I'm no expert.

S: Yeah, me neither. Do you ever perform at all?

Mk: Me? Ha ha! No, no. I'm definitely not good enough for that. I'm just doing this for fun really. How about you?

S: Yeah, same really. It just seemed like a fun thing to do. Anyway, who's leading the group tonight?

Mk: Uh, Lucy, I think. She's actually a professional musician, so we're in good hands.

S: Well I certainly need all the help I can get!

Conversation 2

F: Excuse me, could you tell me where the changing rooms are?

A: Sure. I'm going there now if you want to come with me. I'm Alana by the way. You're new to the Get Together, aren't you?

F: Uh, yeah I am. I've just moved to the area. I was a member of the running Get Together before I moved here.

A: Where were you living before?

F: I was living in Chicago but I got a new job, so I moved to New York. I'm living in Rochester right now, but I might actually move.

A: Oh, really? How come?

F: Well I like Rochester but my apartment is a really long way from the train station and I don't really get along with my roommates.

A: Fair enough. Why don't you like them?

F: Well, one of them works night shifts so he always comes home really late and the other just spends all his time in his room. Maybe I should just look for a place on my own.

A: Maybe, although living with roommates can be pretty fun if you can find the right people.

F: I suppose so. Who do you live with?

A: A couple of friends I've known since college. They can definitely be annoying sometimes, but I wouldn't want to live with anyone else.

F: Sounds fun. Anyway, have you been running long?

A: Uh, no, not long really. I just wanted to, you know, get more into sports and I loved running in college, so I thought I'd give it a try.

F: I see. Are you planning to enter any races this summer or is it a little too soon?

A: Well, I was actually thinking of signing up for the 10K at the end of September.

F: The one in Richmond, Virginia? You definitely should. Ten kilometers sounds like a long way, but it's actually not too bad. I just put in a lot of time training and was completely fine on the day.

A: OK, good to know. Maybe we could do it together?

F: Ha ha! Maybe. I'm doing a half marathon the week before though, so I might not have the energy for another race!

Conversation 3

Mn: Excuse me, could you tell me where I sign in for the book club Get Together?

Y: Uh, yeah, right here actually. I'm running the group tonight. Can I take your name, please?

Mn: It's Martin Pajak.

Y: Oh, yes. I remember your name from your emails. Could I ask you to fill out this form when you get a chance? No rush to return it. Have you had time to finish the book yet?

Mn: Uh, just about! I really like Haruki Murakami.

Y: Oh, really? Me too. Which is your favorite Murakami novel?

Mn: Um, probably *Norwegian Wood*, but I also loved *After Dark*.

Y: *Norwegian Wood* was the first Murakami book that I ever read. I thought it was amazing.

Mn: Oh, well if you like Murakami, you'd probably like Banana Yoshimoto. Especially her first novel, *Kitchen*.

Lesson 1.2 Listening, Exercise B

1.5 **P = Presenter R = Richard**

P: Now we all know that friends are important, but according to our next guest, the type of friends we choose can have a dramatic impact on how successful we are. Here to explain why, is the psychologist Richard Bonnel. Richard, welcome to the show.

R: Thanks for having me.

P: So Richard, we all have hundreds of friends these days ...

R: Well, we all know hundreds of people on Facebook, Twitter and other social media sites but how many are actually our friends is debatable. Realistically, research tells us that we can't maintain a friendship group of more than 50 people and, you know, in fact it's probably much smaller if we consider just the people we regularly communicate with.

P: So what type of friends are important to have in your life?

R: Well, our research shows that very successful people surround themselves with six different types of friends. Not six friends but six types. We all need a loyal best friend. Someone who will support us no matter what happens. Someone who knows everything about you. They know all of your secrets but they still love you anyway.

P: I definitely have one of those. There's no way I'd ever let them on this show. They have far too many stories about me!

R: You probably don't need to worry. You can trust them to keep any embarrassing secrets private! Well, they might let one or two things out just for fun ... The next type is really important to make your life more interesting. This person is an open-minded adventurer. They always force us into new and different situations. They challenge us. They push us to try new things. They are easy-going and open to new ideas, cultures and activities. None of these things stress them out. Basically, they break us out of our normal routine.

P: I actually think I'm that friend to a lot of people. I'm always taking people to new places and making them do new things.

R: I don't doubt it. These people, they're usually great with people, self-confident and like the attention of others.

P: Are you saying I'm arrogant?

R: No, these people aren't arrogant. They just have a lot of self-belief. Other people probably love it because they are much more cautious than you. You add a little spice to their life! Another type of friend that people need, is one they probably don't always like or want. That's someone who is really honest even when it upsets you.

P: How is that useful?

R: Well, this person will tell you when your hair looks awful or your clothes look terrible. They'll tell you when you're being self-centered and should think about others more. Or they'll tell you you are being stubborn and need to be more flexible. It's tough to hear, but it's usually true.

P: I do have a friend like that. She's very down-to-earth. She just does everything in this very sensible, practical way. I guess she is a helpful person to have around!

R: Right, exactly. Equally, it's important to not just surround ourselves with like-minded people. We should have some friends who are the complete opposite of us.

P: Why would you want to do that? Surely you'd just argue?

R: Maybe, but it opens your mind to different ways of seeing the world. It makes you a more accepting person.

P: True. So, are there any other types of people we should surround ourselves with?

R: Well, the last two are not really types of people but friends we should try to make because of our circumstances. We all move around much more these days and typically have no idea who our neighbors are, but they are important to know. Dependable neighbors can help in difficult situations and make you feel happier about where you live.

P: That is so true. I'm really happy where I live now and it's mainly because of the people living near me.

R: How about work? Are you happy at work?

P: Well, I think I'm pretty lucky. I actually love my job.

R: It's vital that you do. Successful people always work with people they like. Most people spend at least 50% of their waking hours at work. On top of that, people commute to work, work overtime, and think about work. It can take over your life. Imagine feeling isolated at work. No one to talk to. Having no witty people to have a laugh with would make work very boring. A depressing thought, isn't it?

P: When you put it like that, I think I might need to find a new job!

UNIT 2

Lesson 2.1 Listening, Exercise C

2.1 **P = Presenter**

P: OK, let's move onto our next topic. Now, according to a recent survey conducted by The Institute for Social Research, the public, in general, is terrible at sticking to their New Year's resolutions. Apparently, 43% of people surveyed broke their resolution within the first month and 86% lasted less than a year.

To test the accuracy of these results, we sent reporter Emily Hussan out onto the city streets to see just how many of you have managed to successfully give something up for the New Year.

Lesson 2.1 Listening, Exercise D

2.2 **P = Presenter S1 = Speaker 1 S2 = Speaker 2 S3 = Speaker 3 S4 = Speaker 4 S5 = Speaker 5**

Speaker 1

P: Sorry, excuse me. We're interviewing people about whether they've managed to stick to their New Year's resolutions. Did you make any this year?

S1: Yeah, I did actually. Well, the whole family did really. My family and I felt that, well, we really didn't spend enough time together. You know, I found we hardly ever spoke to each other. We, uh, just sat around using our various devices in our own little worlds. We've been living without smartphones and tablets for a couple of months now. I bought everyone really old-fashioned phones that you could only call and text on.

P: How did your children feel about that?

S1: Oh, well, the children went crazy! They were really mad at us!

P: Was it worth it?

S1: Definitely! It was really hard to cope with at first, but since then our lives have, well, changed for the better. We've been spending more time together as a family. And, um, I think we have a better relationship. And you know what? We are all sleeping better as a result of giving up technology.

Speaker 2

P: So, did you try to give anything up for the New Year?

S2: Yeah, I've actually given up coffee.

P: Oh, really? Why?

S2: Well, at the end of last year, I was really stressed at work and it had started to affect my sleep. I was only getting about two or three hours every night and this put me in a bad mood the next day. I thought about exercising more, but I've never really been a gym kind of person. Then I thought, 'Maybe I drink too much coffee'. I used to drink, like, four or five cups a day, but I cut this down to two, then stopped entirely to try and help me sleep better.

P: Good job! And did it work?

S2: Absolutely! I've been living without coffee for months now and get at least seven hours sleep every night. You should try it!

Speaker 3

P: Did you make any resolutions back in January?

S3: Well, I always knew that I didn't have a great diet but didn't realize just how bad sugar is for you. Obviously it can affect your weight, but it can also lead to heart disease, diabetes … even some forms of cancer. Anyway, I read this article that said you should only have a maximum of six teaspoons a day, and I was having way more than that.

P: What, like cakes and chocolate and stuff?

S3: Well yeah, but there's also a lot of sugar in things you wouldn't expect like yogurt, bread …

P: Bread?

S3: Yep! Most processed foods have added sugar. Anyway, I've managed to lose a little weight since cutting down and it's really made me think about my diet in general. I've only had three chocolate bars this month!

Speaker 4

P: So have you made any changes since the New Year?

S4: Not by choice! My car's in the garage right now, so I've been riding my bike to work for the past two weeks.

P: No … sorry, I meant resolutions.

S4: Oh, I see. Yes, well this is going to sound weird, but I've stopped using shampoo.

P: Um, really?

S4: Ha ha! Yep. I've only washed my hair twice this month. Pretty disgusting, huh?

P: It doesn't sound great to be honest.

S4: Well, my hair was pretty greasy at first and I'm sure I didn't smell too great either, but after a few weeks my body seemed to adjust.

P: So why did you decide to give it up? To help the environment?

S4: Uh, no. A lot of people say shampoo contains harmful chemicals, but I don't really think that's true. I actually gave it up because of a friend. She said that my hair was in really bad condition and suggested I try washing it less. I haven't used shampoo since December and my hair feels great. And I've saved a lot of money!

Speaker 5

P: Did you try to give anything up for the New Year?

S5: No, not really. I haven't given anything up for a long time.

P: When did you last give something up?

S5: Um, I'm not sure really. Well actually, I've been vegan for five years now. I wanted to reduce my carbon footprint, which I've managed to do.

P: Oh, really? How's that possible?

S5: Well, it takes so much more water to produce meat.

P: Really? Why?

S5: Well, obviously the animals we eat need to drink water and a surprisingly large amount of water is used to grow their food.

P: Oh, right. How do you feel personally?

S5: I feel healthier. I've lost weight and have more energy.

Lesson 2.2 Listening, Exercise B

2.5 **I = Interviewer F = Frank K = Katie**

I: Many of us have dreamed of escaping the rat race and getting away from our stressful lives, but few of us have ever actually taken the plunge. Well, on today's show we have one family who has done just that. Joining us from their beachfront home is Frank Gerrard and his daughter Katie. Thanks for joining us today. It looks beautiful there! Can you hear me OK?

F: Yes, I can hear you.

I: Now, you've made a dramatic change to your life. What were you doing before?

F: I had a terrible job! I used to work long hours and it was stressful. I was exhausted and overworked. I used to dream of living a quieter and more peaceful life … You know, getting back to nature and that sort of thing. So, I quit my job, sold the family home and we moved here.

I: Wow! That's really a dramatic change! How's it all been going?

F: It's been amazing! We have a small plot of land next to our house and we grow a lot of our own food. I go fishing and hunting every day.

I: Is there a local store?

F: There is, but we hardly ever go. I want to grow or catch everything.

I: So was the change easy for you?

F: Actually, it was a lot harder getting used to the new lifestyle than I thought it would be. When I worked in an office, I was so physically tired all the time because I just sat at my desk all day writing emails. I never really got up and walked around until it was time to go home, and even then I just walked to the station and sat on a train for half an hour. Now I have so many more physical tasks to do to produce the food we need. I'm used to getting up at six o'clock every day now and working hard until it gets dark. Financially, it has also been much harder but we're getting used to it.

I: Would you make the same decision again?

F: For me, definitely! I wouldn't change a thing. As for my family, well I'm not so sure. They miss New York a lot and actually, I'm so busy all the time that we don't really spend that much more time together. We also have way less money now – not that there's much to spend it on!

I: Well this seems like a good point to bring in your daughter. Katie, how did you feel about the decision?

K: I understand why Dad did it. Back in New York, he'd complain about his job constantly. He hated it. Mom just wanted him to be happier. But, well I think it was a stupid idea. He's just having a midlife crisis! Why would anyone want to move here?

I: So, you're not happy there then?

K: No. I used to see my friends all the time in New York. We'd go shopping or hang out in the park. What is there to do here? Walk up another mountain? The internet is terrible too. When I was bored in New York, I used to watch Netflix on my phone or listen to something on Spotify. That kind of thing is just out of the question now because our internet connection is so bad. We also don't seem to have any money now, which is weird – shouldn't we be better off?

I: OK, and what's school like there?

K: It's the worst thing ever! I'm homeschooled now. There's a small school on the island, but my parents want me to take US exams, so Mom is teaching us. I never ever leave the house!

I: Do you think you'll grow to love it?

K: No! I'm really stressed actually. What job can I do here? Where will I go to college? I'm getting used to being isolated from everyone, but I need to think about my future. In New York, I would always think about the exciting jobs and opportunities I could have in the future. I don't want a life like this – all day gathering food. It's boring!

I: Are there any positives about the move?

K: Seriously? No. Well, to be fair, I do enjoy swimming and sunbathing every day, but generally no, I'm bored a lot of the time. I guess I'm not used to it yet.

F: Well, our youngest loves it here. New York isn't great for young children. I was always too worried to let him play outside alone. Now he's out there all day! He would hate to move back to New York. It isn't great for teenagers though, so it might change as he gets older.

K: It definitely will. He's going to be so bored!

I: Well, thank you both for joining us.

UNIT 3

Lesson 3.1 Listening, Exercise C

3.1 **I = Interviewer P = Paul H = Hayley L = Lee**

I: OK, welcome back to the show. Tonight we're talking about extreme sports. Why do so many people take part in such dangerous activities? Where's the fun in putting yourself at such risk? Maybe our next caller can help answer some of these burning questions. Paul, what dangerous sport do you do and why?

P: I'm into climbing. Especially free climbing.

I: When did you first get into climbing?

P: When I was four years old, my dad took me walking in the foothills of the Alps. I can still remember the snow crunching under our feet as we walked together. We always had a lot of fun, but I didn't really get into climbing until I was 17. I remember standing in front of a really steep rock face and thinking, 'Can I do this?'.

I: When did you move onto free climbing?

P: Probably about ten years later. By that point I'd become a pretty good climber and wanted a new challenge. I love the excitement, fear and challenge of it. My father thought it was a great idea because he'd been a good climber too, but my mother was terrified.

I: Have you ever had any accidents?

P: Well, I've had a lot of terrifying moments. Once, I was high up the side of a mountain in Argentina, when the wind started to pick up. It was too dangerous to climb down, so I just had to hold on and wait. In some places, there are also these tiny wooden bridges attached to the side of the mountain to help you get from one ledge to another. Sometimes the wood groans under your weight, which can be a little scary, but so far none have ever actually broken!

I: OK, so what's the most dangerous thing that's ever happened to you?

P: Well, a few years ago I was in South Africa with a few of my friends and we'd almost finished the first part of an all-day climb. I was just pulling myself up when I saw a huge snake right in front of me. I am terrified of snakes, so I just froze as it started to hiss and arch backwards. I waited for another few minutes, not moving, and then it just seemed to get bored and slithered back into a crack in the rock. It was the most terrifying moment ever and it had nothing to do with climbing!

I: Thanks for calling in, Paul. Hope you don't meet any more snakes on your climbs.

I: We have our second caller, Hayley, with us now. Hayley, what dangerous sport are you into?

H: Potholing!

I: What, climbing through caves and things?

H: Yeah, that's right. It's a lot of fun, actually.

I: Hmm …, not sure I'd enjoy it. Anyway, how long have you been potholing for?

H: I first got into potholing in college. There was a climbing and caving society that I joined. I had done a lot of climbing but I'd never done any potholing before. It was amazing!

I: How does it compare to climbing?

H: With climbing, you can see a lot of the route in front of you. Potholing is so dark, and the spaces can be really small, so it's difficult to plan your next move. Usually, you start at the entrance to a cave and simply walk in, but within a few hundred meters you have crawled on your belly, swum underwater, and squeezed your body through tiny gaps. The challenges are just so much more varied.

I: And is it a dangerous sport?

H: It's more dangerous than it sounds. You can suffer from a lack of oxygen or too much carbon dioxide. You can get trapped. You can drown when there's a sudden storm. You can even fall to your death climbing. There are literally hundreds of ways you can die!

I: Sounds scary! What was your most terrifying experience?

H: Once, I got lost when I was deep underground in Mexico. It can be silent for just a few minutes and all you can hear is water trickling around you. It's actually very worrying because you have no maps and no way of communicating with people outside and getting help. Luckily, we managed to get back out the way we had come. By then we had been lost underground for several hours. It was terrifying and took me weeks to get over it!

I: Thank you, Hayley. I have to say, potholing sounds terrifying! So now on to our last caller, Lee. Good evening, Lee.

L: Good evening!

I: So, Lee, what extreme sport are you into?

L: I'm a free runner.

I: OK, so when did you first get into it?

L: It started when I was a child. I used to do gymnastics when I was young, so I was always into climbing and jumping. Then a friend at school showed me a video of a group of people free running and I thought, 'Why not give it a try?'

I: What do you enjoy most about free running?

L: Well, it makes you look at cities in different ways compared to other people. People usually don't even look up when they walk around a city. They focus on everything at eye level – stores, people, cars. You actually really appreciate the architecture more from up high. Every city is a new physical challenge. I get excited and my adrenalin starts pumping!

I: How dangerous is free running?

L: It can be very dangerous. You need to be very aware of your own ability and try not to push yourself too hard. Unfortunately, because it is competitive, people are always pushing themselves to do more and more dangerous things. I have broken a lot of bones. Once, when I jumped between two buildings, I slipped and fell 20 meters. Luckily, I didn't break anything. This other time though, I fell just a couple of meters and I broke my ankle. I can still hear my ankle snap as I landed. It was so painful!

I: Oh, wow! That sounds horrible. Anyway, thanks for joining us, Lee. OK, listeners – we're just going to a short commercial break before we take our next caller.

Lesson 3.2 Listening, Exercise B

3.5 **N = Narrator**

Chapter 2 – Phobias and rational fears

Suddenly, you see something in the corner of your eye. Your palms start sweating, your heart beats faster and your muscles become tense. A tiny spider is crawling across the bathroom wall …

Why is it that many of us fear things that are, relatively speaking, completely harmless, yet don't think twice about real, everyday risks such as driving to work or heart disease?

The ability to calculate risk is essential to the survival of any species. Indeed, one of the most primitive human instincts is to assess our environment for potential threats. This heightened awareness of our surroundings is controlled by a section of the brain called the amygdala. It is responsible for our fear, anger, sadness, and our levels of aggression. It determines how we should react to the things we see before us. Is that a tiger waiting in the bushes or just a trick of the light? Should we run away or stay and fight? This response – commonly referred to as 'fight or flight' – is what makes our heart beat faster and our palms start to sweat. This is actually an essential human instinct, but it's worth noting that for some, the response seems to be overly sensitive. They perceive threats where most people wouldn't and are generally far more anxious as a result. A little like an overly sensitive car alarm that goes off every time somebody walks by.

So it is the amygdala that triggers our initial reaction to a perceived threat. But how do we determine whether the threat is real or not? For this, we rely on the hippocampus and the prefrontal cortex. They compare contextual information with our memories and experience, and decide whether we should be afraid or not. This is useful, because it allows us to decide, for example, to run away when we see a snake in the jungle but remain calm when we see one in a zoo. Essentially, the decision-making part of our brain can tell the emotional part to relax when there is no real threat.

The fact that we rely on our knowledge and experience to determine our emotional response is key to understanding our fears. If, for example, you had a terrifying experience with a dog when you were younger, this is highly likely to influence your reaction to them now. Similarly, if your only knowledge of an airline company is that one of their planes crashed recently, you might well be too afraid to fly with them, even if their overall safety record is very good. Although we are capable of remembering facts or statistics, humans tend to focus on the emotional and the dramatic. For example, according to a cancer research study, skin cancer leads to around two and a half thousand deaths every year. Statistically, this is definitely something worth worrying about. In comparison, there are very few plane crashes every year. Yet when we go on vacation, many of us worry more about the plane crashing than whether or not we remembered to pack our sunscreen.

While our brains are constructed to help us identify, assess and react to potential threats, the heighted levels of anxiety this may cause can actually have a hugely negative effect on our bodies. For example, high levels of stress have a negative impact on the immune system, potentially leading to an increased risk of depression, heart disease and diabetes. And unfortunately, it seems that modern society is designed to increase stress and anxiety. We've become accustomed to 24-hour news coverage, instant access to information and a constant flow of messages, yet it could well be that instead of improving our lives, these all have a negative impact on our physical and mental health. If this is true, how we adapt to our increasingly connected world will be fundamental to our continued survival as a species.

UNIT 4

Lesson 4.1 Listening, Exercise C

4.1 **P = Presenter L = Lucy H = Hadiyah F = Frank**

P: Lenox is a small town in Massachusetts, in the US. Like many other towns in this area, not a lot has changed here over the years, but for these three residents, life is about to change forever.

Lucy Warner has just graduated from high school and is going to start studying for a law degree at Harvard in the fall of next year. However, since she's never left Lenox, she wants to take a year off to go traveling. When I spoke to her, she was busy packing her bags.

L: Can you pass me that bag? The red one behind you …

P: Sure. First of all, congratulations on graduating!

L: Thanks!

P: So, when do you leave?

L: Next Sunday!

P: Wow! So soon.

L: I know! Scary!

P: So, anything specific planned?

L: Well, um, I'm flying to Paris because I have a friend there. Then I'm taking the train to Spain, where I'm staying for a couple of months.

P: Oh right. Why so long in Spain?

L: I want to improve my Spanish. I speak a little, but it's well, just tourist Spanish really. I'm starting a month-long course in Spanish in September. The classes are three days a week from nine to four.

P: That sounds great.

L: Yeah, I don't know. It's just a little fun really. I don't really need another language – everyone there speaks some English anyway!

P: Sounds cool though. Any other exciting plans?

L: I'm really excited about taking the Trans-Siberian Express across Russia into Asia. I think it'll be amazing, a once in a lifetime experience. After that I'll probably spend a lot of time in China. Then, I'm going to visit as many countries as I can.

P: All without flying?

L: Well I'm definitely flying to Australia! I want to work there for a few months and then I might go to the United Kingdom. I don't know if I'll have enough money, though.

P: Another person from Lenox about to have a massive life change is Hadiyah Khan. Hadiyah is expecting her first baby. When I spoke to her, she was busy decorating the nursery. So, big changes ahead for you.

H: Yeah, I'm a little worried about it all actually!

P: Yeah, I think that's only natural. When's the baby due?

H: At the end of May, although apparently first babies are always late! A lot of our time is going to be spent getting things ready for the baby.

P: Do you know if it's a boy or a girl?

H: We don't – we wanted to keep it a surprise. My husband thinks it's going to be a girl, though.

P: Oh really? Why?

H: Everyone in our family has had girls!

P: Have you chosen any names yet?

H: No, we can't decide. There's the possibility of naming her Farrah after my grandma or Nabila after my husband's grandma. If it's a boy, who knows?

P: So, how do you feel?

H: I'm so excited! I've always dreamed of having children. I can't wait for everyone to meet our new baby. I know it's going to be exhausting, though. My sister has two children and I can see it isn't easy. But, you know, it'll be a lot of fun too. I'm honestly just really excited! One thing I am worried about though is getting everything done. Parents are always really busy, so I'm definitely going to have to get better at managing my time.

P: At another stage of their life is Frank Schmitt. Having worked in the local bank for the last 30 years, Frank is now finally retiring. When I caught up with Frank, he was busy buying fishing equipment.

F: What do you think of this fishing rod?

P: Um, I have no idea – I don't know much about fishing to be honest!

F: Me neither. It's just something I finally have time to do.

P: That's right, you're retiring soon.

F: I am, I am, and I can't wait!

P: Do you think you'll miss work?

F: I suppose there's the risk of getting bored, but I doubt it. Everyone wants to retire, don't they? I'll probably just spend the first few months at home relaxing but then we're planning a big vacation.

P: A cruise?

F: No, but another typical senior citizen trip! We bought a huge RV and we're going to travel to different places in the US for a year.

P: Great! Where are you going to go?

F: We haven't planned it exactly. I'm excited to see some of the famous landmarks – the Statue of Liberty, for example. I've been to New York several times, but I've never seen the Statue of Liberty! We're going to start in New York and head down to Florida. After that I'm not sure. I'm looking forward to being more spontaneous!

P: I loved Seattle. You should go there.

F: Really? That's a good idea. I'll add it to the list!

Lesson 4.2 Listening, Exercise B

4.5 **P = Presenter M = Mark S = Sarah**

P: Good morning, everyone. Welcome to today's debate. Transportation is changing rapidly around the world. More and more cars are becoming electric. Drones are being used for deliveries. So, of all the future predictions about transportation and travel, which are most likely to come true? Here to discuss this with me today are Sarah Atkinson, technology blogger and editor at *The Neo Futurist*, and Mark Edwards, transportation correspondent for *The Evening Express*. So, first, let's talk about driverless cars – do you think we will see these on our roads any time soon?

M: Definitely! The way we get around is going to be entirely transformed. It's not a matter of *if*, but *when* this happens. These are incredibly exciting times!

P: Sarah, what do you think?

S: Sorry, but that is absolutely ridiculous. I firmly believe there is no chance driverless cars will become popular. How can a car make a decision about what to do in a dangerous situation? Should it protect the driver at all costs? What if doing so might mean injuring somebody else? What does it do then? I just think it would be incredibly dangerous to have driverless cars on the road.

M: People's reactions and decision-making are absolutely terrible! It's undoubtedly true that driverless cars will have more consistent and quicker reactions than most drivers.

S: Maybe, but it's still slightly concerning. Driverless cars frequently crash during testing. A driverless bus crashed in its first *hour* of tests in Las Vegas! It's a dangerous development and we simply don't need it.

M: But it would greatly improve our lives! We could work in the car on the way to work. We could have a second car that took the kids to school. You could jump in and out of driverless taxis just paying with your card.

S: The level of associated risk is crazy! Imagine if the car taking your kids to school had an accident. It's a terrifying idea, but fortunately I think it's highly unlikely to happen any time soon.

P: OK, so what about the Hyperloop? Elon Musk's vision of future trains? A pod travels through a tunnel with no friction or air resistance, making it a very fast and efficient way of traveling.

M: Well, I for one think they're an incredibly safe alternative to our current train systems. They could also cut trip times down by 80 to 90%. Imagine that. A four-hour train ride could be completed in less than an hour!

S: Yes, they are very safe, but it won't happen. A Hyperloop train has to be in a fixed tunnel using air pressure and magnets to move the train. The big problem is that they are likely to run just between a few points that are miles apart and go past all of the other big places in between. They will literally go straight past millions of passengers. Governments simply won't spend the money and companies won't either because it will be hard to make a profit.

M: Nonsense! Hyperloop train systems are widely expected to happen. Countries all around the world are investing time and money into their own Hyperloop systems. They're undoubtedly cheaper than building a normal high-speed train and travel times will be greatly reduced. Dubai to Abu Dhabi, normally a two-hour drive, would take just 12 minutes on a Hyperloop train! Why wouldn't cities invest in it?

P: I can imagine some of these developments happening – especially things that save significant time, like the Hyperloop train, and things that free up personal time, like driverless cars. I can imagine companies investing in and developing these ideas because they could make a lot of money, but what about something more futuristic, like the flying cars we see in movies?

M: This always seems like something purely from science fiction, but I don't think flying cars are actually that unrealistic. The technology isn't that far off …

S: Oh, come on. I think you're exaggerating there! We're at least 25 years away from anything like a flying car.

M: Hmm, I don't think so. Dubai police already have self-driving cars and robot police officers. Now they're adding a flying bike to their force. It will greatly improve response times in cities with serious traffic problems.

S: The laws and the health and safety issues here would be frightening!

M: Yes, but society has dealt with major changes before. Imagine what it was like on the early passenger planes taking people on vacation.

That must have been surprising to society and a lot of rules and laws must have been needed, but society coped and moved on.

P: Actually, that brings me to my next point. What about the travel industry? How do you see that changing?

M: Well, I think we're likely to see hypersonic jets and space tourism in the not too distant future.

S: Space tourism? I can't see that really taking off – if you'll excuse the pun! There may be a small market for it, but only among the super rich.

M: Well, we'll see about that. But when it comes to hypersonic jets, I have no doubt that the technology is improving all the time and it's very likely it will become significantly cheaper over time. That means it would be affordable for most people. The Sabre jet developed in the UK could get you from Britain to Australia in four hours. That's almost 20 hours quicker!

S: You seem incredibly focused on speed! I'd be much more interested in a solar plane that was better for the environment. Even if it took me an extra day to get somewhere! In general people think more about the environment today. It's a bigger concern than speed.

M: That could happen as well. I absolutely love the idea of getting places quicker, though. Who wants to sit on a plane for two days? I somewhat agree with your opinion on space travel, though. It's an experience rather than a vacation.

P: Thank you both. Now let's move on to the Q&A section of the debate. Does anyone have any questions on driverless …

UNIT 5

Lesson 5.1 Listening, Exercise A

5.1 **P = Presenter E = Emily H = Harry**

P: We continue this month's focus on going green with a look at eco-friendly homes. Emily Montague reports from a green housing renovation project in Los Angeles.

E: So, Harry, you've decided to make your home much more eco-friendly. What prompted the change?

H: Well, I used to live in a small apartment and I moved into this house a year ago. I was shocked when I got my first energy bill. Three months here cost almost as much as I spent in a whole year in my apartment! I realize that it's a much bigger place, but I just couldn't believe how much more the bill was.

E: So how did you get started?

H: Well, I did some of the easy things myself first. I put energy-efficient lightbulbs in every room and put new attic insulation in, but I wanted to make a lot more changes. If you come out into the backyard, I'll show you what we're working on now.

E: Ah, I can see you're having solar panels installed.

H: We are. By having these, we can produce about 50% of our own energy every year. In the summer, we'll produce more than we need and then we can sell it back to the energy companies. There's something else that's interesting about this roof though …

E: Oh, really? What's that?

H: The company also transformed the roof into a small garden. They put in wild flowers that attract bees. We've had a bee hive put in at the end of the garden and now we produce our own honey. This will make our roof an energy source and a food source!

E: Amazing! Oh, and what's that over there?

H: That's a rain barrel, but it's not just for the garden. We've had our toilet system changed. Our toilet now flushes with rainwater. Any extra water comes down here to this rain barrel for the garden. We save a lot of water this way. These windows are new as well.

E: Aren't they just double glazing?

H: They are, but they are much more modern and energy efficient. They have a type of glass fitted that reflects energy back into the house. They also have a different type of gas in between instead of air. This helps to further reduce heat loss.

E: I can hear a lot of work going on as well. What else are you having done?

H: You see this box here? It takes heat from the ground into the house. Come into the living room … We're getting underfloor heating fitted. It reduces our energy bills and it looks a lot better than radiators! And, here's the kitchen.

E: Wow! That is one modern looking fridge!

H: I was fed up with throwing out so much food, so I bought this fridge. We order our food online and the fridge knows what we have in it. It then recommends food to cook! It's amazing really and we waste less food.

E: I can hear people working upstairs. What are you having done up there?

H: Come up. We're having a new energy efficient shower installed. It limits how long you can shower for and how much water is used. It obviously saves energy and stops water wastage, but it also saves time.

E: How so?

H: It turns off automatically once you've used a certain amount of water. It means some people can't spend all morning in the shower!

E: Not sure I'm too fond of that idea! Any other plans?

H: Yes, we need to get the walls better insulated. I want to use a natural product though, so we're just waiting for it to be delivered. We're also getting a smart meter installed. Hopefully, it'll help us keep an eye on how much – or how little – energy we're using!

E: Thank you, Harry, for showing us around your home. I have to say, it looks amazing!

5.2 Listening, Exercise B

5.7 **I = Interviewer A = Agatha T = Tim B = Bernie**

I: For centuries, man has been obsessed with the idea of going to Mars. Indeed, for a long time, our little red neighbor was the focus of almost all science fiction but now for some it might become a reality. We spoke to three of the Mars One candidates hoping to take part in the first manned mission to Mars. I caught up with one of the candidates, Agatha Nowak, in the library of her university. Agatha, nice to meet you. Why do you want to sign up?

A: Well, partly this will be a break, you know, a break from the usual day-to-day stuff. Like cleaning, shopping, studying … Also though, I'm a PhD student and I think it's important to advance science whenever the opportunity presents itself. To me, the Mars One project is exactly this kind of opportunity. The technological advancements made after the moon landings were amazing and I think this project could have the same effect.

I: But this is a one-way ticket. You'll never come back to Earth! Isn't that scary?

A: It is, but I'm also really excited.

I: So, why do you think you would be a good candidate?

A: I'm a really positive person with a lot of energy. I work really well as part of a team and get along with everyone. That's going to be key.

I: Surely, being a scientist is the most important thing you bring to the team?

A: I don't know. Maybe. Being a scientist isn't enough, you need to be able to live in a small space with other people for a very long time! We can't, you know, just pack up and leave if we're not happy.

I: True! How are you preparing yourself for it?

A: Can you prepare yourself? I don't know. One guy I know is eating just dried and canned food to get used to the lack of fresh things. I'm not sure that's a great idea. We need as many nutrients as possible before we go!

I: What are you expecting when you first land on Mars?

A: A lot of hard work! We'll have limited food. We'll have to eat dried and rehydrated food at first. Once we establish a community, I think we'll have to attempt to grow our own food, which is going to be challenging. And we also need to build somewhere to live. I've watched people try to build a shelter in the wild on TV and they really struggle. Imagine trying to do it in a spacesuit!

I: What are you going to miss most?

A: I really appreciate drinking a good cup of coffee every morning. Can anyone live without coffee? I read about the coffee machine on the International Space Station, so I'm hoping we get one!

I: Another candidate hoping to join the mission is Tim Davis. Tim loves to challenge himself and is hoping this will prove the ultimate challenge.

I: Can you take a short break?

T: Sure.

I: How far will you run later?

T: Just a short 30K run. Nothing too hard.

I: That sounds pretty far to me!

T: Not really. I've run a lot of marathons and a few ultramarathons. I'll never forget running across the Sahara Desert for seven days. I've always tried to challenge myself physically. I've climbed the tallest mountains in three continents of the world.

I: You like a challenge then?

T: Who doesn't enjoy a challenge? There aren't many left for me on this planet, so why not go to another one?

I: Are you worried or scared at all?

T: Why would I be scared? There's risk in everything we do, and people are just bad at assessing it. Some people worry about flying but you're much more likely to die driving to the airport.

I: True. So, you seem very driven.

T: I am. Everyone wants to leave their mark behind, don't they? Most people choose to have children as their legacy. This will be mine. I'm going to Mars to be a part of history. I'm excited, not scared.

I: What are you going to miss?

T: Well, probably just the simple things in everyday life. I'll miss my friends and family a lot. I'll definitely miss fresh food and just being able to pop into a store to buy something whenever I want.

I: Are you ready?

T: As ready as I'll ever be. I'm not worried about the physical aspect, but emotionally I think it's going to be tough.

I: The last candidate I spoke to is 50-year-old Bernie Johnson. Bernie is an environmentalist from the south. When I caught up with him, Bernie was doing a little last-minute shopping.

B: … yeah, maybe. Can you pass me a bag?

I: Sure, here you go. So, why do you want to sign up anyway? It's such a long way.

B: It's vital for the future of humans! We have to learn to live independently of planet Earth. The world is not going to end anytime soon, but we have made a real mess of things.

I: Why do you think we've been so terrible?

B: Well, you know, we've made a mess of Earth! We've used a lot of natural resources, driven species to extinction and chopped down most of the forests of the world!

I: So, what are you doing to prepare yourself for the mission?

B: I'm trying to live a more isolated life. Some people get really stressed when they forget to take their phone with them. I'm turning off my phone, and permanently disconnecting the internet. For my vacation this year I'm not going away anywhere … I'm staying at home for a month.

I: Is that why you're buying a lot of canned and dried foods?

B: That's right. I'm going to spend a month not talking to anyone except my wife. I'm buying enough food to last for four weeks and we aren't going to leave the living room.

I: Is your wife happy with that?

B: Well, she'd rather be going to Greece or somewhere nice, but, you know, she supports me. It's going to be difficult to live just inside one room, but I think it will be great preparation. I have promised her an amazing vacation next year to make up for it!

I: And how does she feel about you going to Mars?

B: Actually, she seems pretty happy about it …

I: Fair enough. So, if you did get selected, what would you miss about Earth?

B: Well, my wife, obviously. But in general, I think I'll miss being connected to other people. Our world is so small now, really. When you feel lonely you can pick up your phone to connect with a lot of people in seconds.

I: True. Anything else? Like food or something else?

B: Um, I don't know. Actually, yes. Strangely, I think I'll miss everyday noises. I'm used to living in a big city and there are so many sights and sounds to keep you stimulated. In space, all you can hear is endless silence. That could be very disturbing!

UNIT 6

Lesson 6.1 Listening, Exercise B

6.1 **P = Presenter J = Jessica A = Andrew**

P: Hello, and welcome to another edition of *Society Today*. I'm your host Rachel Baxter. So the global school rankings are out again, and they seem to indicate that stricter schooling systems get better results. Here to discuss whether it's time we moved toward a stricter schooling system in the US are Andrew Jones, head of the Lighthouse Academy in Michigan, a school well-known for its 'no nonsense' approach, and mother-of-two, Jessica Wilding. Jessica recently removed her children from a school in Grand Rapids, Michigan because as she thought the rules there were simply too strict. Good morning, both of you.

J and A: Good morning.

P: So Jessica, you went to a very open and relaxed school where children were allowed to pretty much do whatever they wanted.

J: Uh, yes, that's right. We weren't forced to do anything we didn't want to. Teachers and students were treated as equals. Every semester a vote was held so we could decide on rules together. I loved this system and was disappointed to find my children didn't have this level of freedom.

P: So you put them in another school?

J: I did, and I think it was the right decision. The school they're at now is great. Amazing, in fact. The only rule they have is that their actions must not harm anyone else. Every week they have a school meeting and vote on all sorts of issues together. I thrived under this kind of system and I think my children will, too.

A: I'm sorry, but it sounds ridiculous to me. Students that get to decide their own rules will use it as an excuse to behave badly.

J: I'm sorry, but that simply isn't true. Students don't need to follow old-fashioned rules to understand what they should or shouldn't do. Students behave well when they are given power to decide what they can't do. I think this is really important, especially for teenagers.

A: Well, I couldn't work in such a system! Rules are important.

J: I completely agree, but I think students should have a say in exactly what those rules are. I genuinely feel that most problems with teenagers come because we make them follow rules, but they're growing into adults and simply want more control of their environment. They can make very sensible decisions when given trust.

P: But surely students given this much freedom will just choose not to go to classes?

A: Exactly!

J: I'm not sure. In my school, students weren't obliged to attend classes. We could also move up a year group earlier than normal or stay back a little longer if we felt like we needed more time. We could choose our subjects and didn't have to take ones we didn't like. We could even repeat things if we wanted. People weren't left behind.

A: That's very interesting actually. How did they decide when you took exams?

J: Well, in many cases people took subjects and exams earlier than they were supposed to. If you enjoy a subject, you want to do well in it. I don't think students should be required to go to classes or to study certain subjects. If you struggle in physics and you're not ever really going to use it in the future, why study it?

A: Now that I can't agree with. People end up …

J: Why on earth not? The exam results in our school were excellent. Many students managed to get into excellent colleges and go on to have very good careers.

A: Yes, but people end up working in all sorts of jobs they never thought they would have. If you don't get a well-rounded education, it could massively affect your future.

P: Interesting! Now Andrew, you're head of one of the strictest schools in the US, and you also had a similar experience as a child yourself. Why do you think it works?

A: I believe that young students need structure. They simply need to know what the rules are.

P: Could you give us some examples of the types of strict rules you had as a child?

A: Sure. We weren't allowed to have dirty shoes. Basically, everyone had to look the same – no unusual haircuts, the same bag, the same hairbands and even the same coats. We weren't allowed to talk to each other or look at the clock. We also had to focus on our work and we weren't allowed to misbehave and distract others.

J: Not distracting people and talking – fine. But does it really matter what color your hair is or what bag you have? That seems ridiculous.

A: I've put many of the same rules in place in my school.

P: What happened if you broke the rules?

A: We had to wear a tag around our neck with a message such as 'I have 24 hours to straighten up my uniform' if we looked sloppy. If we behaved badly in class, we had to study on our own. We were forced to do this for five classes. Hundreds of children had to do this. I have similar rules in my school.

J: You're joking! How embarrassing!

A: The students are better behaved.

J: Oh, come on! I don't think the punishment fits the crime there. I agree children are supposed to learn right from wrong but being forced to study on their own for wearing the wrong color hairband! That's clearly unreasonable. The punishment should fit the crime.

P: That seems sensible to me. So, Andrew did you enjoy your experience at school?

A: I did. You quickly learned what you needed to do. You got to know what the rules were and how you were expected to behave. It actually made it really fair having more rules. We didn't have the 'strict' teacher because they were all strict. I was really happy there. We had a lot of fun. We went on some amazing school trips. We had all the usual sports teams and parties. It was great!

J: Just don't break the rules! I suppose I just loved my school. I felt like an equal and included. I think it actually made me more mature when I went to college. A lot of people see that moment as 'freedom', but we had had that for years. That time at school was the happiest time of my life, actually.

A: Me too!

P: Interesting that such different systems made you both happy. Thank you for coming in today.

J: Thanks for inviting us!

A: Great to be here.

P: Next on the show, we have several students from …

6.5 Lesson 6.1 Reading, Exercise A

P = Presenter J = Jane

P: Welcome back. Joining me now to talk about her new movie is the actress Jane Nash. So Jane, you've just finished work on your latest movie, an adaptation of the book *Agnes Grey*. When is the book set?

J: It's set at the beginning of the 19th century, when very few people in England went to school. Children generally had to work to earn money for their family. Only rich families could afford to send their children to school. I mean there were some scholarships for boys from poor backgrounds, but not for girls.

P: Shocking to think that so recently not everyone got an education!

J: I know. And it's not like it was easy to get a scholarship. Only the brightest could pass the entrance exam. If a family was rich, a girl might attend a boarding school but more likely she had a governess who taught her at home.

P: A governess? Sounds like a pretty serious person! And that's who you play, isn't it?

J: Yes, I play Agnes Grey, a governess. A governess was usually a well-educated woman who needed to earn money to support her family. They were pretty much a well-educated babysitter, though.

P: Doesn't sound like a fun job.

J: No, it was tough. You could have some terribly behaved children and no support or help. Life could be terrible for a governess! It was supposed to be homeschooling but it was part parenting, part discipline and a tiny bit of education.

P: Interesting! OK, so now we have a short clip from the movie to show people …

6.8 Lesson 6.2 Listening, Exercise E

I = Interviewer J = Janice Ka = Kayley R = Robbie

1

I: So Janice, you started your own business when you were 70.

J: Yes, it all started soon after I had grandchildren. They're amazing, but exhausting! I live around the corner from my daughter and so I used to do her a favor and take care of the grandchildren a couple of mornings a week. Every time they came over, I would, uh, make up games or do activities and that kind of thing, you know. They absolutely loved doing arts and crafts! Well, to be honest, I enjoyed it as well. If I tried to do anything else, they were just really hard to control. They weren't doing any harm, they were just full of energy – running around and shouting constantly. It was just noise! But with arts and crafts, they would sit there and focus on what they were doing. Taking care of the kids turned out to be a blessing in disguise because it led to me starting my business.

I: How did that happen?

J: Well, I'd kind of always wanted my own business, but never been brave enough. One year, I organized my granddaughter's birthday party around arts and crafts and they all loved it. I was worried about setting up my own business, but I decided to bite the bullet and set up a pottery café in my seventies. The parents love it. They can get involved with the kids or just sit and have a cup of coffee.

I: And how well has the business done?

J: Well, you know, it's hard, but I'm doing my best. Like any business, really, we had a loss in the first year. Now we're making a profit. I'm not rolling in money but I make enough. But really I'm so happy I've made a success out of this. It's the first job I've ever loved! I wish I'd done it sooner.

2

I: Hi Kayley, how old are you?

Ka: I'm fourteen.

I: And you're about to start college?

Ka: Yeah, I know. Weird or what? I'm off to study English Literature in September. I took my school exams four years early and achieved A grades in all of them.

I: That's amazing! Why do you think you are so successful academically?

Ka: I don't know. I think, well, I think most people could do the same if they got their act together. I didn't find school that difficult to be honest. It's not exactly rocket science, is it? Anyway, age is just a number. I think schools should do away with age restrictions for taking exams. Some people are ready much earlier than others.

I: Are you worried about going to college at such a young age? Most people go when they are 18 or 19.

Ka: Definitely! What are the other kids gonna make of me? It's going to be difficult to have a good social life, but that only makes up a small part of the college experience. People are generally nice, and I think they'll make allowances for my age. I hope I make a good impression, but I am a little worried.

I: And what do you hope to do when you graduate?

Ka: I love making up my own stories and really hope to be a children's book author. I write and illustrate stories for my younger cousins and they love them.

3

I: So Robbie, you've always had a terrible fear of heights and flying. You were 28 when you first went on a plane. So, how did you get over your fear?

R: Well, I was getting married about five years ago and my wife really wanted to go to the Maldives for our honeymoon, but she knew that wasn't an option. She cut me a lot of slack and didn't push for a trip because she knew I was terrified! She did start looking for vacation spots in the US, but I could tell she wasn't happy. She was trying to make the best of the situation by doing without the exciting honeymoon, but I felt so guilty. I decided to try hypnotherapy to see if that would get rid of my fear. Amazingly, it worked!

I: But since then you have really embraced not being afraid of heights and flying, right?

R: Yes, I've taken up flying and I'm now a certified pilot. I've done ten parachute jumps from a plane as well, and tried bungee jumping and base jumping.

I: That's amazing. A whole new world opened up to you!

R: Totally! My wife now gets slightly annoyed with how much time I spend doing these things, but we do have a lot more fun and exciting vacations!

UNIT 7

Lesson 7.1 Listening, Exercise B

7.1 **P = Presenter**

P: I grew up in a poor, inner-city neighborhood in Greater Manchester in the UK. This is what my neighborhood looked like when I was a kid – abandoned factories, empty blocks of apartments and playgrounds covered in broken glass and graffiti. I couldn't wait to leave, so I worked hard and got into King's College in London. Life in the south was great, but I couldn't stop thinking about my hometown and what it could have been. So, when I graduated, I moved back to Manchester and started the Open Spaces project. The goal of the project was simple – find buildings and spaces that have been abandoned and turn them into something that would better serve the community.

Our first project was an old industrial estate by the river. It hadn't been used for years and nature had naturally taken over. There was a plan to knock down the old buildings and construct new offices, but we thought it would be better as a space for the local community. We had to fight against developers to keep the land. So, how did we manage to get the local council to give us the land? Well, we approached it from an educational perspective. Many kids in large cities like this never have any experience of the countryside or wildlife, so we campaigned to develop an education center for schools across the city. Now, we have an area of local plants and wildlife for children to explore. We've also built a space for teaching the children about the local wildlife and the importance of protecting the environment in general. There are also bike paths for local people to use. So, was it a success? Absolutely. In fact, if we maintain our current numbers, we will have had 15,000 visitors in our first year. For many of the kids this is their only experience of having been shown nature.

The council was so inspired by the success of the community park that they asked us to look for similar opportunities around the city. When we found this old warehouse north of the river, we decided to turn it into a gallery. We wanted to use it to inspire young people to get into art. We got local artists to produce original pieces for the opening and to contribute any other work they had that reflected the city. We have both indoor and outdoor spaces for people to exhibit their work. To involve the local community more, we also have a section dedicated to art produced by local school children. For two weeks every year a different school gets to exhibit their students' work. The children are so inspired by this. Their work is alongside real artists' work. They come down with their families and friends and they're amazed to see their work on display. If we give kids opportunities like this, what are they going to achieve in the future? That's what I find really inspiring!

So, by this point we'd created a community park and a public art gallery. So what next? Well, in a lot of poor areas there are really high levels of obesity. Families eat takeout and microwave meals. They don't eat fresh produce because they find that it's too expensive. So, when we found a small space of wasteland that wasn't used and was largely full of garbage, we decided to build a large community garden. People are free to take the produce we grow in the garden. They can leave a donation if they want but they don't have to. We built an organic café by the entrance and use the profit to maintain the garden. Everyone who works there is a volunteer. Any leftover food from the café is given away at the end of the day to homeless people. This has been by far the most inspiring project. People are starting to use public land all across the city to start small food gardens. Now, there are nearly 20 such gardens across the city. If you're thinking about starting a garden, speak to me later. A few years ago I'd never grown anything; now I'm somewhat of an expert – especially in zucchini!

If we don't come together as a community, neighborhoods like mine will fall apart. We need people to help us take this forward. To take back our city and transform people's lives. Whether you want to start a skate park, an outdoor music venue or simply another organic garden. If you care about your community, do something to improve it. People like you can help bring back the community spirit we've lost. All it takes is a good idea and a little hard work. Thank you.

Lesson 7.2 Listening, Exercise C

7.5 **I = Interviewer C = Callum**

I: Joining us next is activist and founder of the Free Life Project, Callum Castling. Callum, welcome to the show.

C: Thanks for inviting me.

I: So Callum, for some years now, you've been involved in a movement to set up a moneyless society.

C: That's correct.

I: So, how did you get started? What inspired you?

C: Well, obviously I look up to people like Mark Boyle. He's achieved amazing things. But it sort of all started in my son's bedroom.

I: Really?

C: Yeah, so my wife was pregnant with our first son and I needed to redecorate our spare bedroom. The thing is, I'm an accountant. I'm great with numbers, but not so good with anything practical. Anyway, luckily, I get along really well with my neighbors and one of them is a professional decorator. Anyway, it turned out he was looking for an accountant, so we came up with a plan to help us both. I started to do his accounts and he did some painting and decorating around the house. We've been friends ever since.

I: So, is that what inspired your Facebook group?

C: Yeah, that's right. I just thought there must be a lot of people in the community that could help each other out. So, I set up the Facebook group to give people somewhere to share their skills or give away things they don't want anymore. It actually helps cut down on waste as well.

I: Right, so what kind of things do people get rid of?

C: Anything, really. Old bikes ... couches ... one guy even gave away his ex-girlfriend's stuff she had left at his house!

I: Really? So, has the group been popular?

C: Well, yes and no. We only have about a thousand followers, but they are all pretty active.

I: So, why did you decide to move things offline?

C: Well, social media is great, but it can feel pretty impersonal at times. We had a lot of great ideas that we'd never get around to working on because we rarely met. Basically, we felt like a community with no home. So we scouted around the city, looking for a space to use and found an old abandoned factory. It was great but needed a lot of work.

I: How did you get the money to renovate it?

C: Well, the factory was owned by the council and once we explained what we were trying to do, they offered to let us use it until they were able to sell the land. Then we managed to renovate it for free.

I: For free?

C: Yep. We got all of the materials via our Facebook group. People volunteered their time and skills. It was amazingly easy really to get a lot of volunteer workers. We got building materials, plants, gardening equipment. We even managed to get all of our tables and chairs and kitchen equipment from a local restaurant that was closing down. I couldn't believe it. People were just so generous.

I: And what do you do with the space?

C: It's become our community center, really. Twice a week we have a general networking event. We provide drinks and snacks and anyone who is interested in sharing their skills or needs to find someone with a particular skill can come along. It's great because if you come up against a problem then you can usually find someone here to help. People have started car-sharing systems, food banks to help the poor – all sorts of things really. Or you can just start something you're interested in – a language exchange, clubs, societies. You name it, people are starting it!

I: Sounds amazing!

C: People love it. Let's face it, it's more comfortable meeting someone face-to-face than just talking briefly on the phone or on a website. If something is really popular, many people are happy to run a workshop to teach people. This can be anything from basic bike maintenance to teaching people to find food in the countryside.

I: What else have you done?

C: We used the free kitchen equipment to set up a local café. And we've used the outdoor space for a kitchen garden, so everything in the café comes from local farms or our own garden.

I: I must come for lunch sometime!

C: You should! The food is actually pretty good.

I: So, do you do any other interesting things?

C: One thing we always organize is regular parties. People like to come together to socialize with the people near them. We have two or three big street parties every year. You know, like a barbecue using the produce from the garden.

I: Well, it sounds like you're restoring a good old-fashioned sense of community.

C: I think we are. People move around so much these days, they rarely get to know their neighbors. Groups like ours bring people together and show them what can be achieved when they start to help each other out.

I: Thank you for coming in today, Callum. Hopefully, some of our listeners will take inspiration from your group and start their own community projects.

UNIT 8

Lesson 8.1 Listening, Exercise B

8.1 **I = Interviewer P = Phillip**

I: Hello, and welcome to *Connections*. On this week's show, we're talking about the influence storytelling has on our culture. Why do so many countries have different variations of the same story? How do these stories grow and change? Here to help us answer these questions is Philip Norris, author of *The Myths That Made Us*, a new book about the history of storytelling. Phillip, welcome to the show.

P: Good morning. Thank you for inviting me.

I: Great that you can be here. Now, I'd always imagined that myths and legends were very specific to each culture. I thought they were essentially the mythical stories that people listened to before books. Is that not the case?

P: Well, in some ways it is. You're right that each culture has its own myths and legends that are specific to them, but what we do have is common themes across all of them. These myths appear across places and societies that are thousands of miles apart, at a time when there would have been very little contact between these groups, so they can't have the same origins. However, there are striking similarities between these stories.

I: One story we all hear about in England when we are growing up is the legend of King Arthur and the Knights of the Round Table. A king of Britain who defended the country and led a group of knights against invaders. It's almost certainly not true and there are a lot of different versions with tales of his heroic deeds. Do other countries have such myths?

P: Very much so. This is something I would refer to as a 'Hero Myth'. I think this is common across all cultures. Some of the oldest books in many countries are essentially heroic tales – an individual fighting their way across lands on a mission to save someone or find something.

I: Do you have a particular favorite hero myth?

P: Yes. I love the tales of Sinbad the Sailor and his adventures at sea. In the original stories, Sinbad goes on seven voyages across the seas off East Africa and South Asia where he finds whales the size of islands, giant snakes and rivers filled with diamonds.

I: So, can you tell us a little more about one of the stories?

P: Of course. So the third voyage of Sinbad is probably one of the most exciting. As in many of the stories, Sinbad's ship is caught in a terrible storm and driven off course. They sail toward a small island but are attacked by a tribe of monkeys carrying spears. Fearing for their lives, Sinbad and his crew swim to the island and rush to a castle they see at the top of a hill. Tired and hungry from their escape, the crew falls asleep on the floor of the castle but are awoken to find the ground shaking. In the doorway to their room, stands a giant over 20 meters tall. His eyes burn like fire, his teeth are long and sharp, and his huge mouth has the lips of a camel. Sinbad and his crew try to run away, but one of them is caught and eaten by the giant.

I: Wow! So how does Sinbad escape?

P: Well, you'll just have to read the story for yourself. I don't want to spoil the ending!

I: Fair enough. So it seems that dragons and other strange creatures appear across many cultures. Why do you think that is?

P: Well, I think many of them were inspired by people finding the fossils of ancient creatures. Some are pure fantasy, though. Take the Greek myth of Medusa, who was a winged human with poisonous snakes in her hair. In the myth, anyone who looks at her face turns to stone. King Polydectes decides to send Perseus to kill Medusa. The hero Perseus is able to kill her by looking into a mirrored shield and chopping off her head. This myth also connects to other cultures as well though, such as the Berbers in Morocco. However, monster myths are not only present in ancient legends; we have many that still exist today. One that exists in many cultures is a variation of a giant human-like creature such as the Yeti in the Himalayas or Bigfoot in North America. Even today, we still create new stories that have striking similarities across cultures. We usually refer to these as urban myths or urban legends.

I: So are urban legends just modern tales about mythical creatures?

P: Many of them do involve monsters, but others focus on ghosts or murderers. One of the most popular stories in modern culture is of a person appearing in a mirror or bathroom. In Japan, this is known as Hanako-San, when the spirit of a young girl appears in school bathrooms. People have to knock three times on the third stall door and ask, 'Are you there Hanako-San?'. A small girl or a white hand appears from the stall. This is very similar to the Bloody Mary myth in America and many others around the world. It's largely a game for young children, for whom the stories are very believable, to test their bravery, and it's surprisingly similar across the world. As are various other tales about ghosts, murders and other strange events. I guess it just shows the way our ancestors interpreted the world around them differently.

I: Thank you for coming in today, this has been really interesting. For those of you interested in finding out more, Philip's book, *The Myths That Made Us*, is out this Friday.

Lesson 8.2 Listening, Exercise B

8.4 **L = Lecturer**

L: So, I want you all to think of an event from your childhood. Something that makes you smile every time you remember it. Got it? OK, now try to picture that event in your mind. Think about where you were, who you were with, what you could hear, what you could smell ... most importantly, think about how you felt. I bet you can remember everything pretty clearly, right? Well, I don't want to upset anyone, but when it comes to accurately recalling events, the human memory is pretty awful. We like to think that our memories are like recordings we can access and watch whenever we want. Yet in reality, our memories change over time. Each time we recall an event, we rewrite the memory – adding details, updating things to match our current knowledge. Sometimes we combine two memories into one. Sometimes we even create memories. Sounds far-fetched, doesn't it? But actually, in study after study, a surprisingly high proportion of people have described memories of events that they cannot possibly have personally experienced.

'False memory syndrome' – the creation of entirely false memories – first came to the attention of the public in the late 1980s. At the time, many therapists believed that people who had experienced something terrible in their lives blocked out the memory of it, locking it deep in their minds and that the only way to access these 'repressed memories' was through therapy. Belief in this idea spread quickly, and many people who had gone into therapy looking for help with anxiety or depression were horrified to be told that they had blocked out the memory of a terrible experience years before. However, during the 90s, the theory was heavily criticized and, in the years since, multiple studies have strongly suggested that the therapists were actually encouraging their patients to create false memories. But how is this possible? How can we encourage someone to remember something that never actually happened? To help us answer this, we need to look back at the work of the American cognitive psychologist, Elizabeth Loftus.

Loftus actually first started exploring the idea of false memories in the 1970s. She did this by showing people simulations of crimes and accidents, then asking them what they remembered. In a landmark study in 1974, Loftus showed a video of a simulated car crash and asked one group, 'How fast were the cars traveling when they hit each other?' She asked another group, 'How fast were the cars traveling when they smashed into each other?' Interestingly, when asked the question with the more dramatic verb, *smashed*, witnesses said the car was traveling faster. They were also more likely to say they saw broken glass flying through the air, even though this didn't actually happen. In other studies, researchers changed some of the details when discussing an accident and many of the participants added this information to their memory – they essentially rewrote what they remembered happening, simply because they were encouraged to by the interviewer.

So, why is this important? Well, studies like this clearly demonstrate that the way you ask questions or discuss an event can strongly influence someone's memory of it. Loftus and many others like her suspected that this went some way in explaining why so many people in the 1980s were suddenly remembering horrifying experiences from their childhood. The therapists, whether intentionally or not, might actually have been encouraging patients to rewrite their own memories. But could people have been encouraged to create entirely new memories?

In 1995, Loftus designed an experiment to test this very idea. In the study, participants were given a booklet containing four short stories about themselves, three of which were true and one which never actually happened. The false story described how when they were younger, they'd gotten lost in a shopping mall, cried and were eventually helped by an elderly woman. During the study, participants were asked to write down as much detail as they could remember about each of the four stories. One in three remembered getting lost in the shopping mall, despite the fact that this never actually happened. In the 23 years since the shopping mall experiment, multiple studies have supported the idea that, under the right conditions, it is possible to encourage people to create entirely false memories.

If this is true, then I'd argue that we need to seriously reconsider the use of eyewitness testimony in the courtroom. The information presented by a witness may have been influenced by the way in which they were questioned after the event. On top of that, lawyers could encourage witnesses to add or change details. Think about how many innocent people might have been wrongfully convicted of a crime they didn't commit on the strength of an entirely false memory.

To most of us, our memories form the basis of our identity. They represent who we are and where we came from. But the research of Loftus and others like her shows that we cannot reliably distinguish between real and false memories, and in the courtroom, this could change the lives of innocent people forever. Thank you.

UNIT 9

Lesson 9.1 Listening, Exercise C

9.3 **R = Recorded message A = Amy C = Customer**

R: Thank you for holding, we appreciate your call. A customer service operator will be with you in approximately two minutes.

A: Good morning, Top Books, Amy speaking. Sorry to keep you waiting.

C: Finally! I've been on hold for 40 minutes! Aren't you supposed to answer within five minutes?

A: That is our goal sir, yes, but we've been experiencing an unusually high number of calls today. Again, I apologize for the delay, sir. How can I help you today?

C: I'm calling to complain about the condition of the books I received.

A: Oh, I'm sorry to hear that. What seems to be the problem?

C: Well, whoever delivered them left the box out in our backyard. We were away that weekend and it was raining pretty heavily so some of the books got damaged.

A: I see. OK. Could I just take your name and order number?

C: Of course. It's Harry Jenkins and the order number is 077-ADEP-9261.

A: Thank you. OK, here we are. Right, so it says here that the books were delivered on the 12th, and that your safe place is the backyard. Is that right?

C: Well ... yes, but it obviously isn't safe from the rain!

A: I appreciate that, sir, although according to our terms of service, all deliveries are left in a safe place specified by the customer.

C: I understand that, but at no point did I consent to the books being left somewhere they could get damaged! It shows a complete lack of common sense. Underneath the patio table, that's where they should have been left. Or even in the children's playhouse. At least then they would have been protected from the elements! I'm sorry, but it simply isn't good enough. It's just terrible customer service!

A: I'm very sorry you feel that way, sir. How would you like us to address the issue?

C: A full refund, that's what I expect.

A: Well, while I am sympathetic to your situation, the books were delivered in accordance with our terms of service.

C: I understand that, but I really must insist on a full refund.

A: I'm afraid that since we have adhered to your delivery instructions, the most I'd be able to offer is $10 off your next purchase.

C: Are you joking? Those books cost me $150! More to the point, why would I want to buy anything from you again when my first purchase has been such a disaster? If you can't offer a refund, I'd like all of the books picked up and replaced.

A: I see … And, are all of the books damaged?

C: To a certain extent, yes, although some are much worse than others.

A: Well, maybe we could explore some other options? How about replacing the most damaged books?

C: Absolutely not! Why should I have to pay for damaged books? If your delivery driver had used a little common sense, we wouldn't be in this situation in the first place.

A: Well, as I mentioned earlier, we have followed …

C: Look, I don't want to argue about this anymore! If you don't replace all of the books, I'll take my complaint higher. And I'll be posting about the poor service on social media; I can assure you of that!

A: I'm sure that won't be necessary, sir. I'll register your complaint in our system and someone will be in touch within 24 hours to discuss what happens next.

C: 24 hours? Why can't this be dealt with right now? What is the point of speaking to you if you can't help me?

A: I can only apologize for any inconvenience caused. I'm afraid I'm not authorized to deal with refunds or exchanges over $100 without the approval of my manager. It's company policy.

C: It's ridiculous, that's what it is! You need to make some serious changes to your organization!

A: Thank you for your feedback, sir. I'll raise your concerns to my manager after this call.

C: Yes, you do that!

A: Now, could I get the names of the books you'd like to return?

C: Certainly. There are three books on marketing and one on … anger management.

A: Sorry, did you say, 'anger management'?

C: Yes, that's right.

A: Uh, I'm just going to put you on hold a minute if that's OK?

C: No, it isn't OK. I demand to …

Lesson 9.2 Listening, Exercise B

9.5 **P = Presenter D = Dawn**

P: I'm here today with Professor Dawn Jackson, from BLB University, who has just written a book, *Science Fact or Fiction?*, which focuses on common health myths related to the food industry. So Professor Jackson, can you give us an example of one of the myths you discuss in the book?

D: Well, possibly one of the most common myths is that we need to drink two liters of water every day.

P: Is that a myth? I definitely remember hearing that we should try to drink at least eight glasses of water a day to stay hydrated.

D: Well, yes, that's the claim but there isn't really any evidence to support it. We get plenty of water through food. Even drinks like coffee, which some people believe dehydrate you, are actually a good source of water. The bottom line is – trust your body. It will tell you when you're dehydrated.

P: So, where has this myth come from?

D: Well, I don't know the exact origins, but it's certainly useful for the bottled water industry, isn't it? They make billions of dollars a year.

P: Yes, it's a huge industry these days, isn't it? When I was a kid, no one drank bottled water.

D: Yes, the industry has grown rapidly with flavored water, vitamin drinks and even water that claims to be some kind of energy drink! All sorts of varieties.

P: Surely the added vitamins and minerals help?

D: No, not really. This is another huge myth created by creative advertising. A large number of people think taking vitamin C is a good way of fighting a cold, but there is no evidence this is the case. Actually, once you have a cold it will do very little to help you fight it. Vitamin C is good for you, but increasing your intake once you have an infection won't help fight it in the slightest.

P: So what should people do? How can they tell whether a claim is true or not?

D: Well, it really comes down to thinking critically about the things you read. Don't just take claims made in advertising at face value. If you're interested in a product, especially a health product, do a little research into the claim. Is there any scientific evidence to support it? Have there been multiple large-scale studies that consistently give the same results? Only then can you be confident that a claim is based on real evidence.

P: So we need to do a little homework?

D: Exactly!

P: OK, so we asked our listeners to send in their questions and one topic that kept coming up is yogurts. They're good for digestion, aren't they?

D: Well, depending on the type of yogurt – yes. Most yogurt sold in the US is described as 'live yogurt' because it contains living bacteria. The proper name for this type of bacteria is probiotics, but you've probably heard them described as 'friendly bacteria'. This is because they're widely thought to help your digestive system.

P: But wasn't a large yogurt company – I won't say who – actually taken to court over false claims linking yogurt to digestion?

D: Yes, that's true, but that was largely due to the wording they used in their ads. You just can't say something is 'scientifically proven' if you don't have enough evidence to support your claim. In fact, in Europe, companies actually have to get the approval of the European Food Safety Authority – the EFSA – before they're allowed to make health claims in their ads. In the US, they need approval by the Food and Drug Administration – the FDA. Applications are frequently rejected by the EFSA or FDA because the company simply doesn't have enough evidence to support their claim.

P: So I guess companies have to word their ads pretty carefully?

D: That's right. You can say things like 'may help to aid digestion', but you can't say 'clinically proven to help aid digestion' unless you back this up with evidence.

P: So another hot topic for our listeners is sugar. Is it really that bad for you?

D: I'm afraid so, yes. Overconsumption of 'free sugars' – those that have been added to things like sodas or chocolate – can lead to weight gain, which ultimately is linked to things like heart disease, cancer and diabetes. They're obviously really bad for your teeth, too.

P: But doesn't fruit contain a lot of sugar?

D: Uh, it does, but it also contains fiber which actually slows down the rate at which the body absorbs sugar. You'd have to eat *a lot* of fruit to get the same amount of sugar as you'd get from, say, a soda.

P: So I'm OK to keep drinking a smoothie every morning then?

D: Actually, no. When you blend fruit into a smoothie, the natural sugars are released – meaning you consume more sugar than you would by just eating a piece of fruit.

P: Really? But I always think of them as being healthy!

D: Ha ha! Just another example of creative advertising, I'm afraid.

UNIT 10

Lesson 10.1 Reading, Exercise B

10.1 **S = Sally P1 = Press 1 P2 = Press 2 P3 = Press 3**

S: Good morning. It is with a heavy heart that I announce the discontinuation of *Healthy Me* as a print publication. From our January issue onward, the magazine will be exclusively available in a digital format on all portable devices. I will now take questions from the press.

P1: James Patterson, *CBNR*. What motivated the shift away from print?

S: Well, sales have been falling for five years now. We've gone from a distribution of just over 500,000 copies a month to under 100,000. During the same period, downloads of the *Healthy Me* app have increased by almost 300%. In fact, yesterday saw the total number of registered users reach over one million. It's just clear from the numbers that the majority of our readers prefer to consume content online.

P2: Emily Davis, the *Evening Inquirer*. Will other publications from LMI Media make the same transition?

S: Uh, no, not yet anyway. However, I'm sure all magazine publishers will start to re-evaluate their options over the next five to ten years.

P3: Martin Webb, *CityTimes.com*. What does this trend mean for print media in general?

S: Well, I think that really depends on the type of publication. For example, despite the increased popularity of e-readers, people still seem to love physical copies of fiction titles. Students still seem to prefer printed textbooks over digital. However, for lifestyle magazines, like ours, which are predominantly directed toward a younger audience, it simply doesn't make financial sense to produce print media any longer. Fewer young people are buying physical media, and we have to recognize this if we're to continue publishing our magazine. Thank you.

Lesson 10.1 Listening, Exercise C

10.2 **P = Presenter E = Emily**

P: Fake news is a phrase and a concept that didn't even really exist a few years ago, but today it's one of the biggest buzzwords in the media. To discuss why fake news has become so prevalent and what, if anything, can be done about it, I have journalist Emily Woolf with me here today. So, Emily, what exactly is fake news?

E: Essentially, it is news that is not true. Some of it is clearly written as a joke and is simply there to amuse people, but a lot of it is written in a way so as to trick the reader. The writer wants you to believe that it is genuine news.

P: So, how new is the concept of fake news?

E: Well, it's not new at all, really. There has always been fake news, but in the past it was less common, largely because there was no money to be made from it. All of a newspaper's income was made from advertising and no company wanted to advertise alongside fake news articles because it wasn't good for their reputation. You may have found an occasional fake story in a tabloid because they didn't always have such high standards, but you certainly wouldn't have found any in the high-end newspapers.

P: So, what's changed?

E: In a word, the internet. The internet and social media have been massive game changers. It's so much easier for people to share stories and they don't always check that they're true before they do so.

P: But surely, advertisers still want to be associated with good quality content?

E: To a certain extent, yes, but advertising on the internet is based on search engines knowing what you like to look at and then showing you ads that you want to click on, so the association with the content has been lost a little, I think. These days, advertisements and headlines appear together on your news feed and are tailored to your personal tastes or behaviors online, usually showing you more of the same thing. The problem is it can be difficult to tell what the source of a headline is, so it may look similar to genuine news providers, and when you click through it , it's very difficult to tell if the website is genuine or not.

P: That's true. I frequently click on links to websites just based on the headline and the websites look very professional once you get there.

E: They are, and it can be difficult to tell if the news is fake or real. We're no longer so sure which sources to trust. Traditionally, print newspapers have been held to a much higher standard. In other words, unlike bloggers and people writing on social media, large newspapers can't just lie or make things up. I think we used to have more faith in sources like CNN, but now people don't know who to trust. In the past, we could be fairly certain information from those sources was real. We could also tell fairly easily which articles were factual and which ones contained opinions that could be biased or subjective.

P: So, you think some traditional media outlets could be biased or subjective?

E: Yes. Definitely! Let me rephrase that, personal opinion always comes into journalism so there will inevitably be articles that reflect the views of the writer. In the past, it was much clearer that these were simply opinions. Now, some 'opinions' are presented as 'facts'.

P: This is obviously a huge problem.

E: It is. The problem is that people tend to believe a lot of the things they read. Despite the ease of searching on the internet, people don't tend to check the facts in a story on various other sites or from different sources. They are especially likely to believe stories about serious issues.

P: So if someone writes an article, for example, claiming that climate change is a myth, people will usually believe it.

E: Unfortunately, yes. That's a good example actually. Pretty much all scientists agree that climate change is real and there's a lot of evidence to support it. To be more precise, the only real debate is how quickly it is happening and how bad the effects will be. It's very worrying, and dangerous, that several people might read one article and go away with the conclusion that it isn't happening.

P: So, what can be done about fake news? Who should be responsible for controlling it?

E: Governments need to take a much stronger stance. Anyone writing news should be held accountable to the same standards as a journalist. Editors of newspapers were always held responsible for the content of the newspaper whereas website owners aren't necessarily. In other words, the owners of these sites need to be held responsible for the content of their site.

P: The problem there, is that people read websites from all around the world and there might not be the same rules in one country as another.

E: That's true. One other thing that would be useful is encouraging people, students especially, to think critically. Who wrote the text? What is the source? Why was it written? I know some schools are now training students to spot fake news and I think that could really help. In a recent study 75% of students, excuse me 79%, were unable to accurately identify fake news stories.

P: Wow! That's shocking. Critical thinking is clearly a skill people need to learn at a young age. OK, let's see how easy it is to spot fake news. Here are some headlines. Are they real or fake?

Lesson 10.2 Listening, Exercise A

10.5 **P = Presenter**

P: No doubt many of you have seen videos and posts that have gone viral, such as the mannequin challenge, the running man challenge or silly challenges like recreating the 'Harlem Shake' video. When these things start trending, or get a popular hashtag, they can really take off. Some organizations have been smart enough to realize that this meme concept can be used to help charities.

Many of you have no doubt also heard of Movember and the Ice Bucket Challenge, both of which started off small, but grew to capture the world's attention. The Movember event was conceived in Australia by two friends – Travis Garone and Luke Slattery – who were joking about reviving old trends. Inspired by a friend's mother who was fundraising for breast cancer, they decided to use the idea for a good cause – to raise money for prostate cancer and other men's health issues. In its first year, the event made no money and only had 30 participants. By 2014, it had exploded and garnered 1.2 million mentions on social media, with participants in over 20 countries.

Movember gradually built success over a sustained period of time, but the Ice Bucket Challenge took off much more quickly and, arguably, had a larger overall reach. In 2014, Facebook, Twitter and Instagram were flooded with people challenging each other to throw a bucket of iced water over their head to raise awareness of ALS – a disease that affects nerve cells in the brain. The campaign got over two billion online mentions that year and in the first three months, 15 million videos of willing victims were shared on Facebook. These were viewed 10 billion times by 440 million people in countries all over the globe, which in turn led to a significant increase in donations to charity groups like the ALS Foundation. For example, in 2013 ALS's best week saw them raise $25,000, yet after the campaign it raised $2.4 million dollars in one week.

So, what made these campaigns go viral? Well, research from Sander van der Linden, a psychology professor from the University of Cambridge, tells us that watching an act of kindness performed by a peer makes people want to behave in a similar manner. These effective campaigns also help us to better understand the condition these people are suffering from. They encourage people to act and inspire positive reactions from people.

So, how can we use this research to influence the content we create? In order to create good viral content, you need to understand your target audience. In other words, you need to know who you are trying to reach and how. Campaigns only go viral if they speak to people on a personal level, so you need to create an image that represents the demographic, that is the age and gender of the people you want to reach. For example, if you want to target women aged between 18–24, then it's probably a good idea to try and incorporate Pinterest into your campaign since the majority of the platform's users fit this demographic.

Second, you need to create content that has high levels of engagement. Most social media platforms rank content using incredibly complex algorithms. If you don't create engaging content, it will receive a low ranking and is far less likely to be shared as a result. Short videos typically go viral if they are shocking, memorable or funny because viral marketing is about emotions. People will share content that makes them react emotionally and this is the key to rapid growth. Using a hook that makes people happy or makes them laugh will make the content go viral.

So, once you have a good campaign together, how do you spread the word? One efficient way to promote your campaign is to use social media influencers. Social media influencers have the ability to give brands a reach they wouldn't normally get. We've all seen, and been jealous of, people paid to travel the world and share their experiences online. Most of these are social media influencers who are usually paid to promote brands.

Capturing contact information is also vital because, although it is fairly easy to create a viral success, it is phenomenally difficult to maintain this success long-term. Charities, for example, need long-term regular donations, rather than just one great year. Finding a way to encourage people to give you their email address will allow you to build a relationship long-term and gain regular payments from them. One way to get people to hand over their email address is to offer something for free. The word 'free' is a great way to get people engaged and is one of the best hooks you can utilize. I'm sure a lot of you are here today because the talk is free and we have free coffee!

Finally, some kind of competitive challenge is always fun. This challenge could be fun or silly, but ideally a combination of both, since this tends to be what engages people the most. It also needs to create an emotional reaction to the charity being supported. In just a few seconds, you have taken people on an emotional rollercoaster and gone viral.

Macmillan Education Limited
4 Crinan Street
London N1 9XW

Companies and representatives throughout the world

American Language Hub Level 4 Student's Book ISBN 978-0-230-49731-3
American Language Hub Level 4 Student's Book with Student's App
ISBN 978-0-230-49735-1

Written by Louis Rogers

First published 2020

Designed by emc design ltd
Illustrated by Daniel Limón (Beehive illustration) pp 44, 45, 50, 52, 75, 88, 89, 90, 142, 144, 148, 150, 151
Cover design by Restless
Cover photograph by plainpicture/Westend61/Uwe Umstätter
Picture research by Emily Taylor

Authentic video footage supplied by BBC Studios Distribution Limited
Café Hub videos produced by Sharp Focus

The authors and publishers would like to thank the following for permission to reproduce their photographs:

Alamy/Aldamisa Entertainment pp86–87, Art Directors p54(cm), Everett Collection Inc p43, Fotorince p65, Nino Marcutti pp76–77, Kertu Saarits pp54–55; **BBC Studios Distribution Limited** p46; **Corbis** p31(knife); **E+** p115; **Getty Images** pp15(3), 16(d), AFP p10, AFP/STR p104(tr), Ajr images p147(tr), Aluxum p29(6), Anadolu Agency p70(br), Cecilie Arcurs p147(tl), Atsushi p20(cr), Aurora Open p31(bl), Ezra Bailey p32(b), Thomas Barwick p15(6), Leland Bobbe p147(br), Lorraine Boogich p78(Christina), Dan Brandenburg p3, Niels Busch p155, Peter Cade p4(tr), Caiaimage pp14, 38(c), Caiaimage/Paul Viant p106(br), Matt Cardy p80, Guido Cavallini p150, Chinaface p74, David Colbert/EyeEm p114(br), Cultura RF pp41, 53, Shaun Curry p113, Peter Dazeley pp39, 58–59, 92, Jan Diepeveen/EyeEm p114(tr), Digital Vision pp15(2), 78(Chris), Alessandro Di Ciommo/NurPhoto p67, E+ pp16(a), 32(tr), 38(b), Eternalcreative p153, EyeEm pp102, 160, Flashpop p8, Jamie Garbutt p147(bl), Geber86 p19(tr), Graiki p82–83(background), Mike Harrington p73, Alexander W Helin p49, Hero Images pp37, 93, 106(bl), Ralf Hettler p89(tr), Hill Street Studios p81, Hulton Archive Creative p40(tr), Image Source pp70–71(background), iStockphoto pp4(tl), 16(f), 18–19, 20(t), 31(phone, fishing kit), 66–67(background), 89(br), Juanmonino p116(bl), Jupiterimages p33(bm), Justin Lewis p85, Ulla Lohmann p25, Jacob Lund Photography p154, Dave Kotinsky p7, John Lamb pp10–11(background), Matt84 p89(cr), Nathalie Michel p97, Mikolette p32(tr), Momo productions pp78(Hayley), 110, Morsa Images pp46–47(background), 147(cr), Aleksandar Nakic p38(a), National Geographic Creative p28(3), National Geographic Magazines p28(4), National Geographic RF p34, Rick Neves p28(2), Nikada p94(tr), Leo Patrizi p111, Michelle Patrick/EyeEm pp118–119, Lauri Patterson p16(b), PeopleImages p33(bl), Peter Mason Photography p15(4), Ian Ross Pettigrew p20(cl), Martin Poole p58(tr), Witthaya Prasongsin p82(tr), Real444 pp6–7(background), Tim Robberts p78(Kelly), RooM RF pp13, 98, Selimaksan p116(tr), Claudio Sericano/EyeEm pp106–107(background), Asahi Shimbun p27(tr), Kirstin Sinclair p104(br), Marco Siori/EyeEm p31(lighter), SolStock p5(tl,b), Alexander Spatari p22(br), Steve Cole images p17, Linda Steward p86(l), Michael Stewart p6(tr), Stocktrek Images pp56–57(b), Sturti p62, Svariophoto p16(e), Karwai Tang p6(tl), Taxi p78(Nick), Tetra images p157, Towfiqu Photography p16(c), Julie Toy p61, Urbancow p158, Klaus Vedfelt pp1, 118, Claudio Villa p117, VisualCommunications p28(1), Dennis Wagner/EyeEm p51, AJ Watt p147(cl), Dong Wenjie p112, Westend61 pp78(Sam), 101, Wilpunt p15(5), Dong Wenjie p33(br), Brent Winebrenner p109, WireImage p104(tl), Alex Wong p104(tm), Jacobo Zanella pp94–95, Martin Zwick pp34–35(background); **Guardian News & Media Limited** p46; **Photodisc** pp22–23, 29(5), 42–43(background), 56(tr); **Reuters Images**/Joe Brock p27(bl); **Rex Features**/Shutterstock/Paul Cooper p152; **Shutterstock**/Pressmaster p38(d); **Thinkstock** p31(rope)

Commissioned photographs by Sharp Focus pp11, 23, 35, 47, 59, 71, 83, 95, 107, 119

The author and publishers are grateful for permission to reprint the following copyright material: Extract from 'How Wolves Change Rivers – video' by GrrlScientist. Originally published in The Guardian, 03/04/2014. © 2018 Guardian News and Media Limited or its affiliated companies. All rights reserved. Reprinted with permission of The Guardian, pp50–51; Extract from '2 Most Viral Social Media Campaigns of this Decade so far!' by Salman Aslam. © 2009–2019 Omnicore Agency. All rights reserved. Reprinted with permission of Omnicore Agency, pp116–117

Printed and bound in Brazil

2024

29